The Future

An Owner's Manual

Other books by

ROBERT PONDISCIO

Get on the Net

Books by

ROBERT PONDISCIO and MARIAN SALZMAN

Going to the Net

The Ultimate On-Line Homework Helper

Kids On-Line

The Future

An Owner's Manual

WHAT THE WORLD
WILL LOOK LIKE IN THE
21st CENTURY AND BEYOND

Robert Pondiscio

HarperTrophy®
A Division of HarperCollins*Publishers*

HarperTrophy® is a registered trademark
of HarperCollins Publishers Inc.

ISBN 0-380-80335-6
Library of Congress Catalog Card Number: 99-96354

Typography by Julie Schroeder

❖

First Harper Trophy edition, 2000

Visit us on the World Wide Web!
www.harperchildrens.com

The Future *is for Katie and Henry,*
who will spend the rest of their lives there.

CONTENTS

ACKNOWLEDGMENTS

Above my desk is a series of photos of my daughter, Katie, a toddler, wearing nothing more than a diaper and a smile. I have spent many hours looking at those pictures, and daydreaming: What will the world that she grows up in look like? What inventions, discoveries, and breakthroughs will define her life? I think of the amazing events and inventions that have shaped my parents' times and mine—television, world wars, the civil rights movement, moon landings, the Internet—and wonder what my daughter will see: A cure for cancer? Human colonies in space? My desire to answer those questions drove this book forward.

I make no claim to be a prophet, a futurist, or even what the great science-fiction writer Arthur C. Clarke has called himself, an extrapolator. But with all the breathless news coverage and millennial hype being thrown around lately, there seemed to be a need to sort through it all, separate facts from science-fiction, and come up with a clear-eyed look at the world that today's kids will inherit and shape. The book you are holding in your hands is an attempt to make educated guesses as to what lies ahead.

In offering this glimpse into the future, I am heavily indebted to the work of several other authors and journalists. You will see them cited throughout the book, but there are several works whose influence runs deep in these pages: Neil Gershenfeld's *When Things Start to Think*; Michael Dertouzos's *What Will Be; Tips for Time Travelers* by Peter Cochrane; *Remaking Eden*, Lee M. Silver's outstanding book on the genetic revolution; and *Other*

Worlds: The Search for Life in the Universe, by my former *TIME* magazine colleague Michael D. Lemonick. If the subject of the future interests you, I strongly suggest that you pick up any of these outstanding books.

In addition, I have also borrowed liberally—OK, stolen shamelessly—from the ideas and work of my *Business Week* colleagues, the smartest bunch of accidental futurists anywhere. I'm convinced that business journalism may be our most reliable guide to the future, since very little new science or technology makes it out of laboratories and universities until someone finds a way to turn it into a profitable product or business. There are several other news sources that were very helpful in preparing this book, which I would also recommend to anyone wanting to keep an eye on the future: *The New York Times* (especially the "Science Times" section on Tuesdays), the *Los Angeles Times*, and *ABC News* all do outstanding "big-picture" science and technology stories, all of it available for free on the World Wide Web. *TIME* magazine, where I worked for many years, continues to offer some of the best forward-looking science coverage anywhere. And the "Science Friday" segments on National Public Radio's Talk of the Nation (http://www.npr.org/programs/scifri/) are also a must for anyone interested in staying on top of the ideas and subjects covered in this book.

Ultimately, this book is intended to be less a definitive work on where the future will take us, than to whet your appetite to learn more about the amazing work that is being done in any number of fields from information technology and genetics to transportation and medicine. My very strong hope is that this book will inspire you to learn more about the fields that interest you. Toward that end, you'll find a list of books and online resources at the end of each chapter to guide you in possibly exploring your own future.

Many people helped make this book possible. Ruth Katcher, my editor at Avon, has been a tireless supporter of this project from the beginning and, as always, a joy to work with. Kim Brooks of the Center for Food and Nutrition Policy at Georgetown University contributed several helpful ideas to the chapters on biotechnology and medicine. Seth Shostak of the SETI Institute read the chapter on the search for extraterrestrial intelligence and offered numerous suggestions. Robin Schwartz helped me gather many of the quotes used in the first chapter of the book. And special thanks are due to Takako Yamakura of IBM, who arranged for me to spend the day at the famous Thomas J. Watson Research Center in Yorktown, New York. She introduced me to Mark Bregman, Robert Morris, Mark Lucente, Lee Caldwell, and others, whose work and ideas help shape several chapters in the book.

My single biggest debt, however, may be to Drive Savers, a data recovery company in Novato, California. Less than a month before I was due to turn in the first draft of the manuscript, the hard drive of my computer was almost completely wiped out by a computer virus. I shipped my entire machine to them and within a week, they had recovered enough of my manuscript to keep the project alive. This book would not exist at all—quite literally—without their incredible service. Don't forget: Back up your data!

When I began work on this book, my wife and I had just welcomed our daughter, Katharine Greene Pondiscio, into the world. And just days after it was complete, my editor, Ruth Katcher, and her husband, Jeff Newell, had their first child, Henry Isaac. This book is dedicated to them both.

Robert Pondiscio
Medusa, New York
November 1, 1999
Rpondiscio@aol.com

P.S. Yes, that's my personal E-mail address. Questions, comments, complaints, and criticisms are always welcome. And always answered.

The Future
An Owner's Manual

CHAPTER 1

Here Comes the Future

I have a vested interest in the future, because I plan on living there. —Neil Gershenfeld, Massachusetts Institute of Technology

Think for a moment about the incredible events and changes witnessed by the people of the twentieth century. A kid born in 1900 would have been three years old when the first airplane flew at Kitty Hawk. Yet within his or her lifetime, we not only learned to fly, we flew to the moon. On that kid's birthday, the first cars were just starting to appear alongside horse-drawn carriages, but little more than a half century later, the automobile was on its way to completely changing our lives. The ability to call from New York to Chicago on the telephone was one of the wonders of the day. But by the end of the century, having a cell phone in your pocket was just as ordinary as carrying a wallet or a set of keys.

Life one hundred years ago was totally different. Electricity was fairly common in city homes. But if you were transported back in time to 1900, you might think there was nothing worth plugging in. No TV, no radio, no CDs, no cassettes—not even 8-track tapes. Want to listen to music in your room? Start singing. The first motion pictures were a novelty, rarely lasting more than a few minutes, with no sound. Rock music was over a half century away. Ragtime, played on the home piano, was all the rage. Clothes? You don't even want to know. For starters, there was no such thing as a zipper.

At the turn of the century, the average person didn't even make it to his or her fiftieth birthday. Women were not allowed to vote. Common illnesses, like the flu, were deadly. Kids as young as twelve worked in mines or factories for pennies a day—100,000 in New York City alone. You almost certainly had a full-time job by the time you were a teenager. Most kids of a century ago grew up without electricity, running water, and indoor plumbing. More than half the people in the United States lived in towns with less than three thousand people.

And what would you have done for fun one hundred years ago? How about an exciting game of marbles? A stone-throwing game called Duck on a Rock was also popular. Even one hundred years ago kids played hopscotch and jumped rope. If you could get enough kids for two teams, you might play baseball. But you wouldn't go off to play in an organized league. The first Little League was still nearly forty years away. If you were bored enough and brave enough you might challenge other kids to a game of "mumblety-peg," a game played with a pocket knife and your fingers, and which would make your parents' hair stand on end today. Football, considered bloody and violent, was even worse. It was the extreme sport of 1900. Card games and board games were popular at night. So was singing around a piano, if your family could afford one. Your little brother or sister might have had a teddy bear, named after President Theodore Roosevelt, who refused to shoot a young bear cub on one of his many hunting trips. This ignited a Furby or Pokemon-like craze for the stuffed animal, known in those days as "Teddy's Bear."

Yet in some ways, the world of one hundred years ago was just like ours. People felt they were living on the threshold of an unprecedented era of innovation. The period from the end of the Civil War to the turn of the century was a Golden Age of invention. The lightbulb, the telephone, the refrigerator, the typewriter, skyscrapers, elevators, and the "horseless carriage" all arrived in what must have seemed like an astonishing burst of scientific and technological progress. The people of one hundred years ago must surely have felt as we do today: that anything was not only possible, but probable—even unavoidable.

The twentieth century did not disappoint.

Someone lucky enough to have lived from one end of the century to the other witnessed two world wars, the Great Depression, the Model T Ford, and the invention of penicillin, television, and the atomic bomb. He or she lived to see interstate highways, jet travel, rockets, vaccines against smallpox, polio, and other deadly diseases, the discovery of DNA, men on the moon, heart and other organ transplants, test-tube babies, the space shuttle, space probes to the farthest planet and beyond, the personal computer, the VCR, video games, the Internet, and cloning. And that's just the big stuff. The gadgets of everyday life might have seemed even more miraculous if they could have been predicted one hundred years ago. If you could have demonstrated a microwave oven to a turn-of-the-century family, they would almost certainly have thought it was a clever magic trick.

Was any of this foreseeable? Could a person standing at the turn of the last century possibly have predicted how cars, electricity, and television would so completely alter the daily life of the average person?

Probably not. The future takes unpredictable twists and turns. Just knowing about an emerging technology may not be enough to let us guess how it will affect our lives. People of one hundred years ago knew about the automobile. But who could have predicted how the car would spur the development of everything from highways and suburbs to cell phones and fast food? Even if you had known about radio, compact discs and MTV a century ago, would anyone have predicted the Spice Girls? On the other hand, could they have prevented it if they had?

The book you're holding in your hand does not pretend to predict everything about the future. But from our vantage point in the early days of the twenty-first century—and with a little knowledge of the latest advances in science, technology, medicine, and several other fields—we can certainly report on what's being developed right now, today. And armed with that knowledge, we might be able to make some intelligent guesses of how this will affect the way we live. Of course, the future has a funny way of defying our expectations. When I was a kid, I expected the future to look like the Jetsons. And look what we got instead: the Simpsons.

We can never know for sure what the future will hold, but we can make one prediction that is 100 percent guaranteed to be accurate: The pace of change in the twenty-first century will make the twentieth century look sleepy by comparison. It is often said that standards of living and technology changed more in the past one hundred years than in the previous nine hundred. One hundred years from now, however, we may look back on the twentieth century as just a warmup act for what came next. The amount of information generated by human beings doubles every eighteen months. "If this continues, in fifteen to twenty years, it could double every two weeks—eventually every few hours," futurist Arthur Harkins has said. "Someday, early in the next century, people will encounter more change in one year than in all previous human history."

There are those who wonder if the price we are paying for our progress is too high. The end of the twenty-first century could see twice as many people crowded on our small planet as we have today. Natural resources, like crude oil and water, could be depleted. Earth's environment may not be able to absorb the continued punishment mankind asks of it.

But for better or for worse, change can't be stopped. Proof of that is as near as the nearest antiques store. Step inside and you'll quickly find dozens of strange and unfamiliar items that were common household objects for previous generations, things they used and touched every day. What will your grandchildren find when they visit an antiques store one hundred years from now? The list will be long and probably will include things like paper money, personal computers, videotapes, keys, newspapers, telephones, and beepers.

Objects are not the only things that will disappear. Changes in technology can mean entire businesses and industries can disappear and new ones take their place. This is also nothing new. A hundred years ago, there was a great demand for buggy whips. The turn-of-the-century family didn't pop into the car and drive to the mall. They hitched up the horse to the family buggy and—

after a smart snap of a buggy whip on the horse's flank—they were on the way to the town market to get supplies.

The automobile changed everything, including the buggy whip business. It didn't matter if you made the best buggy whip on the face of the earth. When the buggy disappeared, so did your job. One hundred years ago, the three most common occupations for Americans were farmer, domestic servant, and factory worker. By the end of the century, muscle work had given way to brain work. Today, some forms of brain work might make the endangered species list: travel agents, stockbrokers, insurance salesmen, and people who work in stores, for starters—anyone whose job might be done more quickly and easily by a search engine or "intelligent agent" on the Net.

Once you know what is coming down the technological pipe, it's not hard—heck, it's a lot of fun—to imagine and dream how today's Next Big Thing will totally change our lives tomorrow. And there is no shortage of wild scenarios about what the future will be like. Since the future has yet to happen, all guesses about what will happen are just that—guesses. But in this book, we'll try to stay as grounded in reality as possible. We'll look at what some of the leading experts—men and women who are actually working to build the future—are saying, thinking, and doing. By focusing on trends and technology that are taking shape today, we'll be able to make some reasonable guesses about what the world of tomorrow will look like ten, twenty-five, fifty, and one hundred years from now.

Here are just a few of the major changes ahead in the twenty-first century:

- Computers that become so much a part of the fabric of our lives that we no longer notice they're there.
- A revolution in our understanding of genetics that will change everything from the food we eat to the way babies are brought into the world.
- The new science of nanotechnology, which will give us the power to manipulate atoms, building things from molecules on up.

- A wired world where the television, the telephone, and the Internet collapse into a seamless digital service offering constant information and communications no matter where we are.
- Medical breakthroughs that will tell us the diseases we are likely to get during our lifetime, so doctors can help prevent them from ever occurring.
- Advances in transportation that will allow us to travel from one side of the world to the other in two hours.
- The dawn of a true space age, which will set the stage for permanent human colonies on Mars and the moon.

All of these wonders and more won't come without controversy. History is filled with examples of discoveries that the human race was just not quite ready to handle: Copernicus's discovery that the Earth was not the center of the universe, for example, or Darwin's theory of evolution, or the splitting of the atom. The idea of "test-tube babies" horrified many people when the technology arrived thirty years ago. Today it's often as much a part of having a child as a lullaby. Likewise, many of the things that make us nervous today—genetic engineering and cloning, for example—may be a normal part of everyday life one hundred years from now.

In the chapters ahead, we will look at what is to come in many different areas, from computers and communication to technology and transportation—and everything in between. The most profound changes will almost certainly be in the continuing "Information Age" and the emerging sciences of biotechnology and genetics. Barring the end of the world (a possibility we'll discuss in Chapter 10) new inventions in computers and communication as well as in medicine will almost certainly be the defining changes of the twenty-first century.

OOPS! ALL-TIME DUMBEST PREDICTIONS ABOUT THE FUTURE

It was 1499, and a German astrologer by the name of Johannes Stoeffler had a vision of a terrible flood that would wipe out mankind. He even predicted the date the waters would rise and sweep everyone away: February 20, 1524. The astrologer was apparently taken very seriously. One Count von Iggelheim had enough faith in the prediction that he built himself a three-story ark, just as an insurance policy. The day of destruction came, and it rained. It rained *hard.* It rained so hard that a huge mob formed and fought savagely to board the ark and save themselves. The rain stopped, but not before hundreds of frightened people were trampled to death—including the count.

Some insurance policy.

Predictions are fun to make, and are occasionally enlightening. But when they go wrong they often come back to haunt the people who made them. Or, as in the case of the unfortunate count, the people who believed them. Throughout this book, we'll take a look at a few of history's dumbest predictions. If nothing else, they remind us that the future has a way of making even the experts look foolish! Or worse.

FROM FLYING HOUSES TO THE BOMB

. . . wonderful new materials far stronger than steel, but lighter than aluminum [will mean] houses will be able to fly. . . . The time may come when whole communities may migrate south in the winter, or move to new lands whenever they feel the need for a change of scenery.

—Arthur C. Clarke, "The World of 2001," *Vogue* magazine, 1966

Housewives in fifty years may wash dirty dishes right down the drain. Cheap plastic will melt in hot water.

—*Popular Mechanics,* 1950

The bomb will never go off. I speak as an expert in explosives.
—Adm. William Leahy, US Atomic Bomb Project, 1945

You ain't going nowhere, son. You oughtta go back to driving a truck . —Jim Denny, the manager of the Grand Ole Opry, who fired Elvis Presley after his first performance

THE EXPERTS PREDICT: FROM LIFE ON MARS TO . . . PRESIDENT GATES?

What will life be like in the twenty-first century? What wonders, and perhaps what terrors, lie ahead? To set the stage for our exploration of the future, we contacted dozens of people from scientists to science-fiction writers, college professors and journalists, business leaders and elected officials, actors and news anchors, experts and dreamers—even a Nobel Prize–winner, to get their response to one simple question:

What will be the most amazing thing someone who is twelve years old today will live to see?

The hardest thing was getting most of the experts to pick just one thing! "Children born in the 1980s and early 1990s will see the types of change which their great-grandparents born in the 1880s saw with the advent of electricity," predicts Clement Bezold, Ph.D., president of the Institute for Alternative Futures. "Twelve-year-olds today will face the prospect of genetic preselection of the traits of their children, the end of major diseases like cancer and heart disease, the appearance of major threats through new diseases and biological terrorism, and the threat of major climate flip-flops: For example, Europe's weather becoming like that of Siberia."

Another professional futurist, David Pearce Snyder, also sees too many changes to pick just one. Among the common technologies he foresees between now and 2070 are "conversational computers with amiable personalities [who] will serve as our colleagues and assistants, with whom we will have meaningful, long-term relationships." Instantaneous computerized translation, he says, will enable us to communicate easily with people who do not speak our language. He also predicts that genetic engineering will not only eliminate all birth defects, but "will permit people to 'customize' their children to combine the best features of the parents. Humans will be enabled to regrow severed or damaged limbs." Sound amazing? Creepy? Relax. "These future developments may seem amazing to us, and even to today's twelve-year-old, but, as they incrementally become realities over the next seventy years, they will seem less amazing and more like the natural and normal course of events," Snyder adds.

Ray Bradbury, the legendary author of *The Martian Chronicles, Fahrenheit 451,* and more than thirty other science-fiction novels says the most amazing thing has already happened. "The most important event was man landing on the moon," says Bradbury. "If we succeed in colonizing the moon and Mars, we are halfway to the immortality of the human race." Fellow science-fiction writer R. Andrew Heidel, author of *Beyond the Wall of Sleep,* offers a simple, elegant reply. The most incredible thing you will live to see, he says, is "the Earth shining like a sapphire in the night sky from the surface of Mars."

Perhaps the most amazing thing about the future as we see it now is that serious scientists are dreaming bigger dreams than science-fiction writers. In some cases, their predictions are exactly the same. Dr. Richard Smalley, the 1996 Nobel Prize–winning chemist and a pioneer in nanotechnology, predicts you will live to see "an elevator to space, pretty much as described by Arthur Clarke in *Fountains of Paradise.*" Smalley, who teaches chemistry and physics at Houston's Rice University, thinks we will see a world that looks like the one Clarke imagines in his most recent book, *3001*. In this world, "Earth has become just a very beautiful, very big wildlife preserve, rocket launches are only done on the fourth of July to celebrate a long-distant past, and most of humanity lives in a giant 'ring world' that circles the planet," says Smalley.

Compared to this, the predictions of Thomas P. Vitale, the vice president of programming of TV's Sci-Fi Channel, sound absolutely routine. Today's twelve-year-old, he predicts, will live to see "the cloning of a human being, the first person walking on

Mars, and the ability to translate the human brain into data, so that someone can have their memories—their essence—stored into computers."

"There are two big things that will make my daughter's life incredibly different from ours," predicts Walter Isaacson, the managing editor of *TIME* magazine. "The first is artificial intelligence. We'll soon be able to talk to our machines, and they will understand us. Eventually, they will know enough about our desires and habits to act as intelligent agents and anticipate our needs. This will be really cool, at least until they decide they don't need us anymore and start building their own machines they can boss around," he says. The second is genetics. "Our kids will be able to design the genetic traits of their own kids," he predicts, "choosing things ranging from their eye color to height to perhaps even intelligence, and they will also be able to clone themselves—or even clone us if we're unlucky."

William Gibson, the author of the science-fiction classic *Neuromancer,* the book that introduced the word *cyberspace* into our language, says it's not even possible to think seventy to one hundred years ahead anymore. "We're no longer in a predictable scenario," he says. "We're gonna hit what some people call 'the techno rapture' somewhere down the road." Gibson defines that as "a technological development whose effects are so profound that beyond it everything changes." He cites "functional immortality," where we might live for six or seven hundred years as an example. Nanotechnology, which would allow scientists to build anything from atoms on up, is another example of a technology that could change absolutely everything. "As soon as you have that, the whole basis for the human economic universe and society as we know it disappears," says Gibson. "There's no more wealth; there's no more poverty. Everything goes by the boards. We don't really live in a world where there's 'business as usual' anymore," Gibson concludes, "because everything's changing all the time."

In between now and Gibson's techno rapture, however, we will almost certainly live through some profound social and scientific changes. "My son Benjamin is now twelve years old, and assuming he lives to be eighty or ninety—he'll be around until 2075 or so," says CNN news anchor Judy Woodruff. "I think he'll see a United States where women and people of color will play a political leadership role—a number of presidents who are African American, Latino, and/or female. In a more frightening sense, I think he will see terrible conflicts fought over scarce resources—clean water, clean air, and arable land. Nations abroad will have the worst of it; but the United States will suffer over scarcity as well." Woodruff also thinks her son will live to see "a growing dependence on space, including the mining of resources in distant stars and colonies of earthlings living on other planets—to relieve some of the population pressure here on Earth."

What else will today's twelve-year-old live to see? Take a look:

COMMUNICATIONS John McCain, United States senator: "If I asked my own twelve-year-old son that question, I know what he'd say: palm-sized digital transceivers made to relay instant video, voice, and data to or from anywhere on earth—including video games."

Dr. Lee Caldwell, director of Internet technology, strategy and standards, IBM Corporation: "The whole world is going to be very different than the world we have today. I think the most remarkable thing will be the ability to be in instantaneous, full-sense communication with people all over the world for such a modest cost that a fairly high percentage of the world's population can afford it either directly or through some shared community facility."

TECHNOLOGY Glen Hiemstra, professional futurist and host of Futurist.com: "The most amazing thing a person who is twelve years old will live to see is the creation of a computer chip which is as smart as one trillion human brains. This will happen around the year 2060, when our twelve-year-old is seventy-two, and will cost about one thousand dollars to buy. This computer will enhance and extend the abilities of people in ways that are difficult to imagine but will certainly mean that we [will] have intelligent assistants available to answer our questions. They will seem to be human themselves, having their own thoughts, emotions and experiences. Perhaps we will be partners with a new form of intelligent being."

ENTERTAINMENT Janeane Garofalo, actor and comic: "Kids who are twelve today will probably see their first computer-generated actors in films . . . spawning computer-generated celebrities who'll make 'personal appearances' on-line and do pseudo interviews."

MEDICINE W. Warren Wagar, distinguished teaching professor of history, SUNY at Binghamton, author of *A Short History of the Future*: "The most remarkable discovery that a current twelve-year-old will live to see? Medical science and biotechnology will have the ability to liberate humanity from most diseases, disabilities, and premature deaths, and the power to ensure that all children born into the world will be healthy, intelligent, and sociable. Not every part of the world will be benefiting from this progress by the time our twelve-year-old reaches sixty or seventy, but the know-how will be widely available. Most of this progress will result from galloping increases in our knowledge of the human genome and how it functions."

Elizabeth Weise, Technology Writer, *USA Today:* "I expect the most amazing thing someone who's twelve will live to see will be grow-your-own organs to replace worn-out ones. I think it's probably about fifteen to twenty years away, at this point. The most amazing bad thing will be something like biological weapons based on smallpox."

Therese Littleton, science & nature and science-fiction & fantasy editor at Amazon.com: "I think nanotech medical machines will be the most amazing development that kids today will see in their lifetimes. Imagine microscopic devices programmed to destroy arterial plaques, mend broken bones, obliterate tumors, and sew up wounds, all super-fast and without drugs or hideous pain. They will also be pre-programmed to die and break down into easily eliminated compounds after completing their work."

SCIENCE Dr. Laurence S. Kalkstein, associate director, Center for Climatic Research, University of Delaware: "The most remarkable thing I expect to see in my field is the accurate prediction of severe storms and hurricanes, up to several weeks in advance. Then we will be able to warn the population to stay out of harm's way as these storms approach. Presently, thousands of people are killed by these phenomena each year worldwide. Hopefully, today's twelve-year-old will also see an international agreement to curb the very real threat of a global climate change. It seems to be more and more clear that humans are altering the climate, and this will require international cooperation before we can turn this trend around."

SPACE Harry L. Shipman, professor of science, physics, and astronomy, University of Delaware: "The most dramatic discovery of the twenty-first century will be the discovery of many earthlike planets. This could change our view of ourselves as fundamentally as the astronauts' pictures of the whole earth changed our view of ourselves in the 1960s. (I'm just old enough to remember that.) The most interesting thing a twelve-year-old will live to see would be the first landing of human beings on Mars. Whenever I look up at Mars in the sky and realize that we have the technological ability to get there, I'm sure that we *will* get there."

Mark McEwen, co-anchor, *CBS This Morning*: "Space travel will become like it was in *Star Wars,* where it's no big deal. Where you kick spaceships like the tires of the car. Where you know where to go to get the cheapest rocket fuel. Where you buy a used spaceship and think, 'I'm getting the VX4000 at a steal!' Where it's not 'Aargh . . . pressurized suits, what happens if they break?!' but it's like getting into the car and just driving to the 7-Eleven and back."

ENVIRONMENT William Gibson: "One thing I'd love to live to see would be the restoration of extinct species. Someone fairly recently discovered the embryo of a female Tasmanian tiger preserved in alcohol in a museum in Australia. It's this amazing-looking, marsupial, wolflike critter that's like a carnivorous kangaroo with zebra stripes. The last known one died in captivity in 1935, killed off by farmers because [the tigers] ate the livestock. This wonderfully weird critter has been preserved since 1890, and because it's in alcohol instead of formaldehyde, there's a lot more of its genetic information sitting there. With the adequate technology, we might be able to take the DNA of the smaller carnivorious marsupial called the Tasmanian devil, rewrite it based on the information from the Tasmanian tiger and make the Tasmanian tiger live again. I'd love to see that in *National Geographic*: 'Re-release of the Tasmanian Tiger!'"

SCHOOL Mark Dery, cultural critic and author of *Escape Velocity: Cyberculture at the End of the Century:* "K-twelve schools will be privatized, and their electronic textbooks (produced by Microsoft, of course) will enshrine Information Age robber barons as smiling benefactors, much like the recent Microsoft CD-ROM of Funk & Wagnall's encyclopedia revised an entry describing Bill Gates as 'ruthless' into one characterizing him as 'known for his personal and corporate contributions to charity and educational organizations.' Gates, by the way, will be president."

WAR AND PEACE W. Warren Wagar: "The most remarkable achievement of the twenty-first century? Surviving into the twenty-second century! And surviving as a unified species under a single world law and governance system, rather than remaining split into hundreds of rival sovereign nations and movements to preserve ethnic 'purity' or 'dominance.' I believe that by the end of the twenty-first century, we will have managed to set aside our differences and create a world republic that will make international war obsolete."

SPORTS Robert Wuhl, actor, director, creator of HBO's hit comedy series *Arli$$*: "What's the most amazing thing someone who's twelve today will live to see? The Chicago Cubs and the Boston Red Sox win the World Series . . . maybe."

SOCIETY Clement Bezold: "Today's twelve-year-olds will face the prospect and challenge of creating a world that works for everyone on the planet, as well as major increases in the capacity of each individual to contribute to their communities—local, global, and virtual."

Mark Dery: "The most mind-wrenching development today's twelve-year-olds will witness within their lifetimes (presuming that they live until, say, 2077) will be the gradual devolution of America into a Third World country. For all practical purposes, the America of the coming century will be ruled by a small, super-rich economic elite. The wealthy will live in baronial splendor, in Jetsonian cyber-mansions like the one Bill Gates has already built, in heavily fortified gated communities like the ones already springing up around American cities."

IMMORTALITY Ben Bova, science-fiction author and president emeritus of the National Space Society: "I think the most interesting thing will be the end of death from age-related causes. Together with the elimination of most diseases, including cancer, this means today's twelve-year-old will be able to live for many centuries, and see humankind expand through the solar system and out to the stars."

THE BIG PICTURE Richard Long, professor of chemical engineering, New Mexico State University: "With much fear and trembling, I think your hypothetical twelve-year-old will see cloned humans, self-aware computers, and certainly regenerated human body parts. The science is nearly there, though the ethics of use for these and other technologies needs to be worked out. Personally, I am hopeful that an improved understanding of the universe will come from the Hubble space telescope and its successors."

James Halperin, futurist and author of *The First Immortal* and *The Truth Machine:* "Within the next twenty to two hundred years, medical science will likely find a cure for every known human disease, including the aging process. A person who's twelve today might very well live to see . . . everything."

Want to Know More?

On the Web:

- The World Future Society (www.wfs.org/)
- The Futurist (www.wfs.org/futurist.htm)
- The Futurism Page (www.corvinia.org/futurism/futurism.html)
- Eurekalert! (www.eurekalert.org/)
- Breakthrough! (www.lucifer.com/~sean/BT/)

At the Library:

- *Tips for Time Travelers*, by Peter Cochrane (McGraw-Hill, 1998)
- *Imagined Worlds*, by Freeman Dyson (Harvard University Press, 1997)
- *The Macmillan Atlas of the Future*, by Ian Pearson, Editor (IDG Books Worldwide, 1998)

CHAPTER 2

Computers Disappear

The PC is really just a typewriter shoved under a television screen. I'm not sure that we want to spend our days—years, really—sitting in chairs, staring at screens and fumbling with a mouse. For now it works, but we can do better.

—Mark Lucente, IBM

Spend a little time with the technology wizards at the leading edge of the digital revolution, and very soon you'll realize that they don't seem to like computers very much. It's not the machines themselves they don't like. They just hate, *hate* sitting in front of computers, pecking away at the keys. And don't even get them started about loading operating systems and software! "It's absolutely disgraceful how hard it is to use a computer after all these years of trying to make it easier," says technology visionary Nicholas Negroponte, cofounder and director of MIT Media Laboratory. "We should be doing a lot better."

He's right. You could make a strong case that the best, most useful technology is the kind you never think about. Most people don't spend very much time trying to understand their telephone, for example. You don't have to load your favorite television programs the way you load software. So why should computers be so hard to use? Why should we have to be trained to use them? Why can't they *just work?* And if they're going to make our lives more complicated, maybe they should just go away.

Maybe they will go away and, at the same time, make our lives easier. We're in the early days of the Information Age, so everyone talks a lot about computers and how they are transforming nearly every aspect of our lives. But, if most computer and technology experts are correct, the computer may be about to disappear.

Not possible? Well then, ask yourself this question: How many motors are in or around your house? Three? Four? Would you believe that the average home has more than *fifty* motors in it? They're all around you, squirreled away inside refrigerators, dishwashers, electric mixers, and blenders in the kitchen. Washers and dryers, vacuum cleaners, and fans and air conditioners all have motors. Look in the bathroom. See a blow dryer, an electric razor or toothbrush? Stereos, tape and CD players, and computers with CD-ROM drives also have built-in motors. Motors are all around you, hidden in plain sight, but I'll bet that you rarely, if ever, give them a passing thought. They perform their functions quietly, with little trouble and a minimum of human interaction. They are *ubiquitous,* a word that means they're universal, or everywhere. And when things become ubiquitous, we no longer pay much attention to them. They seem to disappear, because there is no longer anything special or remarkable about them.

Today the motor, tomorrow the personal computer. Many experts compare today's PC to a long-forgotten contraption called the Home Motor, which was sold in the Sears Roebuck catalog more than eighty years ago. Like the PC, the Home Motor was a large gadget that powered many other smaller devices and was supposed to be the answer to dozens of problems. You could hook it to a vacuum cleaner. You could use it to run a sewing machine. You could attach a fan to it and cool your house. It basically ran any gadget you had that needed a motor. If that sounds weird, keep in mind that in 1918, a motor was a serious, expensive piece of high-tech equipment, just like most PCs today. You were lucky if you could afford one, let alone dozens of little ones in different appliances. And many homes of a century ago didn't even have electrical service—just as nearly 70 percent of homes in the United States don't have Internet service right now. Eventually motors got cheaper and smaller and found their way into all those everyday appliances we mentioned earlier. Who needs a big single motor to run a dozen different appliances, when every little gadget can have a cheap, inexpensive motor of its own? Well, technology experts reply, who needs a big single PC when every little gadget can have a microchip of its own?

Like the motor, computers will soon be such a common part of our lives that we will no longer notice them. They will be everywhere, but at the same time, they will seem to disappear.

Computer and technology experts agree that the twenty-first century will begin the era of "ubiquitous computing." In the next ten to twenty-five years, computers will become more powerful than ever; but at the same time, they'll get cheaper and more plentiful, so that you will use them to perform a mind-boggling array of everyday tasks, including thousands of things we would never dream of using computers for today. Everything from clothing to coffee cups will be embedded with tiny microchips, experts predict, all connected and sharing information over a vast, seamless global network built on the foundations of today's Internet. In fact, computers will be so common that we will no more think of something as "computerized" than we think of it as "electrical" today. Just like motors, you may hardly notice computers years from now. They will seem to have disappeared—but they will be everywhere.

The future of ubiquitous computing won't mean computers in every room, the way television sets are often found in living rooms, bedroom, kitchens—even in the bathroom. Ubiquitous computing will simply mean the PC will no longer have a monopoly on computing power. Microprocessors, the silicon brains that power computers, will find their way into hundreds of devices that we won't really think of as computers at all. Basically, if something is powered by electricity, you can expect it to have a microchip in the not-too-distant future.

"Invisibility is the missing goal in computing," writes MIT professor Neil Gershenfeld in his book *When Things Start to Think.* Gershenfeld points out that while we may think of our current computers as advanced, it's their raw power to perform calculations that is most impressive, *not* how easy they are to use. Computers are very good at communicating their own needs but they have no way of knowing what *you* need, he notes. That will change in the next several years.

BEYOND THE PC

Picture a computer. The image that probably comes to mind is the personal computer—a big, boxy, extremely complicated appliance that does dozens of different tasks. You can use it to write a report for school, surf the World Wide Web, send and receive E-mail, play video games, store your calendar and address book, and a whole lot more. The PC is a very useful device, but it won't work unless you have another piece of equipment. No, not a printer or a modem. A chair.

Right now, using a computer means sitting down in front of one. But within a few decades, you'll be computing at nearly every waking moment, whether you're sitting, standing, walking around, or traveling—and usually without even realizing it. To get a sense of what ubiquitous computing will feel like, go for a ride in a new car. As much as 90 percent of some cars' functions are now computer controlled. Yet the average driver is probably only dimly aware that there are so many computers on board, controlling everything from the brakes to the flow of fuel to the engine. What's most important is that you don't need to be a computer geek to drive. The car has changed, but driving has stayed the same. Computers have given the car better mileage and made it safer and easier to handle.

This transition from the desktop to ubiquitous computing is already happening. If you carry a cell phone, a beeper, a Palm Pilot, or some other personal digital assistant (PDA), you are carrying an "information appliance," a small computer that has left the desktop and found its way into your pocket. Today's digital devices will soon be joined, computer experts predict, by a host of new, amazing gadgets and devices:

- A "personal communicator" will play the role that your phone, E-mail, and pager play today. Instant wireless voice and data communication will be available anytime, anywhere in the world.
- Smart cards with "digital cash" will allow you to transfer cash instantly to make a purchase.

- Digital "VCRs" will learn your favorite shows and record them automatically, whether or not you program them to do so.
- Reusable, digital paper will store current issues of your favorite newspaper or magazine. When you are done reading today's paper you won't toss it. The next morning's news will be automatically printed on the exact same sheets of paper without your lifting a finger.
- Digital notepads will convert your classroom notes and other scribbles into digital text, which you can store and retrieve whenever, wherever you want.
- Chips powered by your body's natural electrical field will let you carry vital medical records on you at all times in case of emergency, or exchange personal information just by shaking hands, instead of writing down phone numbers or swapping business cards.

Does it sound like we're going to turn into digital beasts of burden, weighed down by all the gear we'll have to carry around? That depends on how you think about it. "I think we'll be carrying a lot. But some devices you won't carry around. They'll just be *lying* around," says Mark Bregman, the general manager of IBM's Pervasive Computing initiative. "For example, something you do all the time is write. But when you go to the counter in a store to sign a credit card slip, they usually have a pen. You don't have to reach into your pocket. Pens are pretty ubiquitous. You don't think about them very much. They're just there," he notes.

Whether you realize it or not, you probably already carry a large number of devices. Lots of people already carry a cell phone or a pager. But you also probably have a wallet, a set of keys, school ID, a watch, and a pen. Most adults also carry a checkbook, several credit cards, work ID, business cards, and more. Ubiquitous computing means that we actually will carry less. Take credit cards, for example. Many adults now have a half a dozen or more. In a few years, a single "smart card" will link all your banking accounts, credit accounts, and even a few dollars of digital walking-around money in one device like today's credit card.

Soon, networked, computer-driven devices will be in every room of the house. At places like the Media Lab at the Massachusetts Institute of Technology, Xerox's Palo Alto Research Center, and IBM's Thomas J. Watson Research Center in Yorktown, New York, researchers are already developing rooms, even entire houses, where computer chips have been built into walls, furniture, and appliances, and every device recognizes and can communicate with every other device. How would you like a "household manager" that would remind you where you left your keys? Better still, why not throw away your keys altogether, since your car's steering wheel and your front door will recognize you by your touch and will let you in automatically or stay locked for strangers.

Within the next few decades, ubiquitous computing promises to free us from dozens of ordinary, time-consuming tasks. Smart appliances that communicate with each other inside and outside the home might lead to automatic management of everyday tasks, like grocery shopping. MIT's Gershenfeld has described a series of microchips in our homes, in our clothes, and in sensors embedded in the products we buy, all seamlessly networked together. "You can put one in your refrigerator and it can analyze your milk and say, 'Your milk is turning bad.' Then as you walk by, your fridge can tell your shoes, 'You're low on milk and it's turning kind of funny.' Later, when you're walking by the store, the store can broadcast, 'We've got milk on sale.' At that point, your shoes can send a message to your glasses, saying, 'By the way, you're running out of milk and you might want to go in and get some.'"

Gershenfeld stresses that not a lot of new technology is needed to make this happen. What is needed are better sensors and computers programmed to have some commonsense understanding about the world. "But that's not a breakthrough in artificial intelligence," he points out. "It's just a bunch of little pieces connected together, getting the right data in the right place."

Of course, maybe you don't *want* stores to broadcast your grocery list to your shoes. That's ubiquitous, but it's sure as heck not unobtrusive. Perhaps it would be better if the refrigerator checks the calendar in your household manager to make sure you're going to be home for the next few days, then places an order with the grocery store for milk to be delivered. It might even hold an on-line auction to get you the lowest price in the neighborhood for your groceries. What's for dinner tonight? A smart appliance could suggest recipes based on what it knows you have in the house—and what it knows you like to eat. It would know what you have by keeping track of the microchips embedded in every single box, jar and can in the cupboard. Chips embedded in food itself will "talk" to your oven, offering meals that cook themselves. Such devices would do more than the pop-up timer that merely signals when your chicken or turkey is done. You will put the bird in the oven and the chip will tell the oven, "I'm a four-and-a-half-pound chicken and I need to cook for about ninety minutes at three hundred and fifty degrees. Turn on the heat and I'll yell when I'm done."

Since you won't have to program anything, you won't really think of this as computer technology. All of these devices and more will work by themselves. When we say "computer" a generation from now, if we use the word at all, we will probably be talking about the wall screen in the den, family room, or office. It will become the primary way we watch TV, play video games, and communicate with one another face to face—in real time, anywhere in the world (see Chapter 3).

If ubiquitous computing gurus are correct, then your future home—the furniture, appliances, and nearly every chip-laden object in it—will be activated when you walk inside. Perhaps triggered by a personal chip on your body or in your clothes, your home will "recognize" you. Without your lifting a finger, your presence will signal the household network to turn on the lights, set the temperature to your preference, perhaps route any important calls and E-mails to a screen in the room. Sounds ridiculous, doesn't it? Just as walking into a room, turning on an electric lamp, and tuning in to a magic electric picture box for the latest news headlines from CNN would have sounded ridiculous one hundred years ago.

COMPUTERS AS TOOLS

If computers will be capable of doing all this for us in the future, it's no wonder that so many technology experts want to put the PC out of business. Ubiquitous computing will mean devices that are for the most part small, cheap, mobile, and easy to use—in short, everything today's PC is not. You may be comfortable sitting down in front of a computer, but if you stop to think about it, even the most basic computing tasks are not as simple and natural as turning on a TV or dialing the phone. With keys, passwords, software programs, Internet URLs, etc., using a computer requires a level of skill that is somewhere in between programming a VCR and flying a 747.

Think about a simple computer task like reading your E-mail. You have to turn on your computer, wait a minute or more for the operating system to boot up, dial up your Internet service provider with a modem to get on to the Net, open your web browser or E-mail program to get your mail. If that doesn't sound so hard, it's only because you've gotten used to it. How much simpler would it be to just walk up to your computer—or a device that is designed to do nothing but send and receive E-mail—and say, "Gimme my E-mail," and have it appear on screen? Or even have it read your messages to you out loud?

Right now, using a computer is an event. But for computers to become truly ubiquitous, we will have to stop planning our lives around them and start thinking of them as simple tools. Most kitchens have entire drawers full of tools—knives, forks, and spoons, for example. You don't think about them. You just open a drawer, and there they are, ready to use. Computers today can't compare with the simplicity and ease of use of common household tools. The way a computer works now, you'd have to boot it up, open up Fork 2.0 if you needed a fork, then multitask and run Knife 3.1 if you wanted to cut your food. You want a spoon? Was that a spoon for Windows or the Mac?

Computer experts like Bregman want using a computer to be as natural and automatic as using that knife and fork. "That's a very different view of tools than we have today," he says. "When we build a PC today we say, 'Well, it's got to do everything.' It's like a Swiss Army knife, because we don't know what you're going to use it for. You're going to decide which blade to pull out. You're going to decide what application to load," says Bregman. "Therefore we have to make it a platform, as opposed to a product."

The change from a platform to a tool will take place slowly over the next several years, but it's already underway. The first change will be in how we interact with computers. Today, where there's a computer, there's a keyboard. Within a very few years, however, we will communicate with our computers primarily by speech and gestures. Voice recognition technologies have been in development for years. And a lot of progress has been made since the days when you said, "Recognize speech," and the computer wrote, "Wreck a nice beach."

IBM and others are getting closer to the goal that could mark the beginning of the end of the keyboard: computers that understand "natural language." Today's speech recognition programs don't have very big vocabularies. And. They. Require. You. To. Take. Long. Annoying. Pauses. Between. Words. Natural language voice recognition, which should become widely available in the first decade of the twenty-first century, will let you talk the way you do normally. Your computer won't have to train you to speak. It will have to learn the way you talk. "Speech is not just the future of Windows," Microsoft chairman Bill Gates said a few years ago, "but the future of computing itself."

Like beepers and cell phones, speech recognition represents a move toward ubiquitous computing, since it frees us to do other things while using a computer. Eventually, a few decades from now, even voice recognition may prove unsatisfying. Unless you want to walk around the house talking to desk lamps and appliances, computers will have to get smart enough to anticipate what we want when we want it. How hard should that be? A good restaurant waiter knows when you want your glass refilled or your plate taken away. Why can't a computer do the same thing?

Some scientists at the far edge of ubiquitous computing research imagine a network that will be able to sense that you've had a stressful day. If you like to relax with a warm bath and a cup of tea, it will learn your habits and have those things ready for you when you walk in the door. "The home of the future is not a vision of dials and buttons," predicts Neil Gershenfeld in his book *When Things Start to Think*. "It is an environment in which the objects that surround you have an awareness."

CHEAP CHIPS AND SMART NETWORKS

At the heart of every computer is something called a microprocessor, which controls the machine. In the same way that motors got smaller, cheaper, and more powerful over time, microprocessors have done the same thing since they were invented in the 1970s. In fact, there's even a formula called Moore's Law that says the power of microchips will double every eighteen months, while the price of all that computing muscle will continue to fall. It's named after Gordon Moore, the former chairman of computer chip maker Intel, who noticed back in the computer Stone Age (1965) that the number of transistors per square inch of a microchip had doubled every year since it was invented. Moore predicted that this trend would continue, and it has, for the most part.

Moore's Law is important, because in the real world, it's *the price,* not the technology that stands in the way of the era of ubiquitous computing. Nearly all of the ideas we've talked about in this chapter can be done today with existing technology. But there's a big difference between being able to do something and doing it affordably. It's been more than thirty years since NASA put a man on the moon, for example, but you still can't book a flight there. It would be way too expensive. But ubiquitous computing will happen sooner than daily nonstop flights to the moon. That's because two things that are needed to make it happen—fast and cheap computer chips and lots of "bandwidth," or the ability to transmit a whole lot of data all at once over an information pipeline—are well on their way.

A PC that used to cost more than $2,500 just two or three years ago is now well under $500. Some companies have even begun giving away free computers when you sign up for Internet service! And the laptop computer on which I'm typing this sentence is more powerful than the mainframe computers that were used to put a man on the moon thirty years ago. As microprocessors get cheaper and more powerful, the computer will go underground. And Internet access will come into your house just like electricity does right now.

Think of how motors have changed over time. IBM's Mark Bregman observes, "If you talked to an electrical engineer fifty or seventy-five years ago, he would have said, 'We're building an even more powerful, more compact, lower-priced motor. It's going to be incredible, and it'll have all this capability.' But if you'd said, 'Well, do you think there'll be a day when I can put an electric motor in the blinds, and use it to raise and lower the blinds?' he'd say, 'That's a waste of resources! These are very sophisticated, complicated things.' And yet we did it."

"The same thing is happening with computers. If you had talked to the chief engineer at Intel five years ago about microprocessors, he'd have said the same thing. 'These things are going to be so powerful, you're going to have this big powerful computer and you're going to use it for everything. It's going to be your entertainment system, it's going to be your communications system, it's going to run your house. . . .' Well, that's not the way it's going to work. The way it's going to work is you're going to have a thousand little cheap processors all over the place. You're not going to care if they're utilized or not."

Cheap chips are only the tip of the iceberg. If you woke up tomorrow surrounded by thousands of new gadgets, even if everything you touched had a microchip embedded in it, it still wouldn't add up to ubiquitous computing. In order to make it all work, all the chips in all the devices need to be able to communicate and work together.

Bregman says it's the behind-the-scenes stuff that makes it really work. "It wouldn't matter how good cars got, if people hadn't built highways," says Bregman. "If the roads were still dirt tracks, you'd be having a flat tire every five miles. The infrastructure isn't very sexy. If you read *Road & Track*, they don't write articles that say 'Oooh, they just paved I-5 and it's really cool!'

But that matters. It *really* matters! But it's invisible."

As computers become cheap and ubiquitous, another unseen change will occur that is even more important. An "information infrastructure," the next step in the evolution of today's Internet, will be just as common and ubiquitous, and it will work invisibly to connect every device, service, and appliance in our lives. As early as twenty years from now, many experts predict, all the microprocessors in our homes and all the digital devices we carry will be connected to this network (see Chapter 3) through always-on, mostly wireless connections—much in the way that the toaster is always plugged in to an electrical outlet even when it's not heating up Pop-Tarts. A broad, mostly invisible network of fiber-optic cables, satellite transmissions and old-fashioned telephone lines will mean you are "wired" at virtually every moment, no matter where you are.

In order for this information infrastructure to work, says Bregman, it will have to be seamless and smart. "Not because you want to make the device dumb or assume that the user is dumb," he says. "But you want to relieve the user of having to worry about the thing." Today, he says, the infrastructure of the Internet isn't all that smart. Think of all the work you have to do just to get on line. A smart infrastructure, he predicts, will be as simple to use as a telephone. "I can go to Home Depot and buy any telephone, *any* telephone, plug it in and *it works.* It's amazing," notes Bregman. "The same thing is true for cars. They all take the same gas. So I don't have to worry if I pull into a gas station: 'Oh, does this work for GM cars? No, it's only for Volvo.' That's now how the computer industry works today. To build the infrastructure to have a single standard for gasoline, and gas tanks that all have the same nozzles, that's pretty boring. But it's really important."

If Bregman is correct and we end up with a single standard for all our digital gadgetry, it will mean that every device in the ubiquitous computing universe will recognize every other device—just like every appliance you own works in every electric wall outlet in the country. Just plug it in. Your digital television will work with your digital camera. Your refrigerator will work with your computerized shoes. The network in your house will recognize the computer in your car, so that when you drive up, it will automatically open the door and turn on the lights. It will all be simple, easy and seamless. It has to be, otherwise people will never use it. Don't forget, this is still a country whose VCRs are flashing on *12:00!* Actually, the network in the smart home of the future could even solve *that* problem. Every clock in the house, including the VCR, will synchronize itself with the network, which will read the time from an atomic clock on the World Wide Web.

We'll talk more about what it will be like to live in a wired world in Chapter 3.

WHEN COMPUTERS RUN OUR LIVES

At this point, it might be a good idea to take a step back and ask why all this is happening. Why do we need all these gadgets anyway? Maybe your life is perfectly fine without a computerized mug that senses when you want a cup of java and tells Mr. Coffee to get busy. Even if you're not a computerphobe, you might read all about the future of ubiquitous computing and think, "Wait! Stop! I don't want all these computers gumming up my life. It's too complicated!" The point of ubiquitous computing is not to make us slaves to technology, but exactly the opposite. It's to make our computer technology evolve to the point that it pretty much takes care of itself, without us having to worry about it all.

"We do become kind of dependent on computers," observes MIT professor Neil Gershenfeld. "But the World Wide Web is designed around people sitting by themselves typing at a desk. If you think about computing, that's what it forces you to do—either you use the computer or you live the rest of your life." Most people agree that computers are pretty much an irreversible way of life for most of us now. If that's the way it has to be, then ubiquitous computing is all about getting us out of our chairs, away from the computer screen and back to the rest of our lives. Far from being complicated and intrusive, the digital devices and service in our future will effortlessly perform simple chores that free us to do other things. In other words, computers will be like shoes.

When you think about it, shoes are an amazing technological breakthrough. Imagine how difficult life would be if you didn't have shoes. You have much more time to focus on other things because of how easy shoes make it to get around.

In fact, computers will end up *so* ubiquitous that you might one day wind up walking around with one *in your shoes.* Gershenfeld predicts that wearable units are the obvious next step in the evolution of computers. First there was the giant "mainframe," locked away in a distant room. "Then came mini-computers, which could be shared by one workgroup," he says. "From there came the PC, a computer used by a single person. . . .Wearables finally let a computer come to its user rather than vice versa." Eventually we will even end up wearing them in our clothes, if not embedded right in our bodies. Everything that runs on electricity will have a microchip. Once we get used to having instant information and communications, the idea of going out without being wired may seem as strange as walking out the front door without clothes.

So far, most wearable computers have been laboratory prototypes—machines with big, goofy-looking, head-mounted displays or helmets that make their users look like cyborgs. While these have been fun to experiment with, very few people would be willing to wear one to school or work. Maybe for Halloween, but that's about it. But the next decade will likely see a new generation of wearables that are lighter, smarter, and less embarrassing to be seen in. The goal, like everything else with ubiquitous computing, is to come up with a design that only the wearer knows is a computer. For example, there are already early models of wearable computers that respond to voice commands (no keyboard to tote around) and display the computer screen on the inside of a pair of eyeglasses. You won't look cross-eyed trying to focus on the inside of your glasses. The display is built so that the screen appears to float about a foot and a half in front of your face. Turn the display off, and they go back to being an ordinary pair of glasses.

The first uses of practical wearable computers probably will not be as fashion statements among the wired elite, but in work settings. Imagine a builder being able to consult an architect's plans for a new house while handling tools, or a delivery driver checking your address on a map while he drives down the street. Anyone who needs access to a lot of data while moving around could benefit from a wearable computer. If you get pulled over by the cops years from now, the police officer might be able to call up your driving record on the inside of his glasses while looking at your license and registration.

Rosalind Picard, a professor at the Massachusetts Institute of Technology's Media Laboratory, has been working on wearable computers for years. She has described a wearable that would be always on and focused on what the user is looking at, recording everything he or she sees. You could fall asleep in class and play back the whole lecture later. Business people could keep perfect records of what is said at important meetings. Wearable computers could even reduce crime. You'd never have to worry about two eyewitnesses with different memories of an accident or a crime. They'd just play back what they saw.

Actually, that's one of the problems with wearable computers. Many people find the idea of always being hooked up to a machine or recording every waking moment—or *being* recorded—a little creepy. But many experts expect the idea to be adopted over time. Like a lot of other future computer ideas, it will take a while before people accept the idea of walking around attached to computers. But many of us already do. If you carry a beeper, a cell phone, or a Palm Pilot, you're already a wearable computer user.

The sky's the limit for wearables. Researchers at the MIT Media Lab have tinkered with T-shirts embedded with sensors for soldiers to wear into battle. The shirts would tell a medic how badly the wearer is injured. Someday, when you put on your shoes in the morning it might be like having a medical examination. A computer will monitor all your vital signs. "The computer will be part of your clothing and your jewelry," says Picard. "If you want to have a video teleconference, you really could call it up on your watch or on a display that projects directly onto your eyeglasses."

Peter Cochrane, the head of research at British Telecommunications Laboratories, imagines you will one day go to work with not just a wearable computer but what he calls a "wearable office" combining a personal computer, telephone, personal digital assistant, and a head-mounted screen with high-definition video inputs beamed directly into your eye. The idea is not as silly—or as painful—as it may sound. Technology tends to move in one direction, from big to small. Clocks, for example, have evolved over the years from giant pieces of furniture to something you strap on your wrist. Why not shrink everything else we need to the same scale? The problem isn't miniaturization—it's finding a power source to run all these devices and keep us truly mobile. Cochrane's solution? "Sitting still, we radiate approximately sixty watts from our torsos and heads, he writes. "When animated, this can exceed one hundred watts and is a potential power source to drive an office you wear. We are our own power station."

It's going to take years, perhaps decades, before the full promise of ubiquitous computing is achieved. It simply won't do to have computers be sorta, kinda ubiquitous. What if your shoes have a computer, for example, but you want to wear sneakers today, and they don't have computer chips? We won't have true ubiquitous computing until *everything* is wired and it's 100 percent trouble free. Nobody is going to spend forty-five minutes on the phone with a technical support person because they can't get their shoes to work, or their boots to boot up.

NATURAL INTERACTION

In a small, windowless room on the 1st floor of IBM's T. J. Watson Research Center in Yorktown Heights, New York, Mark Lucente is waving his arms and talking to the wall. "Put a shape there. Make it this big. Change the color. Make it bigger. Make it smaller. Change its shape. Make it spin."

No, he's not talking to himself. As he's speaking, a series of geometric shapes come alive on a screen across the room, dancing, spinning, and changing colors as he points, gestures, and issues commands. Lucente is demonstrating the future of "multimodal" computing—natural interaction computers you can use without ever touching a keyboard or reading a manual.

"Give me the world," he says, and a globe appears on the screen. "Make it spin," he commands, and it begins to rotate. "Put it there," he says pointing to the right-hand side of the screen. The globe does exactly as it's told. Lucente points again: "Put a small planet there," and another world appears alongside the spinning globe. He holds his hands a few feet apart. "Make it this big," he says. Suddenly there are two Earths: one big, one small.

Using a video camera, a microphone, and voice recognition software, Lucente has created this computer system, which he calls Dreamspace. It listens to his commands and recognizes simple gestures. "The idea is that I want to be able to interact with visual stuff, but I don't want to have to use a keyboard," says Lucente. "I don't want to *have* to do anything. I want to do it just like I would interact with a person. I want to be able to say, 'Hey, show me this. Show me that.'"

The ability to make a computer recognize not just words but gestures hints at a future where computing is truly universal. "I'm controlling this stuff just by talking and pointing and walking around," says Lucente. "There are billions of people in the world who don't use computers, many of whom say, 'I don't like computers. I don't know how to use them. Natural interaction means that they already do know how to use them." Gestures like pointing, he notes, are nearly universal. Almost everyone does it and understands it.

"Show me the Gulf of Mexico," Lucente commands, and the spinning globe stops at the Gulf. "If I'm a kid learning about the Gulf of Mexico, I can say, 'Hey, what's that over there?' And as I'm moving around the room, I'm moving around the Gulf of Mexico. It interprets your motion as a request to look at things from a different direction."

Speaking, pointing, and gesturing at Lucente's setup feels surprisingly natural. "When you move your hands around, you're not touching anything. And you're not looking at any *thing* either. You're looking at virtual things," Lucente reminds me. "You're moving around things that don't exist without touching anything. That's why I call it Dreamspace. It turns out that people are good at moving things around that don't exist without touching anything. It's called dreaming. It's called imagining. It's fun. It seems like a natural thing."

"The idea of a desktop computer is kind of ridiculous. The idea of a *desk* is kind of ridiculous," says Lucente. "Why do you need a desk? To hold up your computer."

Natural interaction is a vision shared by Neil Gershenfeld, who was Lucente's colleague at MIT before he came to IBM. Once the notion of a computer as a box with a screen on a desk goes away, our physical environment and virtually every object we touch could become our interface with computers. "Then you can live your life and interact with people," says Gershenfeld. "It allows you to be human but not chained to the computer."

And what of the personal computer? What will become of

Oops!

THE DUMBEST PREDICTIONS EVER MADE ABOUT COMPUTERS

I think there is a world market for maybe five computers.
—Thomas Watson, chairman of IBM, 1943

Computers in the future may have only 1,000 vacuum tubes and perhaps weigh no more than 1.5 tons.
—*Popular Mechanics* magazine, 1949

640K (of memory) ought to be enough for anybody.
—Microsoft founder Bill Gates,1981

There is no reason why anyone would want a computer in their home.
—Ken Olson, president and founder of Digital Equipment Corporation, 1977

Twenty years later, Digital Equipment was bought by Compaq, the number-one seller of personal computers.

the machine that transformed so many lives in the eighties and nineties? Depends on whom you ask. Some experts think that by the year 2020 or even sooner, the PC will move from the desktop to the museum. A few diehards might still sit with their faces eighteen inches from a computer monitor, pecking away at the keys, the way some old-timers cling to typewriters today. But for the rest of us, the days of Windows—or the Mac desktop—as our primary interface with a computer are numbered.

"The world," says Gershenfeld, "is the next interface."

ARTIFICIAL INTELLIGENCE

The most remarkable wearable computer yet designed weighs about three pounds, has the ability to process billions and billions of bits of information simultaneously, and it's housed inside a custom-built case covered with hair. Hair? Yes, the most advanced computer ever made is the brain that resides inside your head. Right now, even the most advanced computer can't come close to matching its raw processing power. But the computer is catching up fast. And many experts believe computers will far surpass the human brain a few decades down the road. The result will be computers that "think" very much like we do.

A branch of computer science called artificial intelligence is working to create computers that mimic your brain by processing information in the same way human beings do—by understanding spoken language, for example. Or identifying objects by sight and sound. Thinking machines are among the most common science-fiction fantasies, from R2D2 and C3PO of Star Wars fame to the character Data on *Star Trek*. And in recent years, life has begun imitating art as real-life examples of artificial intelligence prove better and better at out-thinking human beings.

In 1997, for example, World Chess champion Garry Kasparov lost a chess match to Deep Blue, a chess-playing IBM supercomputer built to evaluate 200 million possible moves per second. Afterward, Kasparov said he felt like he had "the fate of all humanity on [his] shoulders." Crude forms of artificial intelligence have begun to appear on the Internet. So-called chatterbots are software programs designed to respond to typed questions from users.

Within the next few years, don't be surprised if a more sophisticated form of a chatterbot picks up the phone when you dial 411 for information, or call a customer-service hotline. The investment firm Charles Schwab & Co., for example, is reportedly working on a chatterbot that would give its customers advice on how to invest their money. Chatterbots technically are not a true form of artificial intelligence. They listen to questions and, using sophisticated speech and language pattern recognition programs, mimic human responses.

The true breakthrough in artificial intelligence will come when a machine successfully passes the Turing test. British mathematician Alan Turing wrote a famous article in 1950 in which he suggested that when a person was unable to tell the difference between a computer's responses and a human's, the machine could then be considered intelligent. Fifty years ago, he predicted that by "the end of the century the use of words and general educated opinion will have altered so much that one will be able to speak of machines thinking without expecting to be contradicted."

Can machines really think? Or, as in the case of Deep Blue, can they merely perform so many calculations of so many variables so quickly that they give the illusion of thinking? Many computer experts insist that since chess is all about computations—figuring out the advantages and disadvantages of various moves—playing chess is child's play for a computer. A better test of artificial intelligence, they say, *would* be child's play—telling a story.

Selmer Bringsjord, director of the Minds and Machines Laboratory and Program at Rensselaer Polytechnic Institute in Troy, New York, is working on a program called Brutus1, which is a computer designed to write stories. Bringsjord's work has led him to believe that true artificial intelligence—machines that not only think but understand and feel—may not be possible. "It is clear from our work that to tell a truly compelling story, a machine would need to understand the inner lives of his or her characters," he says. "Future robots may exhibit much of the behavior of persons, but none of these robots will ever be a person; their inner life will be as empty as a rock's."

That may be true today, but other experts disagree. Ultimately, some believe artificial intelligence will become so advanced that the line between humans and computers will begin to get blurry about fifty years from now—a possibility we'll look at in Chapter 3.

Want to Know More about the Future of Computers?

On the Web:

- IBM Research (www.research.ibm.com/home.html)
- MIT Media Laboratory (www.media.mit.edu/)
- Ubiquitous Computing Page (www.ubiq.com/hypertext/weiser/UbiHome.html)
- Wearable Computers (http://wearcam.org/)

At the Library:

- *When Things Start to Think,* by Neil Gershenfeld (Henry Holt, 1999)
- *Being Digital,* by Nicholas Negroponte (Knopf, 1995)
- *The Society of Mind,* by Marvin Minsky (Simon & Schuster, 1998)

CHAPTER 3

Information Technology: The Wired World

Trying to foresee the future uses of the Information Marketplace is as futile as Alexander Graham Bell's having dreamed that his invention would lead to answering machines, 900 numbers, faxes, and cellular car phones. There was no such thing as a car!

—Michael Dertouzos, MIT Laboratory for Computer Science

The great British science-fiction writer and futurist H. G. Wells once imagined something he called the "World Brain." He envisioned it as a kind of "permanent world encyclopedia" that everyone on the planet could use. "It seems possible that in the near future we shall have microscopic libraries of record in which a photograph of every important book and document in the world will be stowed away and made available for the inspection of the student," Wells wrote. "The time is close at hand when any student, in any part of the world, will be able to sit with his projector in his own study at his or her convenience to examine any book, any document, in an exact replica."

Change the word *projector* to *computer* and what do you have? The World Wide Web. Not bad, considering that Wells wrote *World Brain* in 1937, at a time when the PC was a flight of fancy that would have sounded even more ridiculous than a World Brain. Wells showed a great deal of foresight, but he may have been a better futurist than a student of anatomy. While the Internet is a tremendous information resource, placing huge amounts of data at our fingertips, it's on its way to becoming more of a World Nervous System, covering the planet like a digital layer of electric skin. Soon, it will be a live, real-time network, that can provide instant contact and communications between any two points on the planet. Ultimately it will provide both information and communications—and then some. The Internet—and the high-speed data pipelines now being built on its foundations—will provide endless streams of video, audio, and sensory entertainment, information, data, and voice communications. In the process it will change nearly everything about our lives, from where we live to how we live.

Within ten years, many experts forecast, nearly everyone in the United States will be connected to the Internet or whatever replaces it. "Wireless phones will be ubiquitous. E-commerce will be ubiquitous. Voice-recognition software will be ubiquitous. Genetic identification cards and personal digital certificates will be ubiquitous," predicts *Boston Globe* technology columnist John Ellis. "Virtually every institution in American life will be altered by this convergence of technology and telecommunications services."

"There's obviously going to be a ton of implications that we can't even imagine yet," says Web pioneer Mark Andreesen, the inventor of the first Web browser. "The Internet is used by about thirty percent of American households. It's used by about one percent of people worldwide. Both of those are very, *very* low numbers. Over the next fifty-plus years, we're going to go as close to one hundred percent worldwide Internet usage as I think we can possibly get." And when that happens, we will see the emergence of a true Information Age.

Among the changes ahead in the twenty-first century:

- *School:* Education experts expect "distance learning" and the "virtual classroom" to be big trends once homes and classrooms all have high-speed, broadband access. All students will have access to the best schools and teachers, since they will no longer have to crowd into small classrooms to learn. In theory, at least, every student who wants an Ivy League education—and can afford it—should be able to have it.

- *Work:* The way—and where—we work will change. Many who choose to work from home will either telecommute or become permanent "free agents," selling their time and talents to companies for a few weeks or months at a time, then moving on to the next project or assignment (see Chapter 11).
- *Entertainment:* Our insatiable appetite for entertainment will lead to a broad array of entertainment options. Imagine having any movie, TV show, song, or video game available instantly, on demand. The low cost of digital technology will give us a world in which great numbers of us will not only be consumers of entertainment, but producers as well.
- *Politics*: Wired voters will become a powerful political force. In the same way that presidential candidates now try to come up with programs and policies to appeal to large blocks of voters from the elderly to "soccer moms," they will be forced to come up with ideas that appeal to millions of digital free agents and digital entrepreneurs.

For all the hype about today's Internet and the Web, as a technology, it's still in its infancy. In fact, comparing today's Internet to what's coming is like comparing the Pony Express to Federal Express. Andreesen believes the impact of the Internet will be so profound that it will go far beyond the effect of television, or even the telephone. He compares it to another transforming technology of one hundred years ago: electricity. "But it will also be different from electricity or television in the sense that the Internet is much more adaptable to change," he says. "The Internet is a much more dynamic or quickly changing technology than electricity or telephones or radio or television. The implications of it never stop. It's the world's first software-based medium. Electricity wasn't programmable. Telephones weren't programmable. Television wasn't programmable. But the Internet is programmable, so it's never going to reach a point where we've discovered all the possible uses."

Enthusiasts have described the emerging Information Age as a "communications utopia," a multimedia worldwide network in which the distinctions between the telephone, television, and Internet become so blurry that future generations may not recognize any difference among the three.

THE INFORMATION MARKETPLACE

In his best-selling 1997 book, *What Will Be,* Michael Dertouzos, the head of MIT's Laboratory for Computer Science, calls the coming wired world the Information Marketplace—"a twenty-first-century village marketplace where people and computers buy, sell, and freely exchange information and information services."

Dertouzos, who has been promoting his idea of the Information Marketplace for twenty years, long before the World Wide Web came into existence, draws a distinction between the Internet and his vision. "The press and most soothsayers tell us that we must prepare ourselves to enter Cyberspace—a gleaming otherworld with new rules and majestic gadgets, full of virtual reality, intelligent agents, multimedia, and much more," he writes. "Baloney! The Industrial Revolution didn't take us into 'Motorspace.' It brought the motors into our lives as refrigerators that preserved our food and cars that transported us—creations that served our human needs. Ditto with the new world of information. Yes, there will be new gadgets, which will be fun to use. But the point is that the Information Marketplace will bring useful information technologies into our lives, not propel us into some science-fiction universe."

If you are a heavy Internet user—if you use E-mail frequently and spend a fair amount of time on the Web—you are well on your way to participating in the future Information Marketplace that Dertouzos describes. But today's Internet falls short in several important ways. For starters, the Net as a technology is not nearly ubiquitous and accessible to everyone. When you compare it to the telephone system, electrical power, and even roads and highways, it's pretty obvious that far more people use all of those than the Internet. Electricity, phones, and highways are more accessible and easier to use.

Perhaps the biggest problem with today's Internet, however, isn't the lack of availability and ease of use, but *capacity.* In order for a future global communications network to fulfill the promise of our future wired world, it will need to carry not just digital data and E-mail but voice and video—something today's Internet is ill equipped to handle. But that's about to change. And quickly.

BROADBAND AND CONVERGENCE

Here are two words that, if you haven't heard them yet, you'll be hearing plenty about in the years ahead: *broadband* and *convergence. Broadband* refers to bandwidth, which is simply the amount of data you can squeeze through your Internet connection. The faster your modem, the more bandwidth you have. Broadband is the name experts have given to the next generation of Net connections already being rolled out across the country—connections that can carry so much data they will make dial-up modems obsolete. Using superfast "cable modems" attached to the same cable you get your TV signal from, "digital subscriber lines" (DSL) from the phone company, or even direct satellite connections, you will soon be accessing the Internet at speeds hundreds of times faster than today's quickest dial-up modems. In fact, your days of dialing up anything to get on the Net are quickly coming to an end. Like electricity, future high-speed Net connections will be always on, even when you're not using them. A broadband connection can do much more than handle your E-mail and download Web pages; it can make true multimedia—full motion video, CD-quality sound, and eye-popping animation and 3-D graphics—possible.

If you've ever tried to watch "streaming video" over the Web on your computer, then you don't need me to tell you about why we need more bandwidth. The picture looks jerky, the sound and video sometimes don't match up, and all too often, the whole thing just grinds to a halt. When you reduce a moving picture with sound to digital bits and bytes, it's an awful lot for even the fastest modem to handle. Broadband can handle everything from voice and data to audio and video at the same time.

Convergence refers to a whole range of "information technology" services—personal computers, telecommunications, and television—combined into a single digital service. But more than that just making all of those communications and media tools capable of traveling over the same piece of wire, convergence is all about the cool new things that can be done with these tools. We're talking about video on demand, interactive television, videophones, and more. The fat new voice, video, and data pipeline into our homes, with its huge capacity for digital data, will make it possible to combine communications and information services in ways that are not possible today.

In the last few years, massive amounts of fiber-optic cable have been strung all over the place by cable TV companies, telephone companies, and others. This cable is the foundation for a broadband Net. According to Dr. Lee Caldwell, director of Internet technology, strategy, and standards for IBM, such technical improvements will lead to lower *latency,* or delay—something that's crucial for voice communication. "Today's Internet doesn't do very well with telephone service, for example," says Caldwell. "The quality is not very good over any distance." Another big change will be more ubiquity and the ability of more people and devices to be wired. "We're still kind of in a computer-centric mode," Caldwell says. "I think in the future we're going to be more in an 'everything connected' mode. Televisions, palm computers with wireless service, automobiles, you name it. I think we're going to move into an environment where virtually everything will be connected," he predicts.

It's not just the devices that will converge, but what goes through them as well. Because every kind of information will flow through high-speed networks in a universal format, every device will be able to recognize and read this information. "By making everything digital," says Caldwell, "the services, like voice, video, and data, that have been independent now begin to interact, and you can create all sorts of new ways of providing entertainment, education, work, buying, selling, and everything else."

Of course, the idea of whizzy interactive services transforming our daily lives has been kicking around in one form or another for years. A decade ago, cable TV was supposed to bring us a world of five hundred channels, video on demand, interactive shopping, and video telephones. It never really happened. The Internet happened instead. But if you predict something long enough, it's bound to come true eventually, and now, in the early days of the twenty-first century, convergence seems unavoidable. But it's happening *because* of, not instead of, the Internet.

The convergence race is already under way. Internet companies are developing "Net Phones" that allow you to make long distance calls over the Web. Telephone companies like AT&T are buying up cable television systems all over the country and selling high-speed Internet access. Cable companies are selling telephone service and video on demand. And companies that never gave a second thought about any of this a few years ago are fighting like mad to get in the game. Mighty Microsoft, for example, is no longer just a computer software company. It's now a media company that owns half of the MSNBC cable channel, and an Internet access and content provider through its Microsoft Network and MSN Web site. Everybody wants a piece of everyone else's pie, because in the end, there's only going to be one big digital pie.

In a word, convergence.

Like ubiquitous computing (Chapter 2), convergence is all about interactivity and ease of use. Computers are highly interactive. You don't just sit passively and watch what's on the screen. Television is almost exactly the opposite, unless your idea of interactivity is pushing the buttons on the remote. On the other hand, you need a fair amount of training to use a computer. You can be dumb as a box of hammers and still use a TV. The promise of convergence is bringing us communications, media, and entertainment with the power and richness of computers and the ease of television.

As this happens, the world around us will begin to look different. Telephones, television, and the Internet will be available wherever we want via a new generation of wireless devices. Things that we now think of as separate—cable TV, broadcasting, telecommunications, and the Internet—will come through the same gadgets. Even what we do with all these devices—communicate, inform, educate, and entertain will converge.

Several futurists and technology experts predict that many of us will one day carry a pocket communicator that combines the qualities of today's cell phone, PC, and television. "Wherever you have a phone, a television, or a computer, each of those places will have a screen," futurist Glen Hiemstra predicts. "To each screen will be attached a variety of pointing, speaking, and clicking devices. All of those screens will be capable of receiving what we call television today."

Many futurists and technologists predict that we will live in a media- and communications-soaked environment, surrounded by screens and interactive devices that will feed us information constantly. One Silicon Valley company has already created a prototype microwave oven with a built-in screen that would allow you to read E-mail or go on the Web while you cook dinner. Every device will be able to share information with every other device—and with you. As speech recognition technology improves, it is likely that they will all respond to spoken commands as well.

Within the first years of the twenty-first century, it is quite possible—even likely—that your family will start to receive a single "information" or "digital services" bill, instead of paying for telephone, cable, and Internet service separately. You may purchase, for example, five hundred minutes of digital services, then decide how you want to use it—to make phone calls, surf the Web and send E-mail, or watch movies on demand.

When will this happen? Mark Andreesen guesses that the shift will take place gradually over the next several years, almost without our noticing it. "In ten years or twenty years, we will be talking about the Internet less and less," he says. "And we will be talking about its uses and implications throughout our lives more and more. It will fade into the background. When we stop talking about the Internet so much it will be a good sign that it's becoming sort of ubiquitous and we're using it all the time. We're not there yet."

LIVING IN A WIRED WORLD

Less important than the technology itself is the effect it will have on our lives. In a totally wired world, the only thing that will change is *everything.* Before the era of jet travel, most people lived their entire lives rarely, if ever, traveling more than a few hundred miles from where they grew up. A "citizen of the world," someone who traveled extensively and felt as comfortable at home or abroad, was among the rarest and most sophisticated of creatures. But the new information technology, if we choose to take advantage of it, will make nearly all of us citizens of the world.

"Among the people who created the Internet there's a core set of beliefs that our world will be better if somehow we can get people communicating. That we'll break down the barriers between cultures and build a world community," says Caldwell. This is especially true, he says, for young people. "One of the things I notice about the current Internet is that young people love 'chat.' Teenagers really want to be connected somehow. They're developing a sense of themselves, and a sense of the community. Suddenly presenting them with the *world* as their community—not just if they go out of their way, but where it's naturally at their doorstep—I think that has to help in many key ways," he says.

Information technology will transform every imaginable human task. "If you have an interest you want to pursue, you can pursue it immediately," Caldwell predicts. "If you want information, you'll be able to get it almost immediately. If you want to buy something, you can buy it any time of the day or night. There's just no limit to what can be done and the kind of devices that can be created to let you do that."

Ultimately, each of us will live in two places at once: the global community where we work, learn, and play, and our local community, or what one cyberwag has called *meatspace*. In fact, balancing our lives between the two may prove difficult. "The global community could become dominant and the local community could suffer a great deal," says Caldwell. "I think something we're probably going to have to pay a great deal of time and attention to is keeping an adequate personal investment in local community activity."

Another serious concern involves who will be the winners and losers in a wired world. "The downside of convergence is that those who are left behind will be marooned," predicts Ellis. "In the wired age, you're either on line or you're not. If you're not, your horizons recede and your options narrow. Roughly half of America and three quarters of the world will be so marooned."

Others are more optimistic. "One of the things that we've struggled with in this generation is the information haves and have-nots," says Caldwell, who points out that up until now, Internet access required an expensive piece of equipment—a personal computer. "As we get this working across the television system . . . I think we'll be able to leverage more and more of the community," he adds. Then the debate will shift from who are the information haves and have-nots to who are the content producers and who are the content consumers. "We're going to have a different set of issues to deal with. And it's very important that we help young people to think in terms of producing content, producing products and services that can be sold on a worldwide basis," says Caldwell. This way it's not just about what they can buy."

THE FUTURE OF ENTERTAINMENT

"Entertainment will be the first aspect of our lives to be drastically affected," predicts Michael Dertouzos. "Because people crave it, because there are more TVs than computers in the world, and because companies see enormous profits in delivering immediate access to every movie ever made and every concert and song ever recorded. This will be the first major commercial use of the U.S. Information Marketplace," he says.

The generation that has grown up with the Internet, "can look forward to a lot more entertainment. I think that's one of the things they look for out of the Web today," says Caldwell. "For a long time we talked about how the Information Superhighway was going to deliver six hundred channels of interactive multimedia. I really think it's going to blow the top off that. We're going to be looking at thousands of channels from all over the world that will be available to individual people."

You can get a glimpse of what this entertainment universe will be like by looking at on-line radio broadcasts today. Because audio needs a lot less bandwidth than video, radio has already colonized the Net. Today, there are well over two thousand radio stations from 140 countries broadcasting on the Internet. But new bandwidth capacity that's anywhere from 100 thousand to a million times faster than what we have today will be able to handle thousands of TV stations being watched simultaneously. In fact, there will be so much bandwidth that there will be room in the pipe for more than just audio and video. We soon could have entertainment that we not only see and hear, but *feel.* "I think you'll see more and more devices that have tactile response," says Caldwell. "These force-feedback joysticks that people have been touting lately are just the tip of the iceberg of what can be done with the sense of touch."

This fully interactive, on-demand world of entertainment will bring about many subtle but important changes in the next several decades. The biggest change is that it gives the audience—that's you—an incredible amount of power. Take television, for example. Right now, the networks and cable channels treat us like sheep. They decide what we'll watch and when we'll watch it. And we all gather around to be force-fed the same diet of TV shows and commercials at the same time. In a world where we take in what we want when *we* want it—or produce our own entertainment if we can't find something we like—some experts even predict that you will get paid to sit through advertising! There will be no other choice. In a world with virtually unlimited entertainment options, the people who make a living delivering an audience to advertisers will have to go to extraordinary lengths to gather enough eyeballs to sell.

Caldwell also foresees a much higher degree of interactivity in entertainment. "There could be a lot more opportunity for people to add creative components on their own," he predicts. "I hope we can find a way where we can get a higher percentage of people actually contributing creativity and intellectual content, as opposed to just becoming consumers of these products."

Of course, not all future entertainment will become interactive, any more than all sports have become participatory sports instead of spectator sports. There will still be plenty of opportunities to kick back and put your brain on hold. Indeed, some futurists are skeptical that more than a few us even *want* more interactive entertainment. "I don't see us becoming tremendously more active as viewers," predicts Hiemstra. "There's still a big market for passively viewed entertainment, whether you're viewing it on the big screen in the den or on the small screen on the microwave."

Some experts say that could be a problem. "As greatly enhanced entertainment comes to our living rooms, will we derive greater enjoyment, or become lazier couch potatoes?" wonders Dertouzos. "Will we surrender physical human interactions to the artificial virtual-reality cocoon?"

Stay tuned.

WIRED SCHOOLS

When the whole world goes interactive, education will be no exception. Distance education—the idea that students and teachers don't need to be in the same place—will be big. "The last generation of distance education was either correspondence courses or what was called video in the can," notes Lee Caldwell. "I think this time, what we'll see is the ability of students to actually pull up video and information that is tailored to them and what they need at that particular point in time. Drawing on vast stores of video information and other data, and having it come up—just exactly what they need right when they need it—will hold their interest a lot more by tuning it to them better."

Information technology has the potential to make the classroom that *your* children attend—even your younger brothers and sisters—look very different from the one you are familiar with. The world of teachers, chalk, and talk will give way to a classroom where much of students' work is self-directed, and teachers act as guides or facilitators, helping kids research and explore different subjects via computer. Straight instruction of single subjects—math, science, English—will disappear, with integrated studies taking its place. Technology and problem-solving skills will be taught to better prepare kids for the world outside the classroom.

The traditional school year, which was designed over a hundred years ago to let kids work on family farms during the summer months, will give way to year-round schooling, much of it from home or wherever the student happens to be. Perhaps most important, the idea that schools turn fully educated graduates loose on the world will give way to an understanding that education is

Oops!

DUMB QUOTES ABOUT COMMUNICATIONS

This telephone has too many shortcomings to be seriously considered as a means of communication. The device is inherently of no value to us. —Western Union internal memo, 1876

Radio has no future. —British scientist Lord Kelvin, 1898

The wireless music box has no imaginable commercial value. Who would pay for a message sent to nobody in particular?
—A response to David Sarnoff's request to invest in the radio in the 1920s

Who the hell wants to hear actors talk?
—Harry M. Warner, Warner Brothers, 1927

People will soon get tired of staring at a plywood box every night. —Darryl F. Zanuck, head of Twentieth Century-Fox, on television, 1946

a lifelong process—aided by continual access to educational tools and information.

PRIVACY IN A WIRED WORLD

The convenience of living in a wired world will be extraordinary. Everything you want—information, entertainment, shopping, and more—will be available on demand, whenever you want it. There's just one problem, and it's a big one. As more and more of our time is spent on line or interacting with digital devices and services, what we gain in convenience we risk losing in personal privacy.

Every time you read a book, rent a video, visit a Web site, watch a TV show, or buy something, you're making a small statement about your tastes, habits, and interests. Gather enough of that kind of data, and pretty soon a picture starts to emerge about who you are and what you're all about. In a completely wired world, everything you watch, read, listen to, buy, and do can be tracked, stored, and analyzed, revealing more about you than you ever dreamed possible. It's the kind of information businesses are drooling to get hold of. Who will have access to your personal data, from medical records and report cards to your purchases and entertainment habits, and what they can do with that information will be one of the most serious and troublesome issues of the twenty-first century.

The problem is that we surrender our privacy willingly, bit by bit. Visit a Web page, and you've just given out your E-mail address. Buy a book or a video on line, you've surrendered your name, address, and purchase habits. Thousands of people have already agreed to give up details on their income and spending habits in exchange for free PCs and other goodies given away by E-commerce shopping sites on the Web. You're already in lots of different databases from schools, doctors, catalogues, banks, and more. What happens when all of that data gets merged into one giant database?

"Personal details are acquiring enormous financial value," *Business Week* noted recently. "They are the new currency of the digital economy." It doesn't help that some of the people who should be most concerned about privacy see it as a business opportunity, not a problem. "You already have zero privacy. Get over it," said Scott McNealy, the CEO of Sun Microsystems Inc., one of the biggest manufacturers of gear for digital networks, when asked about privacy concerns at a computer conference a few years ago.

Privacy advocates spin hair-raising scenarios about what could happen as more and more of our lives go digital. It starts with simple annoyances like junk mail and E-mail "spam." Once a company knows your tastes and habits, they could blitz you with ads and offers aimed at you personally. They won't have to guess your interests. They'll *know*. If your shopping habits show you're not a big spender, however, you may get second-class service—or none at all—when you call a help line or make a purchase. If your medical records fall into the hands of insurance companies or employers, you may not get health insurance—or a job. We could even see a Big Brother scenario, where digital networks will always know where we are—and where we've been.

Consider the privacy ramifications of just one simple example: MIT professor Neil Gershenfeld's idea of networked "computer shoes" (see Chapter 2). Let's say that the day comes when microchips in your refrigerator are able to communicate with your shoes, as Gershenfeld predicts, so that when you walk past a grocery store, the store's computer, detecting that you need milk, lets you know that they're having a sale. Convenient, right?

If only it were that simple. Imagine that night, while you're at home drinking your milk, you check your E-mail and find a dozen unsolicited messages from other stores and companies offering you discounts next time you need milk. That's annoying. But what's this? An E-mail from your doctor's automated healthbot reminding you that you're on a restricted low-fat diet and that drinking whole milk is a violation of your dietary agreement that could result in the cancellation of your medical insurance. That's *creepy*. What's that sound? Someone's pounding on the door. It's the police! Apparently there was a robbery in front of the grocery store and they're checking out everyone whose computer shoes were recorded in the vicinity at that time. They're *very* curious about you, because your shoes recorded that you made a number of purchases right after the robbery and made a deposit at the bank.

That's downright frightening.

Striking a balance between making your life simpler and safeguarding your privacy will be very, very difficult. It really is convenient, for example, to let an on-line store have your name, address and credit card information and have your purchases sent right to your door. And in a networked world, it's quite possible that we won't be able to effectively decide who we will or won't give our information to. Give it to one, and you might be giving it to all. Says Stanford University law professor Constance Bagley: "The ability to establish a digital trail is unlike anything we've had so far in history."

Want to Know More?

On the Web:

- The Innovation Network (http://innovate.si.edu/)
- Privacy in the Information Age (www.princeton.edu/~kdmukai/begin.html)
- The Digital Revolution (www.rbjones.com/rbjpub/cs/dr000.htm)

At the Library:

- *The Road Ahead,* by Bill Gates (Penguin, 1996)
- *The Death of Distance : How the Communications Revolution Will Change Our Lives,* by Frances Cairncross (Harvard Business Press, 1997)
- *Growing Up Digital : The Rise of the Net Generation,* by Don Tapscott (McGraw-Hill, 1997)

CHAPTER 4

Science Gets Small

The best way to predict the future is to create it.

—Ralph Merkle

What's the difference between a lump of coal and a diamond? To our eyes, no two things could be more different. One is a hard, black hunk of carbon, the other a brilliant, valuable piece of stone that catches light and makes it dance. But if you were able to look deep inside at the atoms and molecules that make up both diamonds and coal, you couldn't tell the difference. There wouldn't *be* a difference.

The same thing is true of sand and silicon chips, healthy cells and cancer cells, notes Eric Drexler in his groundbreaking 1987 book, *Engines of Creation.* "Throughout history, variations in the arrangement of atoms have distinguished the cheap from the cherished, the diseased from the healthy," he writes. "Arranged one way, atoms make up soil, air, and water; arranged another, they make up ripe strawberries. Arranged one way, they make up homes and fresh air; arranged another, they make up ash and smoke."

What if we had the power to rearrange atoms any way we wanted?

Actually, we already do. We're just not very good at it. Everything we've ever built is made up of atoms. To construct something, you take raw materials—wood, iron ore, sand—and work it into parts—lumber, steel, silicon chips. Then you put those parts together and make something—a house, a car, or a computer, for example. Think of how a sculpture is created: The artist takes a big chunk of stone and chisels away patiently, whittling away what he or she doesn't need, until a finished figure starts to emerge from the rock. That's how things are built today. We move atoms around trillions at a time.

But what if we could move them around just a few at a time? Instead of starting with the raw materials found in nature, then sawing, cutting, molding, and shaping, perhaps we can find a way to create finished products from the atoms on up. Some scientists think we can. There's even a name for it: *molecular nanotechnology.* It's an emerging science that has as its goal nothing less than using atoms as building blocks, to make anything, *everything,* we need.

Using atoms and molecules like bricks and mortar, nanotechnologists think they can become nothing less than masters of the molecular world, making atoms dance, sit up, form a line, and assemble themselves into everything from food to furniture. "Science and technology on the nanometer scale is very likely to be one of the most important technologies of the twenty-first century," predicts Nobel Prize–winning chemist Richard E. Smalley of Rice University in Houston, Texas. "It may even be the most important."

When you're talking about nanotechnology, you're talking small. Really small. The word *nanotechnology* itself refers to a unit of size called a nanometer, which, in the metric system of measurement, equals one billionth of a meter—about as long as one dozen atoms lined up end to end. To imagine how small an atom is, think of a Ping-Pong ball. If one atom were as big as a Ping-Pong ball, then a Ping-Pong ball would be the same size as the planet Earth. Or look at it this way: Every word in this book could be engraved on the head of a pin if each letter were one nanometer wide. And you'd still have room left for every word in the twenty-eight-volume Encyclopedia Britannica!

We're talking *small.*

The very idea of nanotechnology is enough to make even a science-fiction writer's head spin. It inspires fantastic-sounding ideas: devices that turn dirt into food, and miniature medical robots that seek out and destroy viruses in our bloodstream. But the idea is based on very sound science. All the material in the universe—solids, liquids, and gas—is composed of the same atoms. Getting the atoms to move around individually is very difficult, but it's not impossible. It was first proposed by the legendary physicist Richard Feynman, who predicted back in 1959 that we might one day create materials from the "bottom up," starting from mere atoms and molecules. "The principles of physics, as far as I can see, do not speak against the possibility of maneuvering things atom by atom," said Feynman, who some regard as second only to Albert Einstein as the most brilliant scientific thinker of the twentieth century. "It is not an attempt to violate any laws; it is something, in principle, that can be done." In fact, Feynman predicted that "in the year 2000, when they look back at this age, they will wonder why it was not until the year 1960 that anybody began seriously to move in this direction."

IT'S A SMALL, SMALL WORLD

One of the first big nanotech breakthroughs occurred in 1989. Using a scanning tunneling microscope (STM), a device that lets scientists see individual atoms and move them around, scientists at the IBM Almaden Research Center, in San Jose, California, rearranged thirty-five atoms of xenon to spell out the letters "IBM" on a nickel plate. It was more than just a cool way to suck up to their bosses. It was very important, because it proved that Feyman was right—we really *can* rearrange atoms one at a time. The problem is that, well, it doesn't really do any good to move around a few dozen atoms. For nanotechnology to become a useful way to build things, we'll need to move billions—no, trillions—of atoms into place quickly. There are more atoms in a grain of sand, for example, than there are grains of sand on the beach. The breakthrough will come when nanotechnologists figure a way to build nanotech "assemblers"—tiny, self-duplicating machines that would make billions of copies of themselves. Armies of assemblers would then manipulate matter at the atomic and moleculular level to build whatever we wanted.

Sounds far-fetched, huh? It is. In fact, it would be downright crazy if it weren't for the fact that there are already nanotechnology factories all over the planet. One common type of nanotech factory manufactures wood for use in new home construction. Perhaps you've heard of it. It's called a tree. Nature is full of examples of nanotechnology at work. Animals, insects, and people all have the ability to make new animals, insects, and people cell by cell. This is what nanotech enthusiasts refer to as the "existence proof." We know nanotechnology will work, they argue, because it *already* works. Just as aviation pioneers knew that heavier-than-air flight was possible because they saw birds do it every day, nanotechnologists see every cell in every living creature as a tiny molecular machine whose job is to make copies of itself over and over again. *Life is nanotechnology.* And if nature can do it, they argue, why can't humans? "Every living cell in our bodies is chock-full of nanomachines of molecular perfection which we are having great fun in understanding," says Smalley. "And now we're beginning to play the game ourselves."

LEGO BLOCKS AND BOXING GLOVES

So what would it be like if scientists could figure out a way to manipulate atoms quickly and easily? How would it change your life? Hungry? Imagine a black box the size of a microwave oven in your kitchen. Throw in a pile of dirt, old rags, tin cans, and dryer lint, set the box for "steak" and hit the start button. The box hums and whirs and rearranges all the atoms so they form a perfect piece of beef? Ridiculous, right? But the fact that cattle make beef sounds pretty ridiculous, too, as Ed Regis, the author of *Nano: The Emerging Science of Nanotechnology,* points out. "What materials do they have to work with, after all, but grass, air, water, and sunlight?" he asks. "Not one of these things looks remotely like steak. Cattle make beef by placing the required molecules into the necessary configurations."

A "universal assembler"—a device that could rearrange atoms exactly the way we want—is the Holy Grail of nanotechnology. The assembler, basically an atom-sized robot, would do two things:

It would make billions of copies of itself, then it would pull molecules together in a preprogrammed pattern. "The properties of materials depend on how their atoms are arranged. Rearrange the atoms in coal and you get diamonds. Rearrange the atoms in soil, water, and air, and you have grass," notes Ralph Merkle, a leading nanotechnology expert with Xerox PARC. "Even in our most precise work, we move atoms around in massive heaps and untidy piles—millions or billions of them at a time. Theoretical analyses make it clear, however, that we should be able to rearrange atoms and molecules one by one—with every atom in just the right place—much as we might arrange Lego blocks to create a model building or simple machine."

That's the goal of nanotechnology, but needless to say, the idea of getting individual atoms to line up and do what you want is a bit of a challenge. You can't exactly tell them, "Sit! Stay!" Smalley says there are two problems that need to be overcome: fat fingers and sticky fingers. "If your dream is to have a little robot that picks up atoms and sticks them in particular patterns, you have to have fingers that are smaller than the bricks you're putting in. And you have to be able to let go," he says. "Since the fingers have to be made out of atoms themselves, they're not small enough and they're sticky," says Smalley. Imagine trying to build something out of Lego blocks while wearing boxing gloves, he says, and you get the idea of the challenge of turning nanotechnology into a useful everyday science.

A challenge, yes, but perhaps not impossible. Merkle points out there may be an easier method than rearranging atoms one at a time. "Imagine putting some wires, transistors, and other electronic components into a bag, shaking it, and pulling out a radio—fully assembled and ready to work," he says. Sounds strange, but "self-assembly" is exactly what happens in chemical reactions, like when you mix baking soda and vinegar in science class to make carbon dioxide. "Mixing solutions in a beaker, a chemist lets the intrinsic attractions and repulsions of certain molecules and atoms take over," Merkle observes. It's possible that the same principles can hold the key to turning atoms into building blocks.

If science ever perfects nanotechnology, it would be nothing less than the greatest technological achievement in the history of the human race—greater than fire, more important than the wheel, bigger than the printing press, more awe-inspiring than human flight, and more revolutionary than the Internet. "We're talking about the miniaturization of everything you can imagine," said Smalley said in a recent interview. "Eventually, we will be designing tiny devices so that every atom is there for a particular reason." This is a Nobel Prize–winner talking!

The only limit to what we can build would be our imagination:

- Computers the size of a speck of dust. Nanotechnologists say it is theoretically possible to shrink a mainframe supercomputer the size of a phone booth to fit into a single human cell.
- Ultralight jumbo jets and manned spacecraft no bigger than a minivan.
- Space probes full of billions of nanoscale robots that would land on an asteroid, mine the rock for metals to produce billions more robots, then begin transforming the asteroid itself into a space station.
- Miniature robots that could be injected into the human body to correct defects at the genetic level and wipe out all known diseases.
- Nanotech robots that would sniff out and purify pollutants in the air and water, spelling the end of environmental pollution.
- Superstrong carbon building materials as hard as a diamond and much stronger than steel, making five hundred–story buildings possible.

If nanotechnology were to be perfected—and it's by no means certain that it can or will be—it would give mankind the power literally to play God, creating anything we can imagine, atom by atom. Some nanotech enthusiasts have even imagined a "utility fog" that would hover over our house to fix a leaky roof, or materialize on command into furniture or any other household item. Or fleets of nanotech robots that could travel through our bodies, revitalizing old and decaying organs or repairing even the most horrific injuries. "Human diseases are caused by damage on the molecular level," says Merkle. "One day we're going to be able to build molecular-scale surgical tools and instruments guided by molecular computers." Will this happen in the twenty-first century? It's hard to say. Many of the far-out dreams of nanotech enthusiasts may never come to pass. Still the promise of nanotechnology is unlike any other dream mankind has dared to dream. It would make us masters of the physical world.

The godfather of nanotechnology, Eric Drexler, envisions a universe in which we have "complete control of the structure of matter." Think of what that means. The elimination of poverty, hunger, and disease. Any object you desired—food, clothing, a new car, a new heart or liver—could be built cheaply by billions of invisible "nano-robots." The Rumpelstiltskin fairy tale would be true: You could literally spin straw into gold. Or steak, for that matter. Control the atoms and you control the universe.

So when can we expect the dawn of the nanotech age? A lot of progress needs to be made before you'll be turning dirt into beef in a box in your kitchen. "The proper unit of measure for 'when' is decades: maybe half of one, maybe two or three. If we really run into trouble, then ten or twelve," predicts Al Globus, a NASA scientist. "The number of decades is strongly a function of the amount of work we put into this. Perhaps a better answer to the question of 'when' is, 'Just before we colonize the solar system.'"

Go ahead, laugh all you want. Just as your grandparents laughed when someone predicted men would walk on the moon one day. "When you start thinking what you can do if you could really position atoms wherever you dream of them," says Smalley, "it looks like a wonderful future."

MEMS THE WORD

Whether we can ever manipulate individual atoms on a mass scale in a useful way or not, you can bet that for science and technology, the twenty-first century will be a small world after all. Already, a lot of progress has been made in building miniature machines. In 1988, researchers at the University of California built a working electric motor less than the width of a single human hair! Not to be outdone, Japanese scientists a few years later built a miniature Toyota the size of a single grain of rice. More recently, Cornell University scientists built a working six-string guitar one hundred nanometers long.

What's the point? While much of the promise of nanotechnology remains a dream, engineering on a very, very small scale is already having an impact on the world. The emerging field of *micro-electromechanical systems* (MEMS) offers a glimpse of what is possible when engineers start thinking small. Forerunners of the coming world of nanotechnology, MEMS marry computer chips to mechanical devices to create miniature tools capable of working with an incredible degree of precision. MEMS are also sometimes referred to as *smart matter*.

MEMS are made using the same kind of microscopic etching techniques that pack millions of transistors on to the silicon chips that power your computer. Instead of just miniature electrical circuits, MEMS have microscopic motors, valves, nozzles, gears, and other mechanical parts. "As a rule, when you make things smaller, they're generally faster, smarter, and ultimately a lot cheaper," Joel Nice, manager at the University of California at Berkeley's Sensor and Actuator Center (which makes MEMS) told *USA Today*. "And this is certainly the case with MEMS. They represent a new level of smaller, faster, cheaper."

What can MEMS do? If the microchips that run your computer can "think," then MEMS can go one step better. MEMS process information like a microchip, but then *do something* with the information. MEMS can think *and* act. And while nanotechnology remains an astonishing idea and an incredible scientific parlor trick, MEMS are already here. Super-small MEMS sensors are what make car air bags inflate in a crash to save lives. And since MEMS are "smart" they can monitor where people in the car are sitting, how much they weigh, and how fast the car is going. This determines if the air bag should inflate completely at full speed, or just partially, offering exactly the amount of protection needed for maximum safety. "Smart tires" are now being developed that use MEMS to monitor the tires' air pressure and temperature. They can also be found as tiny sensors in intravenous tubes that monitor blood pressure in hospitals. But there's more to come—much more. In fact, many experts believe MEMS are the computer chip of the future. They compare the current state of MEMS technology to the silicon chip of thirty years ago—prepared to make a big leap in the next several years. This leap will completely change the way everything is made. "We are seeing the end of inert matter," asserts Paul Saffo of the Institute for the Future in Menlo Park, California. "We'll put computers into things nobody ever thought of before."

Nanotechnologists dream of skyscrapers, made of diamonds, built by nanobots hundreds of stories above the ground. The engineers who work with MEMS have the more practical dream of smart building materials that can sense high winds or earthquakes and react. Stress sensors and actuators embedded in the material would stiffen or strengthen to prevent buckling or collapse.

In the first decade or two of the twenty-first century, you may even fly in a plane that is completely covered with MEMS. Instead of steering the plane with big, mechanical wing flaps, billions of tiny MEMS sensors will change the surface from smooth to something like peach fuzz, altering the airflow over the wings and turning the plane. Scale models of such planes have already been built and flown.

How about speaker paint? Mark Weiser, the chief technologist at Xerox PARC has described paint that is filled with tiny electronic components. "Suppose you're in your house, you bought a stereo and you need speakers," he said in a recent magazine interview. "With smart matter you would buy speaker paint. You would paint the walls where you wanted speakers. The paint is filled with smart matter or chips. It's kind of science-fiction. But we're close," he insists. Other scientists have toyed with the idea of "smart paint" that releases chemicals to douse a fire when it detects extremely high temperatures.

Ultimately, MEMS will allow scientists to create miniature products like a cell phone the size of a wristwatch, and "smart materials" that will go into everything from airplanes to cars. In the next few decades, look for MEMS nearly everywhere:

- Miniature global positioning sensors that will allow packages to be tracked anywhere in the world—no more getting lost in the mail.
- Electronic paper coated with MEMS devices that would change from black to white and back, allowing today's newspaper to automatically change into tomorrow's after receiving a radio signal, or information downloaded over the Internet. The paper could also be used for billboards that change displays on command.
- "Smart dust"—tiny monitors dropped from a plane—that could be used for military reconnaissance, checking for dangerous levels of air pollution, or even broadcasting information about traffic down below.
- Spy MEMS that will monitor the movements of enemy troops and terrorists.
- Tiny sensors that will change color or glow when they detect hairline cracks in the skin of an airplane, alerting mechanics to structural problems long before they would normally be detected.
- Car bodies that would "collapse intelligently" in a crash, absorbing the impact and diverting the energy of the crash away from people inside the car for maximum safety.

Richard Feynman, who died in 1988, imagined all of this and more, forty years ago. "It would be interesting in surgery if you could swallow the surgeon," he once said. "You put the mechanical surgeon inside the blood vessel and it goes into the heart and 'looks' around. It finds out which valve is the faulty one and takes a little knife and slices it out. Other small machines might be permanently incorporated into the body to assist some inadequately functioning organ."

Like computers, MEMS will be ubiquitous within a generation.

Indeed, when computers become truly ubiquitous (see Chapter 2) many of the microchips embedded in everyday objects will actually be MEMS. "Microprocessors defined the 1980s and cheap lasers allowed the telecommunications revolution of the nineties," says Paul Saffo. "MEMS and sensors generally will shape the first decade of the next century."

NANOTUBES AND BUCKY BALLS

While many of its imagined uses remain just that—imaginary—nanotechnology has produced its first Nobel Prize–winner, and, just maybe, a new material that could change everything from buildings to space travel. The "Bucky ball" could be to nanotechnology what Orville and Wilbur Wright's plane was to aviation.

For decades, scientists have known about two types of carbon molecules: graphite, which is what makes a pencil write; and diamonds, which are forever. But in 1985, Rice University's Richard Smalley (the perfect name for a nanotech guy) won the Nobel Prize in Chemistry for his discovery of a new form of carbon. He and some fellow scientists zapped a small bit of graphite with a laser, and the result was a tiny soccer ball–shaped carbon molecule. The molecules were named Bucky balls after Buckminster Fuller, a futurist who was famous for his work with geodesic domes, which is exactly what Bucky balls happen to look like.

What's so special about Bucky balls? A few years after his discovery, Smalley and his colleagues figured out how to get their new toys to roll themselves into long tubes that look like rolls of chicken wire. These Bucky tubes, or "nanotubes," could be the first useful product born of nanotechnology. They are 100 thousand times thinner than a single human hair, one hundred times the strength of steel (and only one sixth the weight) and virtually indestructible. "You can do anything you damn well want to with these tubes and they'll just keep on truckin'," says Smalley. Squish 'em, stretch 'em, bend 'em, tie 'em in knots. "Whatever you do . . . when you let it go, it goes right back to the way it was."

Nanotubes are so strong because, atomically speaking, they are perfect. No flaws, no imperfections like those that weaken steel, for example. Figure a way to manufacture enough nanotubes, and you can create a bulletproof vest no thicker than a plastic bag. And that's just for starters. Nanotubes could be the most nearly perfect conductor of electricity ever known, which would enable computers to be miniaturized to the point where a computer the size of a sugar cube could hold every book *ever written.* Superstrong, ultralight nanotubes could be the "supermaterial" of the twenty-first century, making it possible to build a car that weighs less than the person driving it—and could withstand getting hit by a Mack truck—and spacecraft that weighed no more than the family car. Fewer pounds means that less of a boost—*much* less—is needed to get it into space, which would drastically reduce the cost of space travel.

In fact, space scientists are among those most interested in nanotubes and other supermaterials, because they could usher in a day when ultralight spacecraft make traveling in space safe and affordable. Says Al Globus, a NASA scientist: "If you can buy a sixty-thousand-dollar vehicle and stuff your family inside for a little field trip into space, then colonization [of the solar system] will happen."

ROBOTS

Here we are in the first days of the twenty-first century, already talking about miniature nanotech robots that will build other robots. Did we miss something here? What happened to ordinary, everyday household robots? The kind of robots that futurists of a generation ago promised would be freeing us from everyday chores right about now?

OK, so maybe the future isn't what it used to be. But robots are with us, even if not exactly the way they were envisioned on the Jetsons or the World's Fairs of your parents' and grandparents' generation. Industrial-strength robots are commonly used for building cars and other precision assembly-line work. Mobile robots are used for dangerous tasks like handling hazardous materials and disposing of explosives for police bomb squads. One of the most visible robots in recent years was the twenty-four-pound

Sojourner rover that roamed the surface of Mars on the 1997 Pathfinder mission.

But don't look for household robots to cook your dinner or take out the garbage anytime soon. The problem isn't technology, but cost. "NASA might be willing to pay millions for a robot capable of wandering around the surface of Mars and grabbing soil samples," *Discover* magazine noted in a recent issue, "but how much are you going to pay to avoid taking out the trash? As always, researchers tend to go where the money is."

It's still possible that we may one day share our homes with robots, but not the kind science-fiction writers imagined years ago. Years of science-fiction movies have conditioned us to think of robots as mechanical human beings like C3P0 in *Star Wars.* But practical robots will have more in common with household appliances than walking, talking droids. "If we think of a robot that looks like us and does what we do in the kitchen, we are thinking in the wrong direction," says MIT professor Michael Dertouzos in his book *What Will Be.* "What is easier and more likely to work is a collection of dedicated and far simpler robots that are part of the microwave, stove, and sink and have bearings and levers that can manipulate foods, pans, and utensils." In other words, future robots will have more in common with a washing machine that Rosie the Robot from the Jetsons. "Mechanical hands don't scrub and squeeze our clothes and pin them on clotheslines, Dertouzos points out. "Instead, motors, agitators, squirters, blowers, and revolving cages perform the washing and drying functions. Ditto in the kitchen."

Of course there's another possibility. You may not ever get a robot of your own. But maybe—just maybe—you'll become one yourself.

HUMAN? MACHINE? OR IN BETWEEN?

From a technologists' point of view, your brain is a piece of computer "wetware," a collection of billions and billions of neurons that store data and form electrical connections with other neurons. Work is under way now to develop artificial neurons that could replace our own. Ultimately, some experts predict, we will see everything from augmenting the human brain with data chips (no more math class after your brain is fitted with a calculator of its own) to uploading every thought, idea, and memory your brain has ever had into silicon form for permanent preservation. Researchers at British Telecommunications have described a device they call the *Soul Catcher,* which would capture your nervous system's electrical impulses—including your thoughts and emotions, allowing future generations to converse with you, just as if you were alive.

"The next step is the one where you have a stroke or a bump on the head, and we actually take those little electronic connections and replace brain cells with it," Danny Hillis, a famous futurist, told *ABC News* last year. "And in that case, you could actually think a thought, and you wouldn't notice that some of the electrical signals which make up that thought are actually happening with your little piece of electronics." Ultimately we might opt for chips that would boost the capacity of our brains, says Hillis, not just replace damaged neurons.

While it seems quite likely that human beings will begin to take on some of the qualities of machines in the twenty-first century, the opposite is also true. Computers will become so powerful that they will appear to think. Indeed, some experts say they actually *will* think. "The computational capacity of the human brain is only a few decades away from being duplicated on an affordable computing machine," says Colin McGinn, a professor of philosophy at Rutgers University. What this means is at once exciting and frightening. "Brains are about to be outpaced by one of their products," he says.

Once computers are literally smarter than the human beings that created them, it is not out of the question, some scientists say, that they could displace us altogether. In his 1999 book, *The Age of Spiritual Machines,* Ray Kurzweil predicts that not only will computers surpass our intelligence within the next few decades, but that human beings will someday willingly accept computer implants that give them instant access to information. He also believes that we will one day be able to scan the contents of our human brains and "upload" ourselves into a computer as a way of extending our lives.

The twenty-first century, Kurzweil predicts, will see astonishingly rapid advances in computer technology. He believes a computer will pass the Turing test within twenty years. Within thirty years, computers will claim to be conscious, and, echoing what Turing himself said years ago, these claims will be accepted by most people. And, within one hundred years, says Kurzweil, computers will far surpass human intelligence.

"By 2019, a one-thousand-dollar computer will match the processing power of the human brain—about 20 million billion calculations per second," says Kurzweil. "By 2030 it will take a village of human brains to match a one-thousand-dollar personal computer. By 2055, a thousand dollars of computing will equal the processing power of all human brains on Earth. OK, I may be off a year or two," he says.

And that's only the beginning. "Once a computer achieves a level of intelligence comparable to human intelligence, it will necessarily soar past it," he explains. "For one thing, computers can easily share their knowledge. If I learn French, or read *War and Peace,* I can't readily download that learning to you. But if one computer learns a skill or gains an insight, it can immediately share that wisdom with billions of other computers. So every computer can be a master of all human- and machine-acquired knowledge."

Since we can't beat 'em, Kurzweil predicts, we may as well join 'em. Within our lifetime, he believes we will see "neural implants" that will enhance memory and reasoning, allow the blind to see and the deaf to hear. This may sound like pure science-fiction, but a surprising number of serious people are saying exactly the same thing. "At some point in the future it is almost certain our technology will be able to transfer human minds into silicon form," says Peter Cochrane, Head of Research at British Telecommunications Laboratories, in his book *Tips for Time Travelers.* "It is not too difficult to envisage a creeping evolution toward a cyborg world of partially artificial people. It already looks as though some thirty percent of our bodies can be replaced, artificially repaired, or modified to some advantage." And Hans Moravec, founder of the Robotics Institute at Carnegie Mellon University, places the crossover point where machines will exceed human intelligence at around 2050. "Rather quickly, they could displace us from existence," he writes in his book *Robot: Mere Machine to Transcendent Mind.* He foresees a day when people will "personally transcend their biological humanity" by uploading themselves into a computer. Kurzweil calls this *reinstantiation,* and predicts we will see it by the 2030s.

This raises the intriguing possibility that future generations—your great-great grandchildren, for example—may be able to "talk" to you, interacting with you as if you were still alive. But would you be? If every thought, idea, and experience you ever had was stored in an interactive computer program that would respond precisely as you would if you still inhabited your body, would it still be you? Or would it be just a really advanced form of artificial intelligence? Scientists don't even fully understand human consciousness, so it will be a long time before we know the answer. But the possibilities are very intriguing. Ultimately, computer technology could force us to redefine what it means to be immortal, and even what it means to be alive.

Kurzweil, Cochrane, Moravec, and others see our part-man, part-machine future as a natural, if very rapid, phase of our evolution as a species. "Keep in mind that this is not an alien invasion of intelligent machines," says Kurzweil "It is emerging from within our civilization." And if the idea of merging or being replaced by a robot frightens you, Moravec says, relax. "These future machines are our progeny, 'mind children' built in our image and likeness, ourselves in more potent form," he writes. "Like biological children of previous generations, they will embody humanity's best hope for a long-term future. It behooves us to give them every advantage and to bow out when we can no longer contribute."

Others, of course, are not so sure that humanity is about to go out of business. Are we all going to be replaced by silicon chips and networks sometime in the next century? What will the relationship between computers and humans ultimately be? "I think we have no idea," says Richard M. Shiffrin, director of cognitive science at Indiana University. "People who claim they really know are probably fooling themselves."

Oops!

THE DUMBEST PREDICTIONS EVER MADE ABOUT TECHNOLOGY

Everything that can be invented has been invented.
—Charles H. Duell, commissioner, US Patents, 1899, urging that the patent office be closed

There is no likelihood that man can ever tap the power of the atom. —Robert Millikan, Nobel Prize–winner in physics, 1923

Nuclear-powered vacuum cleaners will be a reality within ten years. —*The New York Times*, 1955

Want to Know More about the Future of Technology?

On the Web:

- Foresight Institute Web page (www.foresight.org)
- Xerox PARC Nanotechnology page (www.nano.xerox.com/nano.html)
- MEMS clearinghouse: (www.mems.isi.edu/)
- Nanotechnology Institute home page: (www.nano.org.uk/)
- Nanotechnology FAQs: (www.lucifer.com/exi/faq/nano.html)
- Paul Saffo's home page (www.saffo.org/)

At the Library:

- *Engines of Creation,* by Eric Drexler (Anchor Books/Doubleday, 1987)

- *The Emerging Science of Nanotechnology,* by Edward Regis (Little, Brown, 1996)
- *The Age of Spiritual Machines: When Computers Exceed Human Intelligence,* by Ray Kurzweil (Viking, 1999)
- *Robot: Mere Machine to Transcendent Mind,* by Hans Moravec (Oxford University Press, 1998)

CHAPTER 5

The Age of Genetics

We, as human beings, have tamed the fire of life. And in doing so, we have gained the power to control the destiny of our species. —Dr. Lee M. Silver, Princeton University

From a scientist's point of view, the twentieth century was the Age of Physics. Rapid advancements in our understanding of matter and forces of nature enabled us to fly, split the atom, send men to the moon, and build our emerging digital world. When the history books are written about the twenty-first century, however, it will probably be remembered as the Age of Biology. We have already taken the first bold steps toward manipulating the fundamental building blocks of life to cure disease, prevent birth defects, produce abundant food—even stop pollution. The key to these breakthroughs and countless others is our emerging ability to manipulate genes, the building block of every form of life on Earth.

Can special foods be grown that will keep us healthy or cure illnesses? Can doctors stop a disease even before it starts? How many people can the planet Earth feed? Can every acre of farmland be made to grow even more food to keep up with Earth's exploding population? These are just some of the questions scientists are asking at the dawn of the new era of genetics. The answers includes unfamiliar terms like *biotechnology, the human genome, genetic engineering,* and *gene therapy.* These terms will become household words in the next decade or two. And no household will ever be the same.

What is biotechnology? It's a term scientists use to describe techniques that manipulate the nature of living things to achieve a desired result. What are the desired results? Babies born free of the risk of inherited diseases that afflicted their parents and grandparents. Food crops that are resistant to frost, protected against insects, and immune from disease. Replacement organs, grown from scratch or harvested from animals, that take over when our natural ones become diseased or break down. Some researchers, in fact, believe there is a genetic cause behind nearly every known disease. If so, the more we know about our genes, the closer we will get to effective treatments for any and all diseases. These incredible breakthroughs will not come about without great controversy, however. Critics of biotechnology and genetic sciences worry that by altering the fundamental building blocks of life, mankind is on the verge of grasping God's infinite power, but without God's infinite wisdom. They worry that we may not understand the full impact of the Genetic Revolution until it's too late.

THE HUMAN GENOME PROJECT

Every generation—if it is lucky—gets to witness an event that completely changes the world or captures the imagination. For your parents, it was seeing men walk on the moon in 1969. For your grandparents, it might have been the day the atomic bomb exploded over Hiroshima. Today's generation of kids and teens are the first to grow up with the Internet, perhaps the defining technological breakthrough of the age so far.

In your lifetime, however, something will happen that has the potential to make all of these events seem small by comparison. Sometime in the next three to five years, a group of scientists is scheduled to complete a massive scientific project launched by the U.S. Department of Energy and the National Institutes of Health in 1990. It's called the Human Genome Project. Every one of the 100,000 genes in the human body will have been identified and mapped. Scientists will then have nothing less than a periodic table of the human body, a working genetic blueprint of a complete human being. Once they have the map, they'll be able to explore how every single gene functions, including the roles individual genes play in causing deadly diseases like heart disease, cancer, and more. In fact, many experts believe the ability to "read" genes and learn which are linked with different diseases will be the most revolutionary advance in medicine *ever.*

What's a *genome?* A genome is a complete set of genes in an organism's chromosomes. The nucleus of every cell in your body contains two sets of 23 chromosomes—one from each of your parents. The goal of the Human Genome Project is to find the precise location of every one of the genes we carry. Every gene carries instructions to make a specific protein. Eventually, researchers want to figure out the purpose of each protein, including possible links to diseases. Mapping the entire human genome is a huge scientific undertaking. It has kept hundreds of scientists in labs all over the world busy for more than a decade now. It's a bigger and more breathtaking effort than the Manhattan Project, the World War II effort to split the atom and build the atomic bomb, or putting a man on the moon. And its potential effect goes far beyond both.

The Human Genome Project, however, will not be the finale of the genetic revolution. It will be the beginning. Having a complete genetic map, one scientist has said, "will be like having a whole history of the world written in a language you can't read." Knowing the location and sequence of our genes won't immediately tell us what each of them does. Years of painstaking research lie ahead to find the links between a particular gene and the symptoms of a disease.

Once those links are discovered, however, doctors will have a roadmap of your future health. Think of genes as nature's diary. But instead of telling us what has happened, genes may tell us what *will* happen. That can be both good and bad. For example, your doctor may discover you have a gene that increases your risk of getting cancer or heart disease. That would be a scary piece of news, but he or she may be able to prescribe simple changes in diet or lifestyle that will reduce your risk for developing the disease. Indeed, many experts believe that genetics has the ability to completely change the practice of medicine from a science that treats illness to one that helps prevent it, a possibility we'll discuss in the next chapter.

DNA: THE BUILDING BLOCKS OF LIFE

All living creatures—plant, animal, and human—share the same chemical structure. DNA, which is short for deoxyribonucleic acid, is the fundamental building block of all life. You have DNA to thank, or to blame, for all the traits and talents you inherited from your parents—curly hair, blue eyes, the ability to hit a curveball. Chemically speaking, DNA is the same in every organism, it's just rearranged differently from creature to creature. In other words, if you could see all the way down to the molecular level, you'd look no different from the way a daffodil or a dachshund looks. It doesn't matter if we're talking about the DNA from plants, animals, or humans. Chemically, it's all the same DNA. It functions as a kind of code, instructing cells to make the proteins that are the basis for every kind of life.

What is DNA, and how does it work? DNA is made up of four different sugars called nucleotide bases: adenine (A), thymine (T), cytosine (C), and guanine (G). Think of those four letters as the alphabet of life. Link those four bases, or letters, in a sequence, say . . . er . . . GATTACA, and you get a word; string words together and you create sentences. Each "sentence" is a gene. All the DNA in a cell has enough "words" and "sentences" to act as a blueprint for an entire organism. The secret of all life comes down to the precise order of those A's, T's, C's, and G's. Put them in one sequence, and you're a human being. Rearrange them and you're a mold spore. An organism's genes carry information for making the proteins it needs to live. These proteins determine, among other things, how the organism looks, how its body works—and sometimes even how it behaves.

The fact that every organism passes on traits from one generation to the next has been well known for centuries. It's pretty obvious, really—there's a reason kids look like their parents, after all (genetics cannot explain, however, why dogs look like their owners). Once humans began cultivating crops and domesticating animals thousands of years ago, it became clear that traits and characteristics were passed from one generation to the next, just as in humans. Exactly how it worked in plants and animals, however, remained something of a mystery until 1856, when an Austrian monk named Gregor Mendel began carefully cultivating pea plants at a monastery in Brno, Czechoslovakia, and conducting experiments in *hybridization*—crossbreeding different varieties of plants.

Mendel studied 28,000 pea plants over eight years, carefully studying their basic characteristics. He crossed tall plants with short plants, smooth seeds with wrinkled seeds, yellow peas with green peas, and so on, in an attempt to see what traits got passed on to the plants' offspring. His systematic study offered the first description of how inherited genes worked over several generations. The importance of Mendel's experiments went virtually unnoticed at the time, but today, he is recognized as the father of genetics.

BUILDING A BETTER TOMATO

Armed with a basic knowledge of genetics, plant breeders over the years have learned how to produce plants with specific traits and characteristics, such as flowers with different-colored petals or jumbo tomatoes. The traits that make a flower red or yellow, for example, are carried in the genes of the plant and get passed on to future generations in its seeds, encoded in the plant's DNA.

Traditional plant breeding, however, is a time-consuming process, done almost completely by trial and error. A plant could have up to fifty thousand different genes, and in trying to make sure that a particular gene gets passed along, a gardener might also end up passing along thousands of other less desirable genes. With conventional plant-breeding techniques, for example, it could take years to grow a new strain of tomato that produces bigger fruits, or one that ripens faster than an ordinary tomato.

Modern biotechnology techniques jump-start the process. Gene splicing, a technology pioneered in the 1970s, allows geneticists to cut small segments of DNA into tiny pieces that can be inserted into the cells of another organism. Using such techniques, scientists can isolate a gene responsible for bigger fruits or quicker ripening and insert it directly into a plant's DNA, eliminating the guesswork and cutting years off the process. All its offspring will then have that trait. When this happens, scientists are said to have used *genetic modification* to shorten the process that Gregor Mendel studied in his garden.

Gene-splicing techniques let researchers create new varieties of fruits, vegetables, and grains with specific desirable traits, such as a resistance to disease and insects or the ability to withstand drought or cold temperatures. Plants can be "engineered" to produce their own pesticides, or to grow in dry or poor soil. The genes that allow a cactus to grow in the desert, for example, might be used to create a variety of wheat that could grow just as well in Arizona as in Kansas. Farther down the road, genetically modified foods could be developed that are much more nutritious than what we have today. Some scientists are even experimenting with crops that have special properties to fight diseases in the people who eat them. Supporters of biotechnology say that these techniques can solve a huge number of problems, from eliminating disease to guaranteeing more than enough food to feed the world.

What's more, biotechnology literally allows scientists to improve upon nature (at least from the perspective of mankind), taking genes from different species to create plants that resist disease, fight pests, and grow in almost any climate. Nature limits the potential for crossbreeding. You cannot, for example, cross a cow with a pig or a flower. You can crossbreed only cows with other cows, or close relatives of cows. So unless purple cows occur naturally or through a genetic mutation, you can breed cows from now until the last cow dies and never see a purple cow. Genetic modification, however, means you could theoretically make a purple cow as long as purple genes are available somewhere in nature. Remember that DNA is DNA is DNA, no matter what kind of organism it comes from. So if you could isolate the gene that makes a flower, eggplant, or angelfish purple, those genes could possibly be used to create a purple cow.

From its humble beginnings in a garden of peas, the Genetic Revolution has the potential to completely change our relationship with nature, controlling the kinds of plants and animals that exist on earth. And that, it should be noted, scares the pants off some people. Critics fear that, by manipulating the building blocks of life, science may end up doing more harm than good. Nature has achieved a balance over millions of years, they say, and we have to think very carefully before we disrupt it by fiddling with the basic blueprints of life. The debate between those for and against biotechnology will probably be one of the most critical—and loudest—arguments of the twenty-first century.

10,000 YEARS OF BIOTECHNOLOGY

You may think of biotechnology as a twenty-first-century science, but its roots are ten thousand years old. That's how long we have been domesticating and breeding animals, cultivating crops and trying otherwise to "control" nature for our benefit. You could even define biotechnology as using living organisms to act upon other living organisms in a way we find useful (This is true at the genetic level only. Hiring someone to beat up your brother is *not* an example of biotechnology, no matter how useful that might be to you). Using that definition, the first genetically altered food was bread. By mixing live yeast organisms with flour and water, our ancestors were actually practicing a crude form of biotechnology. Bread simply doesn't exist in nature. Wine, which has also been with us for thousands of years, is another example. It uses a natural biological process called fermentation to turn grape juice into something more potent. Over two thousand years ago, the Greeks became the first people to develop plant-grafting techniques, another early biotech breakthrough, which let them produce fruit and vegetables in greater abundance than grew in the wild.

Today, your refrigerator is probably stocked with a number of foods that can be described as "traditional biotechnology" products: cheese, pickles, yogurt, vinegar, and more. None of these foods occur by themselves in nature. It takes an act of human intervention to turn milk into cheese, cucumbers into pickles, and so on.

While farmers and gardeners have been crossbreeding, grafting, and creating hybrids for centuries, until very recently, there were limits on our ability to manipulate genes. We had to work within a plant or animal species and use trial and error until we got the results we wanted. With modern biotechnology, though, scientists can now transfer specific genetic traits from one plant to the next in a far more precise way than could be done by traditional techniques. As biotechnology critic Jeremy Rifkin points out, the working unit is no longer the organism, but rather the gene. "The implications are enormous and far reaching," he says.

It's not hard to see why its critics call biotechnology playing God with nature. Genetic engineers make us engineers of life itself. We decide which genes we want plants and animals to have, and which we don't. Our needs and desires govern creation. We no longer just live on Earth. We control it, and we shape it however we want.

Biotechnology is also controversial because some genetic modifications go beyond what could have occurred in nature. Fish genes have been inserted in plants, for example. There are big benefits to having tomatoes that are as protected from the cold as a codfish swimming in the freezing waters of the North Atlantic—no more losing crops to surprise frosts. Still, critics worry about complications that we can't predict right now. One thing is certain, however, biotechnology is already having a profound impact on food, medicine, and dozens of other fields.

The products of biotechnology have already found their way out of the lab and onto the dinner table. Dairy cows are routinely injected with the genetically engineered bovine growth hormone BST, enabling them to produce more milk than ordinary dairy cows. Tomatoes that ripen without growing soft and rotting are now commonplace in the vegetable aisle of your local supermarket. By 1999, an estimated 100 million acres of genetically modified crops, mostly corn, soybeans, potatoes, and cotton, were being grown worldwide. And there's more to come. Much more. Within twenty years, experts say, virtually every food product you eat or drink is likely to be, at some level, a product of genetic modification.

Of course the phrase *genetic modification* strikes fear into the hearts of millions of people by conjuring up images of mutant tomatoes and strange new strains of super-strong plants. Are we supposed to eat this stuff? Or is this stuff going to eat us? The biotechnology revolution has attracted little attention or concern so far in the United States, but in Europe, it's another matter. Lingering fears over mad cow disease and a general distrust in government food safety agencies have created an atmosphere where people are very concerned about the food they eat. Protesters have burned potato fields in Ireland and dumped truckloads of genetically modified vegetables in front of the British prime minister's door. News reports are full of scary stories about "Frankenstein foods."

THE BENEFITS OF BIOTECHNOLOGY

Supporters worry that such scare stories blind people to the benefits of biotechnology. The upside for agriculture and the world's food supply are incredible. If plants and trees can be genetically engineered to withstand drought and frost, that would reduce crops lost to bad weather. Plants that can be engineered to produce natural pesticides reduce the need for environmentally harmful spraying. Just like humans, plants can get deadly viruses, but biotechnology techniques can make those plants resistant to disease. Techniques have also been developed to protect any number of crops from bacteria and funguses that attack them.

One of the most common uses of biotechnology is to create crops that are resistant to plant-killing herbicides. Why would a farmer want to grow such a plant? A major threat to food crops is weeds. Even a small number of weeds can reduce the yield of a farmer's field. But killing the weeds can also kill the crops. Biotechnology techniques are commonly used to produce plants that are immune to specific herbicides. Such plants allow a farmer to spray his fields, so the weeds die but not the crops. Critics worry, however, that herbicide-resistant plants could cross-pollinate with weeds, creating a strain of "superweed" that can't be killed.

One of the strongest arguments in favor of genetically modified crops is increased yields of fruits, grains, and vegetables. By 2050, the world's population could hit twelve billion—twice what it is today. That's a lot of mouths to feed. During the so-called Green Revolution of the 1950s and 1960s, increased use of fertilizers, irrigation, and hybridization of crops boosted corn yields from 20 bushels per acre in 1920 to 120 bushels per acre today. But that number probably can't go much higher through conventional farming methods. Biotechnology techniques that increase the amount of food yielded per acre of land could be the key to ensuring that there is enough food for everyone, greatly reducing the risks of famine and food shortages that have plagued mankind for centuries. Biotechnology also can be used to produce not just more food, but more nutritious food. Rice can be genetically modified using genes from pea plants, to pick one example, resulting in a higher amount of protein per grain of rice—a boon to developing countries where malnutrition from lack of protein is a big problem.

Biotechnology can also be used to increase the shelf life of fruits and vegetables, thus reducing waste. Many fruits and vegetables are picked when still green, then sprayed with a chemical so they ripen in the truck on the way to the grocery store. Genetically modified tomatoes whose gene for softening has been "turned off" have been developed. This means they can ripen on the vine, then be picked and shipped without getting too soft—or being sprayed with chemical ripening agents—on the way. Slow-softening apples, raspberries, and melons also have been developed.

Much of what is grown on farms never reaches your dinner table at all. It ends up in silos and food troughs as animal feed. Genetically engineered feed corn and other crops could lead to more nutritious animal feed—thus more nutritious chicken, beef, and pork. Raise a pig on low-fat, high-protein feed, and what do you get? A low-fat, high-protein pig. And low-fat, high-protein hot dogs.

Indeed, plant biotechnology starts on the farm, but its impact will be felt throughout the food chain, touching our lives in an extraordinary number of ways. Here are just a few examples:

- Food Allergies: Allergic reactions to foods can be annoying. Some, like peanut allergies, can be deadly. If the enzyme that triggers peanut allergies is someday eliminated from peanuts, kids who grow up today avoiding peanuts and foods cooked in peanut oils would be able to consume goobers in the future.
- Clothing: Blue genes for blue jeans? Cotton needed for jeans could be *grown* blue rather than dyed after being picked and spun. Result: cheaper blue jeans.
- Drugs: Naturally occurring chemical compounds used to produce pharmaceuticals can be grown and harvested from plants. Insulin for diabetes patients, for example, is synthesized from the pancreas of a pig. If genetic engineering can find a way to make plants produce insulin, the supply would increase, making it *much* cheaper for patients.
- Energy: Scientists are also developing *biofuels*—strains of bacteria that will consume garbage and convert it to ethanol to run machinery.
- Disease fighters: Lycopene, a substance found in tomatoes, seems to be effective in helping to fight cancer. "Designer tomatoes" engineered to have high levels of lycopene are being developed. Also on the way: bananas and potatoes that can deliver a dose of vaccine (see Prescriptions You Eat, Chapter 6).
- Plastics: Plastics made from plant polymers will replace those made from synthetic polymers, meaning lots of stuff that clogs our landfills—packaging, car tires, Styrofoam cups—will be made from biodegradable substances.

The list of possibilities is endless. Plant biotechnology will mean that plants will be transformed from simple crops to living factories for food, drugs, and dozens of resources. Money still may not grow on trees in the twenty-first century, but lots of other things will.

THE BIOTECHNOLOGY DEBATE

The familiar Old Testament account has God spending days three through six creating the fish of the sea, the fowl of the air, and "every creeping thing that creepeth upon the earth." On the seventh day He rested. But here it is a couple days later, and a bunch of biotechnologists have snuck into the kitchen, thrown all that into the blender and hit "frappe." At least that's the view of some biotechnology critics, who worry that the promise of abundant food and medical breakthroughs—not to mention the chance to get insanely rich—is blinding society to what may be enormous risks.

Much of the work of geneticists involves manipulating the fundamental building blocks of life. And it raises questions that will have to be answered not in a laboratory, but in the grocery store, the hospital, and ultimately perhaps at the ballot box. The benefits are incredible: Biotechnology could help us feed the world and end hunger. But is a plant with fish genes still a plant? Gene therapy could end disease before it starts. But . . . but . . . but . . .

The ability to isolate, identify, and manipulate genes does something that until just a few years ago would have been unthinkable. It turns genetic material, the blueprint for every human, animal, plant on Earth, into raw material—modeling clay that we can bend, twist, and shape into almost any combination we choose. God couldn't cross a fish with a tomato (or at the very least decided against it), but we can. He couldn't clone a sheep, but we did. And not everyone thinks it's a good idea. Jeremy Rifkin, perhaps the most outspoken dissenter, calls biotechnology nothing less than "the wholesale reseeding of the Earth's biosphere with a laboratory-conceived second Genesis, an artificially produced bioindustrial nature designed to replace nature's own evolutionary scheme."

Critics of biotechnology have three main concerns: that genetic manipulation is "unnatural" and therefore wrong or dangerous; that genetically modified food is unsafe to eat; and that introducing "transgenic" species of plants could harm the environment.

The first argument is largely a matter of personal preference. Just as some people prefer organic foods, some people may just not like the idea of genetically modified *anything.* Supporters of biotechnology like to point out that there's no such thing as natural crops anymore, since everything that is grown now has been subject to centuries of hybridization. A rose is a rose is a rose? Not after a couple of hundred generations of crossbreeding, it's not. As for the idea that genetically modified foods are bad for you, no scientific tests have proven that's true. If you transfer a gene from one edible plant to a second edible plant, you get a third edible plant.

The third argument is the strongest one, and it could be years before we find out for sure whether it's true or not. We're setting in motion a process we can't control, argue biotech opponents, and it could do permanent damage to the environment. Insects have quite a talent for developing resistance to insecticides, for example. Will growing plants that produce their own insecticides lead to insects that are even harder to control as they become resistant? Even worse, some fear that the genes that make genetically engineered crops resistant to herbicides could find their way into the wild, giving us "superweeds" like something out of a horror movie. Even Britain's Prince Charles has jumped on the anti-biotech bandwagon. In a letter to London's *Daily Telegraph,* he wrote that genetic engineering "takes mankind into realms that belong to God and God alone." Like other critics, he raised the possibility of unintended consequences. "If something does go badly wrong," he wrote, "we will be faced with the problem of clearing up a kind of pollution which is self-perpetuating. I am not convinced that anyone has the first idea of how this could be done."

GENE PATENTS

"Poems are made by fools like me, But only God can make a tree," concludes Joyce Kilmer's famous poem. That may be so, but God left a heck of loophole open by neglecting to apply for a patent on His invention. And biotechnology companies are taking advantage of it. It should be noted that science isn't the only thing driving the biotech revolution. There's lots of money to be made in all the genetic innovations we've described. And biotech companies are locking in their potential profits by patenting genetically modified plants and animals. Patents have been claimed on hundreds of mice, rats, rabbits, birds, fish, a guinea pig, and a genetically altered cow—even human genes. What's going on here? How can anyone claim to have invented a mouse or a cow or a human gene?

The patent system was created to encourage inventions that serve us all. The scientists and companies that have applied for patents on genetically modified plants and animals say that patents are the only thing that makes it possible for them to do their research. They should get paid for any drugs or foods that come from their work, they argue, or else they can't afford to do the work to begin with. The issue of patenting human genes is especially touchy. As researchers identify genes that play a role in diseases, they are streaming to the patent office to claim the exclusive right to use these genes in treating diseases or developing medicines.

Rifkin disagrees. He says genes belong to the public. Granting patents to biotechnology could slow research and give control of food and medicine to a few large biotech companies. Rifkin argues that you don't have any more right to patent a gene than, say, oxygen or any other naturally occurring element. The patent office, so far at least, disagrees. I guess if Kilmer were alive in the twenty-first century, he might have to write a different poem: "People are born, we are not machines. But a biotech company owns my genes."

GENETIC PRIVACY

Within the next several years, you'll probably buy your first car. And that means you'll also be in the market for car insurance. The insurance companies will want to look at many things—do you have lots of speeding tickets? Have you ever been in an accident?—before deciding how much to charge you or whether to insure you at all. *Got a problem with that?* Most people don't. We tend to think it's fair for drivers who are reckless or accident-prone to pay more for insurance than safer drivers. If you're an accident-prone speed demon, you may not like it, but hey, you don't have much choice.

Fast-forward twenty years. Suppose doctors found out you were carrying a gene that could lead to your developing heart disease or cancer. Then suppose you get a letter from your health insurance company telling you they're raising your rates because of your "genetic risk" profile. Or maybe they cancel your insurance altogether. Got a problem with *that?* Oh yeah . . . big time! It's one thing to be penalized for your driving record, but for your genes? It's nobody's fault but your own if you're caught speeding. *But your genes?* You were *born* that way.

Welcome to the dark side of the Genetic Revolution. Should your employers be allowed to screen for genetic defects in the same way that they now routinely ask new employees to take drug tests? What if scientists find a gene for violent or criminal behavior? Should the police be allowed to monitor every move of someone who has it, presuming that he or she is more likely to commit a crime than someone without it? Would you want to know if the person moving in next door to you has such a gene? Should everyone be required to have a DNA sample on file with the police so they could quickly catch criminals with genetic evidence gathered at the scene of a crime?

How you answer these questions reveals how you feel about *genetic privacy,* a term that didn't exist a few years ago, but which will be hotly debated in the twenty-first century. All knowledge is a form of power, but genetic information is a very delicate form of power.

Decoding our genes could make medical miracles commonplace. But it could also unlock a Pandora's box. It may tell us things about ourselves that we don't want to know—things that insurers, employers, and even your future in-laws might *love* to know. One top scientist has described unlocking the secrets of genetics as "a test of humanity's character." Will future generations deal with genetic discrimination the way people today deal with racism or sexism? Some people fear a nightmare world like the one portrayed in the science-fiction movie *Gattaca*, where the "genetically superior" are given preferential treatment, while those deemed inferior have to settle for lousy jobs and second-class-citizen status.

Genetic privacy is an issue that can hit us close to home. Thinking of getting married? Your prospective spouse's genes are going to be passed on to your future children. Aren't you a *little bit* curious about his or her genetic makeup? And forget insurance companies discriminating against you because of your genes. How about your parents? One doctor tells the story of a woman with two children at risk for developing Huntington's disease, a serious neurological disorder. The woman wanted her children tested because she could afford to send only one of her kids to college. She wanted to make sure she sent one who didn't have the gene for the disease.

By offering a glimpse into our medical future, genetic testing has the potential to save lives, but it also runs the risk of completely changing how people treat one another. One of the most important legal and ethical challenges of the twenty-first century will be setting good guidelines for genetic privacy—and not just for fear that some science-fiction nightmare will come true. Privacy concerns could stop the Genetic Revolution dead in its tracks. Doctors predict that within ten years, you will be able to undergo genetic screening that will tell you exactly the diseases you are at risk for. That would be incredibly valuable information to you. But fears that such information will find its way into the hands of everyone from insurance companies to advertising agencies could scare people away from being tested. "I'm quite concerned that if this privacy problem is not fixed in the next two or three years, people won't want anything to do with genetic testing," warns Dr. Francis Collins, the researcher in charge of the Human Genome Project, "because of their fears that the information could be used against them."

CLONING: THE SCIENCE OF THE LAMBS

When it comes to the future of genetics, cloning is the most controversial topic *by far.* Cloning was purely the stuff of science-fiction novels until February 23, 1997, when the news came from Britain that Dr. Ian Wilmut of the Roslin Institute had successfully cloned a sheep named Dolly. Clones were nothing new. Scientists had long been able to clone mice, frogs, even sheep. But what made Dolly different—and what made the news from Britain go off like a bomb—was that she was cloned from the DNA of an *adult* sheep, not from embryonic critters like all previous clones.

The breakthrough was greeted with awe . . . and horror. The technique, long thought to be beyond the ability of scientists, seemed to create a whole new range of genetic possibilities overnight, from cloning endangered species to human beings. People immediately speculated that if an adult sheep could be cloned, an adult human could be next. A poll showed that 90 percent of the American people agreed that human cloning should be banned. That shows the depth of anti-cloning feelings. Typically, 90 percent of Americans can't even agree that the sky is blue.

"It was the idea that humans could now be cloned as well, in a manner akin to taking cuttings from a plant," notes Princeton University molecular biologist Lee Silver, "and many people were terrified by the prospect." This was news that began to sound like science-fiction. News anchors and pundits began to speculate about wild scenarios that human cloning would create: Parents would clone their fatally ill children. People would create clones of themselves to harvest organs for transplant. Movies like *The Boys from Brazil,* in which Hitler clones are produced, would become real. People dying of terminal diseases would achieve immortality through cloning. There were even fears that cloning would replace sexual reproduction as the number-one way for humans to reproduce.

Such terrifying and creepy ideas drove the anti-cloning furor. And they are all complete nonsense. If you cloned someone dying of a genetic illness, the clone would have it, too. If you cloned Hitler, (or Einstein, for that matter) you wouldn't give new life to the original person, since upbringing, environment, and experience has at least as much do with who we are as our genes. A theoretical Hitler or Einstein clone wouldn't even have his parents around to influence him toward evil or brilliance. Sure, you might be able to create a clone for donor organs. But you'd go to jail for murder. You'd no more take your clone's heart for transplant than you would your twin brother's or sister's. Besides, if it's a new heart or liver you need, there are better and much faster ways to get one (see Biopharming in Chapter 6). As for the cloning replacing sexual reproduction, well, you're just going to have to trust me on this one. No *way* that'll ever happen.

Yes, clones might appear identical to their parents at the same age, but they would not have all their parents' memories. A clone has the exact same DNA as its donor parent. If you cloned yourself, all you would get would be an identical twin born many years later. He or she would be an individual just like you and me, with his or her own identity, consciousness, personality, and memories built from scratch. Clones would not be something less than human. They'd be members of our species in good standing.

Many scientists and futurists expect that we will see human clones in the twenty-first century. There is no reason to expect that the technology that created Dolly couldn't be transferred to human cells, says Silver. "On the contrary, there is every reason to expect that it *can* be transferred," he writes in his book *Remaking Eden.* "It requires only equipment and facilities that are already standard or easy to obtain by biomedical laboratories and freestanding in vitro fertilization clinics across the country and around the world."

The mere suggestion of cloning a human being is still enough to make most people today jump in horror. But keep in mind that many people once felt the same way about in vitro fertilization—so-called test-tube babies. Now, tens of thousands of babies are born each year who were first conceived in a laboratory. Couples who are having trouble having children now routinely ask for in vitro—the very same technology that was viewed as unholy just a generation ago. The strong desire for children—and the money to be made in satisfying that desire—seems nearly certain to take human cloning down the same path in the twenty-first century.

"Cloning is inevitable," says Dr. Richard Seed, a rogue physicist who made headlines a few years ago by announcing plans to open a human cloning clinic. "If I don't do it, someone else will. There's no way you can stop science."

On that much at least, there seems to be quiet agreement in the scientific community. "Richard Seed will never succeed in cloning even a single human being," says Lee Silver. "But at some future point, someone else will—working quietly, away from the media lights, in a very-much-for-profit private clinic. . . . The money to be made will be irresistible."

Want to Know More about the Future of Genetics and Biotechnology?

On the Web:

- Human Genome Project Information (www.ornl.gov/hgmis/)
- Access Excellence (www.accessexcellence.org/AB/)
- The Council for Responsible Genetics (www.gene-watch.org/)
- The Biotechnology Knowledge Center (www.biotechknowledge.com/)
- Conceiving a Clone (http://library.advanced.org/24355/)
- The Biotechnology Information Center (www.nal.usda.gov/bic/)
- Food for Our Future (www.foodfuture.org.uk/)

At the Library:

- *Remaking Eden,* by Lee M. Silver (Avon Books, 1997)
- *Biotechnology Unzipped: Promises and Realities,* by Eric S. Grace (Joseph Henry Press, 1997)
- *The Biotech Century,* by Jeremy Rifkin (J. P. Tarcher, 1999)
- *Clone: The Road to Dolly and the Path Beyond,* by Gina Kolata (William Morrow, 1998)

CHAPTER 6

6

The Future of Medicine: Stopping Disease before It Starts

The human intellect has finally laid hold of cancer with a grip that will eventually extract the deadly secrets of the disease. For the first time in my thirty years as a biomedical scientist I now believe that we will eventually cure cancer.

—Dr. J. Michael Bishop, Nobel Laureate in Medicine

You have been blessed to be born in an age where medical miracles are routine. Modern medicine is one of mankind's greatest success stories, nearly doubling our life expectancy in the last century. Rapid advances in health and medicine in just the last several decades have given us a world of organ transplants, wonder drugs, and vaccines that have all but wiped many dreaded diseases right off the face of the Earth. But if those are miracles, then what would you call treatments where cancer is cured or prevented by ridding our body of the genes that cause the disease? What would you call new technologies that allow a disease to be spotted even before it starts? What would you call a world where living well beyond one hundred years is normal? Where doctors have learned to stop the aging process—and perhaps even reverse it?

What is more miraculous than a miracle?

If medical experts are right, we may have to come up with a whole new vocabulary to describe medicine in the twenty-first century. *Miracle* may be too mild a word. Researchers are promising new treatments, even cures, for a whole host of diseases that have plagued us for thousands of years. These changes are *so* radical and profound that we may end up replacing the science of medicine altogether with something new and different—the new field of *Genomics.*

In the last chapter, we learned about the Human Genome Project, the massive scientific endeavor to map every gene in our bodies. Thanks to that pioneering work, the first decades of our new century hold the promise of revolutionizing medical science. We can look forward to a Golden Age of health care, filled with treatments that attack the underlying causes of disease, reducing the number of dangerous drugs, surgeries, and radical treatments we have to use today. All of these could be our reward for cracking the human genetic code.

When you were born, you came into the world with an owner's manual. Inside every cell in your body was a complete set of genetic instructions. It's all still there. These invisible blueprints not only determine the traits and talents you inherit from your parents, but the types of problems you might encounter later in life. Learn how to read this owner's manual, and you have an early warning radar system against any disease that begins in your genes.

Some experts see this emerging ability to decode genes and link them with diseases as having the greatest impact on medicine since penicillin. "In the next five to ten years, everybody who's interested will have the opportunity to undergo some form of DNA testing to predict their future risk," predicts Dr. Francis Collins, director of the National Human Genome Research Institute, and the man in charge of the Human Genome Project.

Genetic research has been put on the fast track as scientists race to analyze our genes and create new drugs and treatments. Controversial private efforts have sprung up to catalogue some of our genetic material even faster than the Human Genome Project—perhaps as early as 2001. Either way, it is nearly certain that scientists will have a working genetic blueprint in the first years of the twenty-first century. Armed with that knowledge, we can expect a flood of medical advances, with new discoveries being made on what will seem like a daily basis. "We are just now identifying these genes and the proteins they produce," Dr. Bert Vogelstein, one of the world's leading gene hunters, told the PBS television program *Nova.* "Their discovery has become a beacon guiding us into a world that was impossible to investigate ten years ago."

Yes, the twenty-first century will give us some astonishing medical breakthroughs. But it may also force us to make agonizing ethical choices. If doctors could tell you that you had a gene for a terrible illness, would you want to know? What if there was no cure? The same technologies that will enable doctors to stop an inherited disease before a child is born will also enable us to influence an unborn child's eye and hair color, athletic ability, personality, and even his or her IQ. Should we? Cloning humans will almost certainly be possible, but should it be allowed? What if cloning your son or daughter was the only way to produce a blood or bone marrow donor to save your child's life? Such agonizing questions will probably not be answered by government policies or laws. They may be decided by individuals like you and me, forced to make highly personal decisions with enormous consequences. Today these are philosophical questions. Tomorrow, you may have to answer them in a real-life situation.

GENOMIC MEDICINE

For a fortunate few, the future of medicine is already here. Parents who carry a gene for cystic fibrosis or muscular dystrophy can use genetic testing right now to keep from passing the gene on to their children. Using in vitro fertilization, doctors can combine a couple's sperm and eggs in a lab to create several embryos. Then they can study the embryos' genetic blueprints. If an embryo carries the gene for the disease it is discarded, and only the disease-free embryos are implanted in the mother's womb. In this way, a crippling disease is stopped before it has a chance to take root in a newborn child.

Take a moment to think about what that means: If a particular disease or condition "runs in the family," you'll have the chance to eliminate it from your genes—and your children and grandchildren's genes—forever. Such tests can already identify about forty inherited problems, including Down's syndrome, cystic fibrosis, muscular dystrophy, and others.

Tests already exist for a genetic mutation that greatly increases the risk of breast or ovarian cancer in women who carry it. Thanks to the screening, women who discover they have the gene can change their lifestyle to lower the risk of developing cancer, including switching to a low-fat diet and exercising regularly. Most important, women with the gene can go for regular checkups much more often and at an earlier age than usual, so that if they do develop the disease, doctors can stop it before it spreads. Catching a disease like cancer in its earliest stages makes the odds of survival much, much higher. So testing almost becomes a form of treatment all by itself.

Both approaches—genetic testing before birth, and looking for genetic danger signs later in life—offer a glimpse of the future of medicine. As genetic research and testing continues to advance, doctors will almost certainly be able to tell us if we are likely to develop any of the four thousand inherited diseases to which humans are subject.

Ultimately, some experts say, doctors will be able to identify possible genetic problems quickly and easily, with a device much like a computer microchip. In the same way that silicon chips let your computer perform millions of calculations at once, a tiny device called a biochip will one day be used to quickly scan your DNA for genetic mutations that cause or put you at risk for various diseases. And just as computer chips get faster and cheaper year after year, experts predict that biochips will one day scan for thousands of diseases—perhaps every inherited disease—all at once. Ultimately, your entire genetic code may be scanned for problems as quickly and easily as a supermarket scanner reads the bar code on groceries. Dr. Wayne Grody, who runs the DNA diagnostic lab at UCLA Medical Center, has predicted that doctors will soon have "tests and ultimately treatments for every disease linked to the human genome."

If Grody and others are correct, the biochip will become as much a standard part of medical checkups as sticking out your tongue and saying "Aaaaaaaahh." If anything, doctors worry that medical technology is racing ahead of our ability to handle what we find out. It's one thing to be screened for a specific genetic problem, but if, as seems likely, we will be able to get screening for many genetic problems at once, many of us will be emotionally unprepared to deal with the laundry list of potential problems we might encounter. Nobody's genes, after all, are perfect.

Of course, testing our genes is only the first step. What will doctors do once they find potential problems? Besides prescribing changes in our diet and other lifestyle changes that will help keep illness at bay, the first advances from genetic medicine will probably take the form of safer and more effective drugs to treat illnesses. In a fast-growing new field called *pharmacogenomics,* scientists are using the latest genetic discoveries to search for differences in an individual's genetic code that cause a drug to work well in one person and not at all in someone else. Your doctor will someday be able to use a genetic test to prescribe drugs tailored to your body. This would be an important breakthrough, because it would take some of the guesswork and danger out of today's medicines. Right now, some commonly prescribed drugs may only work in, for example, 25 or 30 percent of the patients who take them. For diseases like cancer or high blood pressure, time is wasted "shotgunning"—trying one drug after another, sometimes triggering dangerous side effects, until the right one is found. Your genetic profile will help doctors prescribe only the safest and most effective drugs for you. Within several decades, and almost certainly within your lifetime, you will be able to carry a digital version of your genetic code with you at all times, the same way some people today wear bracelets identifying themselves as diabetics, or carry cards with their blood type.

GENE THERAPY

Knowing the diseases we are at risk for will extend our lives by letting us adjust our lifestyles and monitor our health much more closely. Just like a baseball player who knows what pitch is coming, you won't be fooled if life throws you a curveball. Still, people who carry a potentially lethal gene may feel that they're walking time bombs, carrying a gene that could one day jump up and bite them. Isn't there any way that the "bad gene" can be swept away altogether? In time, the answer may be yes. Ultimately, scientists say, genetic medicine, or "gene therapy," will allow us to go beyond merely identifying genetic problems to actually repairing them. For starters, genes will give scientists important clues in developing new treatments. While there are genes that increase the likelihood of developing a disease, there may also be genes that help to *prevent* diseases. Indeed, virtually every disease known to man has at least some connection to our genes. Ultimately, the emerging field of gene therapy will look for ways that genes can be added or replaced in our bodies to prevent and treat disease.

It's hard to describe just what a huge step that would be. Until now, you could pretty much boil down all major advances in medicine to one of three types: Advances in sanitation and public health that helped rid our lives of many of the germs, bugs, and viruses that spread illnesses; surgery, which enables doctors to intervene physically to fix damaged parts of the body; and antibiotics to fight off invading germs in our bodies. Gene therapy promises to go much farther, working at the molecular or cellular level to wipe out the cause of disease. Gene therapy may enable doctors to treat illnesses by inserting new genes into the body's cells that either correct problems with the body's natural genes or make the genes do something new and useful. We may see a cure for cancer or new organs grown from our own cells to replace old, failing ones. There is even a chance that we will find a way to stop, and even reverse, the aging process. In time, gene therapy will be an entirely new and unique branch of medicine.

"Even though we like to think we're fairly sophisticated in medicine, we don't cure disease. We make it more bearable, or we prolong peoples' lives," Dr. Gary Nabel, a University of Michigan gene therapist, told the *Chicago Tribune*. "Genomic medicine is different. You're getting at the root cause of the disease and you have rational new ways of treating it."

Since cells are so small, and genes even smaller, inserting new genes into the body may seem impossible. There are billions and billions of cells in the body, each one with absolutely identical genes. How can doctors change each and every one? Gene therapy will trick the body into doing the job by itself by using viruses, which have been designed by nature to do one thing: burrow into cells. A type of virus called a *retrovirus* has the ability to work its way into a cell and insert its genetic material into its host.

Some scientists are trying to develop viruses that can be injected just like a vaccine. The viruses would be designed to target only the cells the doctor wants to treat. They would work their way in and insert the "good genes" exactly where they are needed, without doing any damage to other important cell functions. This sounds impossible, but viruses do it naturally all the time. Hepatitis B, for example, is a virus that can find and invade liver cells like a smart bomb locking on a target. The trick will be to develop man-made retroviruses that can be made to focus on the genes doctors want to treat or correct and leave the rest alone.

"Today, if you have an infection, you expect to be able to go to your doctor and get a pill or a shot that will clear it up," says physicist and science commentator James Trefill. "Can you imagine doing the same thing if you had cancer? That's exactly the promise of gene therapy." Researchers on the cutting edge of gene therapy research describe a future hospital where you will walk in, give a blood sample for DNA sequencing, get some healthy DNA made and injected, and walk out cured of your disease the same day.

The real breakthrough, scientists predict, will come when we learn how to turn genes on and off as needed. For example, if you were genetically at risk for certain kinds of cancer, you might be given a gene that would destroy cancer cells. The gene would be activated only if you developed the disease. But since the gene would copy itself into every cell in your body, you would pass the cancer-killing gene on to your children, enabling doctors to turn on the gene if *they* need to.

The potential power of gene therapy is mind-boggling. We're talking about altering in an instant the genetic blueprint we've developed over billions of years! In the same way that vaccines helped to eliminate diseases like polio and smallpox, we may be able to undo generations of genetic mutations, literally wiping disease-causing genes out of our bodies and off the face of the Earth.

GENETIC MEDICINE FAQ

The brave new world of genetic medicine can be exciting and confusing at the same time. Here are some basic questions and simple answers to help you sort it all out.

Q: What is a genetic mutation?
A: As cells in your body are duplicated and replaced, an exact copy of your genes is made by each cell. Sometimes a gene gets damaged or deleted, perhaps because you have been exposed to a toxic chemical or some other environmental factor. When genes are damaged it is called a *mutation.* Some mutations have been linked to diseases.

Q: What is genetic testing?
A: Genetic testing is a way to see if a person is carrying a gene that has been linked to an inherited disease.

Q: Does carrying a gene mean you'll get a disease?
A: It depends on the disease. It many cases, it just means you have a higher risk than someone who doesn't have it. Learning that you have a problem gene is different from learning you have a disease.

Q: How are genetic illnesses treated today?
A: It depends on the problem. A genetic illness like diabetes can be treated by regular injections of insulin. Other diseases, like cancer, may call for surgery to physically remove a tumor, or radiation or chemotherapy to kill the cancer cells. Scientists hope to find gene therapies for all genetic diseases eventually.

Q: What's the difference between gene testing and gene therapy?
A: Gene testing is the process where doctors look for potential problem genes that could cause us to develop diseases. Gene therapy, still mostly experimental, is the name for treatments that try to repair or replace bad genes and get them to copy themselves in every cell in our bodies.

Q: Can damaged genes be cured?
A: This is the ultimate goal of genetic medicine. Using gene therapy techniques, doctors hope to replace bad genes with good ones, and get the good genes to keep reproducing in every cell in our bodies.

DESIGNER BABIES?

The genetic revolution in medicine will be nothing short of astonishing. But it comes with profound implications for mankind that we will wrestle with in the twenty-first century. It means nothing less than holding the direction of human evolution in our hands. What can we do with that power? For starters, parents will be able to decide what qualities they want their children to have.

The same genetic testing and selection techniques that will let us "fix" defective genes could also lead to parents' choosing their child's eye and hair color, IQ, and athletic abilities as if they are ordering dinner from a menu. "It's the ultimate shopping experience—designing your baby," biotechnology critic Jeremy Rifkin, who finds the idea appalling, told *TIME* magazine recently. "In a society used to cosmetic surgery," he warned, "this is not a big step." A poll in the magazine showed that 60 percent of those surveyed would choose to rule out a fatal disease in their unborn child if they could—something that is already routinely done. But one third also said that given the chance, they would like to ensure greater intelligence. Doctors can already determine the sex of babies conceived through in vitro fertilization. In the not-too-distant future, gene therapy techniques could make it possible for parents not only to use genetic testing to screen out possible health problems, but to actually insert "desirable" traits into the genetic material of their developing child.

That sounds shocking, but most experts say it probably can't be stopped. Why? The desire to give a child every advantage in life is as old as parenting. If genetic testing or gene therapy can guarantee a healthy baby will be born, few people would blame a parent for taking advantage of it. But is it okay to try to "engineer" a child with a high IQ? Or is it okay to give your child every advantage . . . *but not that one.* Society sees nothing wrong with the father of golfer Tiger Woods, for example, teaching his son to play golf at age two and coaching him to become a pro golfer. But what if a future Tiger Woods can be given genes for extraordinary athletic ability and physical coordination? What makes one right and the other wrong? The fight for success and for an advantage is as old as the human race. Genetic engineering may mean that the fight can be won or lost before birth. "Historically, we've talked about having children," writes Glenn McGee, a University of Pennsylvania bioethicist and the author of *The Perfect Baby: A Pragmatic Approach to Genetics.* "Soon, we'll talk about 'making' children."

Given enough time, geneticists will almost certainly be able to identify genes that affect nearly every trait and talent we have—athletic or musical ability, happiness or depression, assertiveness or shyness. Who will decide which traits are off-limits and which are "treatable conditions" that can be altered on demand? Some decisions seem easy. Most people would agree that we want to eliminate disease and leave things like hair and eye color to nature. Perhaps it will be decided that genetic screening can be used to treat medical conditions but not for lifestyle reasons or to "improve" on nature. But there are plenty of gray areas. If we discover a gene for longevity, would it be OK to make sure a baby is born with it, guaranteeing that child a long, healthy life? And if that's acceptable, how about picking body type? Thin people live longer than overweight people; does that make a gene that affects body type a "medical" gene or a "lifestyle" gene? Where do we draw the line?

Ultimately, many leading experts say, such choices may be too important to leave to parents alone. "As opposed to every other decision made in medicine, this will involve more than the patient, the family, and the doctor," French Anderson, director of the University of Southern California's gene therapy laboratory, told the *Houston Chronicle* recently. "The gene pool is not owned by any one person. It is the joint property of society. And when you manipulate the gene pool, you need the agreement of society."

Easy to say, but agreement may be hard to come by. Today, most experts agree with the idea of using genetic engineering to cure diseases but not to improve on nature. However, medical history is filled with examples of treatments, techniques, and drugs being developed for one thing that ended up being used for something completely different. Plastic surgery, for example, was developed to fix disfiguring war wounds, but ended up being used for face-lifts and nose jobs. In vitro fertilization, or "test-tube babies," shocked and horrified many people when the techniques were developed twenty-five years ago. Today it's not even an issue. You may be thinking right now that this will never happen, but most scientists and ethicists say it's not a matter of if, but when. It is possible, even likely, that you will face this decision when you have children of your own.

Some leading experts see absolutely nothing wrong with manipulating human genetic traits. James Watson, who won the Nobel Prize in Medicine by discovering the structure of DNA, argues it would be cruel not to use our knowledge of genetics to eliminate nearly every human health problem. Most observers agree that whether or not we like to admit it, designer babies will almost certainly be an inevitable part of twenty-first-century life. One of the things we don't know, however, is the full impact of tampering with our genes. We may discover that by eliminating "bad genes" we may cause some unexpected harm. The same gene that causes sickle cell disease, for example, protects against malaria.

"No matter what techniques are ultimately used, genetic engineering of human embryos is sure to become feasible, safe, and efficient by the middle of the twenty-first century," writes Lee Silver, a Princeton University biologist, in his book *Remaking Eden.* "For better *and* worse, a new age is upon us—an age in which we as humans will gain the ability *to change the nature of our species."*

PRESCRIPTIONS YOU EAT

When most people go on a diet today, it's to lose weight. Imagine a diet that was designed not to help you shed pounds, but to prevent or cure a disease. That's the idea behind "nutriceuticals" (think *nutrition* plus *pharmaceuticals*)—foods that provide health benefits beyond basic nutrition. Scientists are doing more than just studying the foods we eat to determine their nutritional value. They're trying to determine the exact medical or "therapeutic" effects of the chemicals in foods on the human body. The goal is to be able to prescribe a designer diet, featuring highly targeted nutriceuticals, that may be able to treat or prevent many kinds of illnesses.

At some level, the link between diet and health has been well known for centuries. It's long been known, for example, that eating citrus fruits like oranges and lemons prevents scurvy, a disease caused by a lack of vitamin C in the body. Even the grandfather of medicine, the ancient Greek physician Hippocrates (doctors to this day still take the Hippocratic oath) said 2,500 years ago, "Let food be thy medicine and medicine be thy food."

Researchers are discovering just how right Hippocrates was. You might have heard TV commercials talking about the health benefits of Omega-3 fatty acids in fish oils that seem to ward off heart disease, and plant sterols in margarine that lower blood cholesterol. Foods including oat and soy products, flaxseed oil, tomatoes, garlic, broccoli, citrus fruits, cranberries, green tea, fish, dairy products, beef, and many more are being studied in a search for chemical compounds that may play a key role in keeping us healthy.

For example, research at the University of Illinois has strongly suggested that a plant-based diet can play a major role in reducing the risk of many diseases. Scientists have identified a number of *phytochemicals* in plants that appear to reduce the risk of cancer. *Lycopene,* for example, a chemical found in tomatoes, seems to reduce the risk of several types of cancers. *Limonoids,* a chemical in citrus fruits, and other compounds found in broccoli and green tea also may help. Other compounds in soy and flaxseed oil are thought to reduce the risk of breast cancer in women.

Garlic and yogurt may prove to be the wonder drugs of the functional food world. Chemical compounds called *organosulfurs* in garlic may offer several levels of protection—fighting cancer, and lowering cholesterol and blood pressure. Plus, it acts as an antibiotic. Compared to all that, what's a little bad breath? Yogurt has "good" bacteria called *probiotics,* which seem to reduce the risk of certain types of cancer, lower cholesterol, and knock out bad bacteria in the intestines.

"In this generation we will be able to deliver 'designer diets' to individuals based on their own personal risk profiles," Linda Van Horn, professor of preventive medicine at Northwestern University Medical School predicted recently. "We are standing on the precipice of jumping into a whole new area of medicine. This is exactly what they must have felt like one hundred years ago when they discovered that vitamin C cured scurvy."

Indeed, with everything researchers are learning about the genetic causes of disease and the link between food and health, you can easily imagine a future where you will meet with a doctor to explore your genetic profile for the diseases you're at risk for, and a nutritionist to design a diet that gives you the best chance of preventing them from starting in the first place. Instead of leaving the doctor's office with a prescription, in the twenty-first century, you may leave with a grocery list!

BIOPHARMING

When I say *drug factory,* what do you think of? Maybe you're imagining a giant steel-and-concrete pharmaceutical plant, with steam belching from a smokestack into the sky. No, the drug factory I had in mind has four legs, a tail, and goes *Moooooo*. In fact, picture a whole pasture full of cows dotting the landscape as far as the eye can see.

You're looking at a twenty-first-century drug factory.

Only, these cows are not quite what they seem. Cloning techniques let scientists insert human genetic material into animal embryos, resulting in "transgenic" goats, sheep, pigs, and cows. Common barnyard animals with transplanted human genes can be used to produce milk with important human proteins, which can in turn be used to produce life-saving drugs. Clone a sheep or a cow with the right human gene, and you can then breed whole herds, creating an enormous supply of drugs that would otherwise be incredibly expensive. The same technique can be used with plants, which can have the human proteins extracted from their cells. The word that describes these techniques is *biopharming.*

When Ian Wilmut cloned Dolly the sheep in 1997, there was a lot of discussion about the potential for human cloning. But that's not why most scientists are interested in cloning. The goal is not to produce carbon copies of human beings, but to use cloning in the practice of biopharming, creating transgenic plants and animals with human genes that help make drugs for human use. In the future, biopharming may also be used to alter the genetic makeup of plants and animals to grow organs for transplant into human beings or to create foods that could prolong our lives.

By combining genetic engineering and cloning, scientists are hoping to create whole herds of animals that produce medicines for humans in their milk, for example. By the time you read this, the first drugs from cloned transgenic animals could already be on the market.

- Researchers at Tufts University School of Veterinary Medicine in Massachusetts cloned three transgenic goats. The genetically engineered goats were given human DNA to make proteins that can be used in a number of drugs for humans, drugs that won't be rejected by the people taking them. Cloning the goats could mean faster and less expensive production of at least one protein, *Antithrombin III* (ATIII), currently drawn from human blood, that's used to make heart medications.

- PPL Therapeutics, a Virginia biotech company, has produced cloned sheep that have been modified to make human clotting factor, used to treat hemophilia, in their milk.
- Genetically engineered pigs are being developed to produce organs that can be transplanted into human patients. Right now, *xenographs* (animal-to-human organ transplants) are difficult because the body tends to reject animal tissue. If a pig's immune system can be genetically engineered to resemble a human's, then the body may accept a transplanted pig organ.
- The American Red Cross has been working with drug companies to make something called human *fibrinogen,* a protein that makes blood clot, in cow's milk. The goal is to make a new kind of bandage that stops bleeding almost instantly. "We're talking about a bandage that could revolutionize emergency medical care," William Drohan of the Red Cross told *Popular Science.*

Why create animals with human DNA to make medicines? Two reasons: cost and safety. A herd of a few thousand cows, sheep, or goats might be able to produce enough human proteins in their milk to make certain types of drugs in far greater quantities than can be made today from human donors. And with concerns about infectious diseases in donated blood, biopharming techniques will let scientists create cloned four-legged walking drug labs that will eliminate the risk of passing along blood-borne diseases from human donors.

Not all biopharming techniques involve transgenic animal milk. Researchers at North Carolina State University are experimenting with inserting human genes into chickens to get them to lay eggs with human proteins. Other research is exploring getting mice to produce human proteins for drugs in their urine.

Of course you don't need to be an animal rights activist to find the whole idea of transgenic critters a little disturbing. Supporters of biopharming point out that creating animals with human traits is not all that different from what occurs in nature through evolution. Remember that all DNA—plant, animal, and human—is exactly the same. When a gene comes along that gives an organism a better chance of survival, it tends to be passed along to future generations, ultimately creating new species. As a result, there are already genetic similarities among species. Humans and chimpanzees, for example, share 95 percent of the same genes.

That doesn't mean the idea of monkeying around with the genetic material of plants and animals isn't going to take a little getting used to, however. I mean, haven't we learned anything from the movies? (Be afraid. Be *very* afraid). The "transgenic express" was nearly derailed in 1998, when a small Massachusetts biotech company called Advanced Cell Technologies announced that it had created a hybrid human-cow "stem cell." What's a stem cell? It's the most basic form of cell. Stem cells have an almost magical ability to develop into any of the more than two hundred different types of human cells—a process that happens naturally as babies develop in the womb. Put it this way: Stem cells made you what you are today. Every inch of you. Learn how to control stem cells and you just might be able to trick the human body into growing any spare parts it needs, from new skin to heart tissue.

But why create a hybrid cow-human stem cell? And why clone them? For starters, cow egg cells are much easier to get than human egg cells. And if stem cells with a patient's own DNA can be cloned, they can in theory be coaxed to grow into any kind of human cell, with no chance of rejection—the body would recognize its own DNA and accept it. So the cow-human hybrid stem cell is a possible first step that could someday lead to growing replacement human organs and tissues of any kind. Donor organs are extremely rare, and thousands of people die each year waiting for replacement hearts, livers, and other organs. An estimated 100,000 die without ever making it onto a waiting list. But even though we're talking about creating human and cow *cells,* not growing a creature that would be half human and half cow (scientists say that's not possible) the very notion of crossing species even at the embryonic stage is enough to give some people a serious case of the creeps. "Many people are going to be horrified by this scenario, others will say 'So what?'" says Thomas

Murray, director of the center for biomedical ethics at Case Western Reserve University in Cleveland. Among those apparently in the horrified camp was President Clinton, who asked his National Bioethics Advisory Commission for a report on the implications of the technique.

The techniques and the ethical issues sound complicated, and they are. But the idea behind it is very simple. In the not-too-distant future, scientists may be able to take a sample of your DNA, and use it to grow tissues and cells engineered just for you, then transplant it back into your body to treat any number of diseases. And using the same techniques, animals can be made to grow organs that can replace a failing kidney, heart, or liver. Since a pig can grow an organ suitable for human use in just a few months, we may no longer have a shortage of donor organs.

Ultimately the benefits of biopharming may be so great that the "ick factor" may disappear. For all the billions of dollars that have been spent on drug research over the years, pharmaceutical companies have gotten around to exploring only a fraction of the chemical compounds the human body produces. "Almost every pharmaceutical company now has a genomics division," notes Dr. Francis Collins, director of the National Human Genome Research Institute. "They see this as their future."

Oops!

DUMB PREDICTIONS ABOUT MEDICINE

Louis Pasteur's theory of germs is ridiculous fiction.
—Pierre Pachet, a professor of physiology at Toulouse, 1872

The abdomen, the chest, and the brain will forever be shut from the intrusion of the wise and humane surgeon.
—Sir John Eric Ericksen, Queen Victoria's surgeon, 1873

BIOTECH BODY PARTS

Pioneering work is being done on creating replacement parts for human beings without swimming around in the gene pool of cows, sheep, and pigs. The emerging field of tissue engineering is already working to create laboratory-grown bone, skin, and other tissues. Further down the road, some scientists believe, ears, fingers, toes, and complete internal organs will be grown in the lab and transplanted into human patients. In fact, there's a teenager in Massachusetts right now who was born without bones on one side of his body. Doctors gave him a lab-grown ribcage in a successful operation when he was twelve years old—a sure sign of things to come.

In the next ten years, predicts *Business Week,* a veritable body shop of spare parts will make its way from labs to patients. An effort is under way at the University of Toronto to produce a lab-grown human heart. And researchers in California and Sweden have reported success in getting nerve cells to regenerate in rats—giving hope to paralyzed people that they may someday walk again.

When tissue engineering becomes common, however, it is most likely to arrive first in your mouth. Treatments are already available that help damaged gum tissue to grow back. And the technology to get the enamel on your teeth to regenerate may not be far behind. All the genes your body uses to grow tooth enamel have been identified and cloned. Some experts predict that within ten years, the nearly 300 million teeth that are drilled and filled each year will be filled not with silver but by lab-grown human enamel.

IMMORTALITY

So, to sum it all up, twenty-first-century medicine will mean that you'll stop disease before it starts, have your failing body parts replaced by pig organs, and have a head full of laboratory-grown teeth. Pretty cool, huh? Growing old in the next hundred years is going to be a breeze! Sounds like you'll be blading and snowboarding well into your nineties, dude!

It's quite possible. Medical science has already extended our lifespan to a point that would have seemed impossible just a few generations ago. As hard as it is to imagine, if you were born 150 years ago, you could expect to live to a ripe old age of thirty-eight. If you're still a teenager, that may strike you as forever. But I'm thirty-seven, and I'm sooooo glad it's not 1850. By 1999, life expectancy had doubled to seventy-six. Is it possible that it could double again. Could the average lifespan be 150 years or more?

Sure, but why set your sights so low?

"The first immortal human beings are probably living among us today," writes Dr. Ben Bova, in his book *Immortality: How Science is Extending Your Life Span—and Changing the World.* "You might be one of them." He's not talking about our immortal souls, life after death, the world beyond. No, he's talking about sticking around forever in *this* life, in this world.

It's highly speculative, but to understand why the prospect of a much, much longer life is worth speculating about, you need to know about something called the *Hayflick limit.* Nearly forty years ago, a biologist named Leonard Hayflick discovered that normal human cells divide about fifty times during an average lifetime. When cells divide, all the genetic material—every chromosome, every gene, every strand of DNA—gets copied. But with each and every division, the tips of the chromosomes, called *telomeres* get a little bit more worn and frayed. Eventually, these telomeres get so short that the cell stops dividing. It's hit the Hayflick limit. Then we start to age and eventually, well . . . buh-bye.

Ever since that discovery in 1961, scientists have looked for ways to beat the Hayflick limit. In 1998, they succeeded. A group of scientists at the Geron Corporation found a way to reactivate an enzyme called *telomerase.* This enzyme *extends* the tips of the chromosomes, and kept test cells dividing more than twenty times past the Hayflick limit. Less that a year later, the scientists scored a potentially more important breakthrough. They used the procedure on human stem cells—those magical cells that have the ability to turn into any type of cell. In theory, rejuvenated stem cells would make it possible to literally make old organs young again with a simple injection.

Well, that's the theory anyway. Could telomerase be the fountain of youth? Will injections of this remarkable enzyme keep our cells happy, dividing, and young *forever?* Time will tell. But I've already begun working on my next book. It's called *The Twenty-Second Century: An Owner's Manual. What Life Will Be Like When You're 118, 130, and 250!*

Want to Know More about the Future of Medicine?

On the Web:

- Scientific American (www.sciam.com/)
- National Institutes of Health (www.nih.gov/health/)
- Innovation (www.wnet.org/archive/innovation/index.html)

At the Library:

- *Who's Afraid of Human Cloning?* by Gregory E. Pence (Rowman & Littlefield, 1998)
- *The Perfect Baby: A Pragmatic Approach to Genetics,* by Glenn McGee (Rowman & Littlefield, 1997)
- *Immortality: How Science Is Extending Your Life Span—and Changing the World,* by Ben Bova (Avon Books, 1998)

CHAPTER 7

From Here to There: The Future of Transportation

To fully realize the potential of space, we need to create the "space highway of the twenty-first century."

—Daniel S. Goldin, Administrator, National Aeronautics and Space Administration (NASA)

Human beings are restless creatures. We're never happy, it seems, unless we're in motion. From the time mankind first walked upright—and probably even before that—we have journeyed far and wide. Actually, you could make a pretty convincing argument that the history of transportation and the history of the human race are exactly the same story. We covered the earth on foot and on the backs of animals, then we conquered the water, sailing to every corner of the globe. Still not content, we taught ourselves to fly. And not satisfied with merely cheating gravity, we defied it altogether, hurtling ourselves out into space.

Our need for transportation began as a simple survival skill. We hunted for food and gathered what we could eat from the land. When the food ran out, we picked up and moved on. Trans-to places far from where they began. Today, global transportation is a key part of our economic survival. We ship our goods to every place on earth. And nearly every other nation sends its own to us.

The need to move ourselves and our stuff from place to place has been a constant throughout history. But the twentieth century was when we got really, *really* good at it. A hundred years ago (a mere blip in the big scheme of things) the most common vehicles on American roads were attached to horses. Today, our collective odometers clock over 2,500 *billion* miles each year on America's highways. Airplanes? No such thing a hundred years ago. Wilbur and Orville Wright were still tinkering in their Ohio bicycle shop, dreaming of building an engine-powered glider. Railroads were the dominant form of transportation one hundred years ago, while steamships were the best way to cross the oceans. The Wright Brothers' first flight in 1903 lasted twelve seconds and covered 120 feet, about half the wingspan of the Boeing 747, which took to the skies in 1969, the same year the Apollo 11 mission sent men to the moon. By the time Orville Wright died in 1948, he had lived long enough to see his invention play a key role in two World Wars, carry passengers across oceans, and evolve into jets that could fly faster than the speed of sound.

Think of the time we have saved because of advances in transportation. A cross-country trip in a nineteenth-century covered wagon was a dangerous six-month ordeal. The transcontinental railroad, opened in 1869, reduced the trip to six days. By the 1950s, it took a mere six hours by airplane.

Can it get any better than this? How much faster, farther, or higher can we go? Well, strap yourself in. The twenty-first century promises revolutions in transportation that will make the pace of change in the last one hundred years seem as fast as a wooden-wheeled oxcart. Imagine cars that drive themselves along digitally wired "smart highways." Hypersonic planes that could cut a transatlantic flight to twenty minutes. Imagine a world where space travel has become routine. Actually, there's no need to imagine. They're all on their way.

First, a reality check. Some of the goofiest predictions ever made about the future have been about transportation. Just ask your parents. Kids in the fifties and sixties grew up with promises of flying cars, hovercrafts, and helicopters in every garage. The World's Fair of 1964 promised rocketships that would carry passengers to all points of the globe. Personal flying scooters and jet backpacks would take us to school. And high-speed monorails would make commuting into cities fast and easy. More than a generation later, those transportation fantasies remain distant, impractical dreams. You still can't buy a ticket to ride the space shuttle. Flying scooters haven't made it past the Jetsons. The only monorail you're likely to ride anytime soon is at Walt Disney World. And airline food *still* makes what's served in the school cafeteria seem like gourmet fare.

But many of the futuristic transportation schemes being hatched today seem almost certain to come true. That's because they're not being driven by dreamers and tinkerers, but in most cases by cost-efficient technology breakthroughs, serious environmental concerns, and most important, by the potential fortunes waiting for people and companies who can move goods and passengers from place to place faster and cheaper than today. If the history of transportation has taught us anything, it's that profits drive progress.

TOMORROW'S CARS

In terms of its impact on our daily lives, the rise of the automobile was almost certainly the most important technology of the first half of the twentieth century. It completely changed the face of the country, as well as the way we live. The car decentralized life, letting us live miles from where we work and shop. It would be hard to imagine what our lives would be like without a car in every driveway. Likewise, the Internet was one of the most important breakthroughs of the second half of the century. In the future, the car and the Internet will meet on the highway, giving us cars with more computing power than the spacecraft that flew to the moon. Eventually, transportation experts predict, cars will use always-on Net connections to communicate with other cars and the highway itself to make trips faster and safer.

Cars will also be filled with enough cool gadgets and toys to make James Bond jealous:

- A *heads-up display* (HUD), just like fighter pilots have, will project the instruments of today's dashboard onto the windshield of the car.
- A *global positioning system* (GPS) will use satellite technology to monitor exactly where you are at all times, giving you detailed directions on demand to anyplace you want to go, as well as up-to-the-minute updates on traffic jams, construction tie-ups, and accidents.
- Advanced radar and "obstacle detection" systems will keep track of other cars and things that dart in front of you, taking control of your car to avoid collisions faster than if you'd had time to react on your own.
- Onboard computers will let you check your E-mail and offer news, information, and entertainment while you drive.

If this sounds like an awful lot of gadgets—and an awful lot of distractions while you're driving—don't be concerned. Why not? Well, you won't be doing as much driving as today's drivers do. Cars are well on their way to becoming computers with tires. They may not be able to drive themselves from one place to another anytime soon, but as we'll discuss shortly, they will be pretty darned close. "In tomorrow's dream cars, brains will beat brawn," predicts the magazine *The Futurist*. "Vehicles with intelligent systems may become more attractive to car buyers than high-performance 'muscle' cars. Consumers will also be looking for cleaner, quieter modes of personal transportation through congested cities."

All of these gadgets, and many more just like them, are already being tested. And some are even available today on expensive model cars. Onboard computers that read your E-mail are already a reality. Systems such as the Clarion AutoPC and Ford's Visteon system look like a car radio and combine a phone, CD player, E-mail, and paging capability and a satellite navigation system in the dashboard of the car. As voice recognition technology (see Chapter 2) becomes a more common way to interact with computers, people will be able to get more and more uses from onboard computers while keeping both hands on the wheel.

However, in the car of the future, some experts predict, you might not have very much to do. You'll pick the music, set the cabin temperature, and maybe, but only maybe, steer.

IMPROVED SAFETY

Car manufacturers are not only dreaming up ways to keep you wired and entertained in your car. They're also using advanced technology to improve safety features. In the years ahead, more and more cars will come with state-of-the-art sensors that will keep track of your speed, how many people are in the car, and even where they're sitting, so that air bags and seat belts will work better in an accident. "If you're in a crash, the car will know it's going eighty miles an hour and you're a two hundred–pound male sitting far back from the dashboard, so the air bag should inflate at full speed," says Dan McGinn, who writes about cars for *Newsweek*. "If you're short and you're very close to the steering wheel, and it's only a fifteen-mile-an-hour crash, maybe the air bag should only go off slightly." Manufacturers are also experimenting with new materials for auto bodies that can withstand the force of even the most severe crash.

A heads-up display that projects the dashboard instruments onto the windshield is also intended to enhance safety. That may sound strange. How can putting stuff on the windshield make driving safer? "I wasn' t glancing down at the speedometer," says McGinn, who has test-driven experimental cars with HUDs. "I could see the instruments as I was looking out at the roadway."

Technology may also solve one of the trickiest safety hazards on our roads: falling asleep at the wheel. Driver fatigue is a serious problem today. The AAA Foundation for Traffic Safety estimates sleepy drivers may cause half of all truck crashes. A National Sleep Foundation survey estimates that at least 1,500 people a year are killed in accidents linked to drowsiness.

Dashboard-mounted devices that monitor the driver's heart rate, head movements, brain-wave activity, even blood chemistry have been built and tested. The U.S. Department of Transportation has tested several high-tech devices that look for signs that a driver is in danger of nodding off, and issue a warning before disaster strikes. One such device shines an infrared light into the driver's eyes and monitors how much of the light, which is invisible to human eyes, is reflected back. Drooping eyelids and a drop in the rate at which a driver blinks are 90 percent accurate in predicting when a sleep-deprived trucker is no longer capable of driving safely, says David F. Dinges, chief of the division of sleep and chronobiology at the University of Pennsylvania Medical Center.

High-tech devices like blind-spot alarms, enhanced cruise control, collision warning radars, dash-mounted computer readouts, and inebriation monitors to stop drunken driving are being tested, primarily in trucks. But they will almost certainly find their way into the family car within the next few years.

SMART CARS, SMART HIGHWAYS

Farther down the road, automation technology holds the promise of solving a host of safety problems while taking a big bite out of traffic congestion. Nearly 90 percent of Americans do their daily traveling by car instead of by mass transportation like buses or trains. Since the first Model T rolled off the Ford assembly line in 1908, the number of cars on highways in the United States and around the world has risen steadily. Over 625 million cars and trucks crowd the world's highways right now. And some estimates say that number will grow to over *one billion* by 2025.

So it's a good thing cars will have so many cool toys packed into them in the future. You might just spend the twenty-first century stuck in traffic. Americans spent 1.6 billion hours sitting still in traffic in 1989. And that figure, some experts predict, will rise to 8.1 billion by 2005. That's the equivalent of more than four million people spending forty hours a week stuck in traffic for an entire year! You think we have a problem with road rage now? Just wait.

What's the answer? Mass transportation? Carpooling? Ho-hum. Nearly all experiments in car and van pooling and so-called high occupancy vehicle (HOV) lanes have been limited successes at best. In the United States at least, we like to drive ourselves, thank you, and that's not likely to change anytime in the foreseeable future. So if you can't stop people from buying and driving cars or persuade them to carpool, you're left with two choices: Build more highways or figure out how to cram lots more cars on the highways we already have. Building additional lanes can cost billions of dollars. The answer could be automated highway systems that let cars, trucks, and buses travel packed together at high speeds, with computers coordinating the movements of every vehicle. So some of the biggest leaps forward in cars won't be in the car at all. It will be in the roads the car travels upon.

Smart highways, essentially autopilot systems for cars, will whisk you along at 100 mph, bumper to bumper, with hands-off driving. Drivers literally will turn over control of their vehicles to a centralized highway computer, which will communicate instructions to each car via an onboard PC connected to the Internet. Within twenty years, transportation experts expect many highways to feature at least one lane of "smartway," just as you now see a HOV lane on many highways.

"A typical freeway lane can handle about two thousand vehicles per hour, but a lane equipped to guide traffic automatically should be able to carry about six thousand, depending on the spacing of entrances and exits," says James Rillings, a General Motors researcher who designed smart highways for the National Automated Highway System Consortium. "The savings brought about by not having to build more roads or not having to widen existing ones should more than pay for the sophisticated electronic equipment needed for cars to drive themselves," he adds. Automated highways may sound like gee-whiz technology, but it's an old idea. In fact, a working model of an automated highway was a big hit at the General Motors pavilion at the 1939 World's Fair!

What will it be like to drive on an automated highway (assuming you still call it driving, not riding)? You will get in your car, tell your onboard computer where you want to go, then head for the smart highway, probably in complete control of your car. Once you're ready to pull into the automated lanes, "devices installed on the roadside would electronically interrogate the vehicle to determine its destination and to ascertain that it had the proper automation equipment in good working order," says Rillings. "Assuming it passed such tests, the driver would then be guided through a gate and toward an automated lane."

The computer-guided system would merge you into traffic smoothly, at a distance that might at first seem frighteningly close to the car in front of you—at least until you got used to it and gained confidence in the automated system. "Once a vehicle had settled into automated travel, the driver would be free to release the wheel, break open the morning paper, or just relax," Rillings says. Traffic would be managed either through a system of "free-agent" vehicles or "platooned" vehicles. In a free-agent system, every car would operate independently, with the computer spacing each car based on its braking ability and the road conditions, making sure that every car could stop in time, even if the car in front of it slammed on its brakes. In a platooned system, groups of ten to twenty cars would be linked together electronically via a network of sensors, computers, navigation systems, and cameras. Trading information about speed, acceleration, braking, and objects in the road, a platoon would act as a single vehicle. "Such constant interchange would enable the vehicles of the platoon to become, in essence, an electronically coupled train," says Rillings. "But unlike a railway train, these chains would be dynamic—forming, splitting, and rejoining again as traffic conditions and individual destinations demanded."

Supporters of automated highways argue that smart highways will not only increase highway volume, but safety as well. Right now in the United States, there are about ten million accidents a year, which kill more than forty thousand people. Automation, proponents say, could reduce that by as much as 80 percent. A car that drives itself can't weave in and out of lanes, pass on the wrong side, or bomb across four lanes to avoid missing an exit. And it's highly unlikely that a computer driver will ever flip the bird to another computer. Automation will also save fuel and reduce pollution. Cars packed tightly together draft behind one another like NASCAR race drivers, cutting wind resistance and becoming more fuel efficient.

Automation will certainly change the way we drive. Tailgating will no longer be against the law, for example. It will be required! And falling asleep at the wheel may be how millions of people get to work every morning. Come to think of it, that raises an interesting question. If you turn the car over to a computer, what happens when the computer is ready to turn it back to you? What if the driver is asleep? Rillings has an answer: The automated highway system "might signal the approach of the exit and observe the behavior of the vehicle while the driver assumed limited duties. If he or she acted appropriately, the computer would release control completely, and the driver would complete the exit. But if the driver was not responding properly, warnings would sound. Should these promptings fail to wake the driver, the automated system would notify authorities of an emergency and bring the vehicle to a safe stop in a nearby holding area."

The number-one cause of car accidents today is human error. If every car on the road is wired to every other car, the chain-reaction collision, where the lead car slams on the brakes and every other car slams into the stopped car, could become a thing of the past. An onboard computer could react instantly, detecting the slowing of the car ahead braking and immediately applying its own brakes—long before a human driver would have time to react. Another plus: Computers are never distracted by the radio, cell phone calls, or kids screaming in the backseat.

There have already been a number of successful experiments of smart highways. And plans are underway for more:

- In August 1997, the National Automated Highway System Consortium (NAHSC) successfully demonstrated a 7.5-mile stretch of automated highway in San Diego, California.
- Transportation officials in Houston are considering adding automation to special lanes running down the middle of the Katy Freeway. Under the plan, platoons of buses would run as electronically coupled trains.
- A 5.7-mile "smart road" linking Blacksburg, Virginia, with Interstate 81 has been proposed as a test site for automated highway technologies, and to relieve traffic on U.S. 460. It's expected to be built sometime after 2002.

- The Japanese car company Honda has demonstrated automated navigation and driving systems on a stretch of the Joshinetsu Highway in Nagano, Japan.

Successful experiments in automated driving have also been achieved *without* smart highways. Researchers at Pittsburgh's Carnegie Mellon University built and drove a car with automatic navigation from Washington, D.C., to San Diego, with the car driving itself for 98 percent of the coast-to-coast trip.

While most future automobile transportation schemes assume individuals will continue to own their own private cars, other ideas have been put forth. One plan championed by some public transportation advocates involves fleets of thousands of electric cars scattered throughout a city. If you needed to travel within the city, you'd grab the nearest available car, drive it where you want to go, then leave it there, plugged in for recharging, for the next person who needed it. Such a system seems unlikely, however, given our love affair with owning our own cars.

Still, it's pretty clear that driving is going to change dramatically in the next few decades. It could mean the end of the big, dramatic Hollywood chase scene. It won't be very exciting to watch the good guy riding in the car with nothing to do. He'd just yell "Follow that car!" (some things never change) then sit back and play video games on the screen built into the passenger seat. At least he'd be able to ask the car to find some exciting chase-scene music on the radio.

GPS AND NAVIGATION

Whether you're travelling by land, sea, or air in the future, your trip from here to there will almost certainly be guided by the global positioning system (GPS), a satellite-based navigational tool. In cars, GPS could become as common as the steering wheel.

Here's how GPS works: Two dozen military satellites hover in orbit twelve thousand miles above the earth. Each satellite carries an extremely accurate, synchronized atomic clock, and beams down a constant signal. Using simple geometry, the GPS receiver in a moving vehicle can precisely pinpoint its location, within a few feet, relative to the satellites. Car owners in Japan have already gone crazy for GPS. Over 2.5 million cars in Japan have onboard mapping devices that use GPS systems to tell drivers exactly where they are and give directions to their destination, compared to just a few thousand in the United States. Japanese drivers also enjoy a state-of-the-art traffic system that gives real-time information on traffic jams. The onboard GPS system helps drivers route around the congestion.

Developed to locate troops and tanks on battlefields, portable GPS units are now carried by boaters and hikers. Mushers in the famous Alaskan Iditarod dogsled race use GPS to know exactly where they are, when all they can see is miles and miles of snow and ice in every direction. Farmers can use GPS to plow their fields—even at night and without a driver in the tractor. United Airlines has done experiments with GPS, performing hundreds of flawless automatic landings in which the pilots never touched the controls. It's so accurate that if you put a GPS receiver in a golf cart, it can tell you how far your ball is from the pin and even suggest a club to use. Of course, GPS still has military uses. Cruise missiles guided by onboard GPS systems, for example, are said to be accurate enough to hit a mailbox when fired from hundreds of miles away.

Fans of GPS imagine dozens of other uses. It could be used to track missing children or the elderly who tend to wander off. Put a small GPS device in a child's sneaker or an Alzheimer's patient's clothing, and you can pinpoint exactly where they are. And the government is requiring that all new cellular phones be equipped with GPS devices that will let police know where a call is coming from. Of course, where some people see great practical benefits, others see threats to privacy. "There's no centralized Big Brother executing a plan to fit us all with GPS dog collars," says Phil Agre, an associate professor of communication at the University of California at San Diego.

Add a GPS system to the MEMs and ubiquitous computing revolutions we discussed earlier, and what could you get? A system so advanced that sensors in your car could alert you to an impending mechanical problem, while GPS gives you directions to the closest service station. When you arrive, the mechanic will greet you by name and already have replacement parts ready, since your car's onboard computer will have called the problem in to the service station's computer and let him know you were on the way.

The uses of GPS, it seems, are limited only by the imaginations of people who work in transportation. "I would say it's going to be in every automobile, says Stanford University professor Bradford Parkinson, a retired Air Force officer often described as the "father" of GPS. "It's going to be in probably half the farm tractors. Open pit mines will be operated robotically. I see it in ships. I see it controlling all the timing in the whole nation. I suspect that within the United States alone there'll be over twenty million users."

BEYOND THE INTERNAL COMBUSTION ENGINE

Auto industry pioneer Henry Ford once joked that he would sell his customers a Model-T in any color they wanted, "as long as it's black." You may be told someday that you can have any color car, as long as it's green. Cars will still come in every color, but they will be "green" because they won't harm the environment. As concerns about greenhouse gases and global warming grow in the twenty-first century, so will calls for environmentally friendly cars, including electric cars, gasoline and electric hybrids, and vehicles powered by onboard fuel cells.

The move to cars that are easier on the air we breathe seems inevitable. "Motor vehicles account for one quarter of all U.S. emissions of carbon dioxide, the chief cause of global warming," says Jason Mark, a senior transportation analyst with the Union of Concerned Scientists. "U.S. cars and trucks alone emit more carbon dioxide than do all combustion sources in any country other than China, Russia, and Japan." The source of all that pollution is the gasoline- or diesel-burning internal combustion engines that power nearly every vehicle on the road today. The twenty-first century seems likely to mean the end of the internal combustion engine.

The technology exists for electric cars that have almost no harmful impact on the environment. In fact, electric cars that run on stacks of rechargeable batteries are already out there, although your odds of seeing one on the road are about the same as getting a snow day in May—in Florida. As of 1998, there were only about one thousand electric vehicles on United States highways, nearly all in California and Arizona. The handful of people who drive electric cars today find plenty of things to love about their cars—no exhaust, no oil changes, no need to ever fill 'er up with gas. And speed isn't a problem. Electric cars can do the speed limit just as well as traditional gas guzzlers. However, today's electric vehicles are practical only for a short drive to and from work, school, or shopping, since you can go only sixty to ninety miles before you have to plug your car in to recharge its batteries. Even the most advanced electric cars on the road today can travel only half the distance that the average internal-combustion-powered car achieves on a tank of gas. But environmentally, they are the best cars on the road, since they emit zero exhaust.

Southern California has the worst air pollution problems in the United States and, not surprisingly, the greatest number of electric cars on the road. To encourage people to try plugging in instead of filling up, there are over 250 free public battery chargers in the region, by far the most in the country. Every one of those free chargers is badly needed, given EVs' limited range. Still, the intrepid pioneers who have bought these early EVs say the ease of owning one makes up for the hassle of recharging, since electric cars are virtually maintenance free.

And expensive. General Motors EV-1, the best-selling electric car, sells for about $32,000. "The drawbacks are the cost, the range, and the recharge time," says Jeremy Barnes, product safety and environment administrator for Toyota Motor Sales U.S.A. in Torrance, California. "Until there is some huge breakthrough in battery technology, which hasn't happened in the last one hundred years, that range is not going to increase appreciably." Most research today focuses not on increasing the range of electric cars, but on reducing the time it takes to recharge a car from a few hours to a few minutes. Right now, some electric car drivers have their ride home from work interrupted for a forty-five-minute recharge stop at a public charger.

Unless the cruising range of electric cars improves dramatically, they may never be fully embraced by our road-crazy culture. Most car rides may only be a few miles, but people are in love with the idea of taking long road trips. We're not about to trade jumper cables for a really long extension cord unless the price of gasoline goes up dramatically, or the world simply runs out of oil.

THE NEXT BIG THING: FUEL-CELL CARS

Whether electric vehicles prove practical or not, major carmakers are already preparing for life after the internal combustion engine. At the North American International Auto Show in Detroit in 1999, Dodge debuted a prototype Charger that runs on compressed natural gas. Honda showed off a hybrid electric vehicle (HEV) that gets seventy miles to the gallon by running on both batteries and gasoline. A tiny Norwegian company introduced the Pivco Think—a two-passenger electric car with a plastic body designed for city driving. And Ford demonstrated a prototype it called the P2000, powered by a "fuel cell" that uses a chemical process to turn hydrogen into electricity to power the car.

If you took a poll of auto manufacturers, they'd probably say that fuel-cell vehicles are be the best bet to replace the internal combustion engine. Some auto industry experts have even described the work under way on fuel-cell vehicles as possibly the most significant change in the automobile since Henry Ford introduced the assembly line.

"A fuel cell is an electric chemical engine," explains Robert Rose, the executive director of the Breakthrough Technologies Institute, a nonprofit organization dedicated to promoting the use of alternative fuels for cars. "A fuel cell actually works very simply by taking advantage of the chemical reaction between hydrogen and oxygen. In the process of that reaction, electrons are released and you can harness those electrons for useful work, such as driving the electric motor in an electric vehicle."

Ironically, fuel cells are far from a cutting-edge technology. In fact, the Englishman Sir William Grove invented the fuel cell in 1839! There were very few practical applications for fuel cells until NASA used them for the Gemini and Apollo space missions. Fuel cells combine hydrogen and oxygen into water—H_20—producing electricity in the process. A device that produces electricity for a space capsule and water for astronauts at the same time has been extremely useful in space, but not terribly practical on Earth.

If you're paying close attention, you might be thinking, "Hmmm. Run the family minivan on hydrogen? Isn't that a little dangerous?" (Think "Hindenburg disaster.") Besides, where would you *get* the hydrogen? Good questions. In 1997, an important breakthrough was achieved with the development of a fuel cell that extracts hydrogen from gasoline, the stuff that nearly all cars and trucks run on already. Suddenly, fuel-cell vehicles seemed like a real possibility. Instead of burning the gas in an internal combustion engine, an onboard fuel cell could produce electricity from the liquid to power the car. Your car would go much farther on a gallon of gas, with no exhaust fumes. In fact, the emission that fuel cells produce is water vapor.

But gasoline? Isn't the point of alternative cars to get away from running our cars on gasoline? In the long run, yes. But even fuel cell backers argue that one way to get people to make the switch from the internal combustion engine to the next generation of vehicles may not be to change everything all at once. Drivers may be more likely to buy cars that they can fill up at the pump just as they always have. Rather than waiting hours to recharge an electric car, fuel-cell car drivers will spend no more time in the gas station than with today's cars. Plus, you won't have to visit as often. Fuel-cell cars will deliver dramatically more miles to the gallon than conventional vehicles.

Here's how it would work: To generate electricity, a fuel cell needs hydrogen and oxygen. The air we breathe has plenty of oxygen, but getting hydrogen is tougher. Gasoline is a type of chemical compound called a *hydrocarbon.* It's basically made of hydrogen and carbon. Many experts believe that unlocking the hydrogen from gasoline could be the key to letting fuel cell cars replace traditional internal combustion vehicles. For now, it's simply not practical to replace every gas station in the world with a hydrogen station.

Fuel cells aren't perfect. They still emit carbon dioxide, a so-called greenhouse gas. But they produce far less of it than internal combustion engines. And fuel cells produce none of the polluting nitrogen oxides that pour out of the tailpipes of today's cars. DaimlerChrysler has announced that it will start producing 100 thousand fuel-cell engines a year by 2005. General Motors, the world's biggest car company, says it will have fuel-cell vehicles in car showrooms by 2004. Toyota also has plans for fuel-cell vehicles, and has already built one that can go over three hundred miles between refuelings.

For now, the cheap price of gasoline and the ease and convenience of the old-fashioned internal combustion engine means drivers will be slow to embrace new car technologies like electric cars and fuel cells. But gasoline may not be cheap forever. And eventually, concerns about air pollution and global warming may force people to buy electric and fuel cell cars whether they want them or not. Environmentalists argue that getting people to switch to cleaner running cars could be easier if drivers get an offer they can't refuse—like taxes on gasoline and car emissions that will mean only Bill Gates will be able to afford to drive a standard car. Many people think that as concerns about the environment and global warming grow in the next century, there will be more and more pressure on both car makers and drivers to switch to alternative cars.

Today, Los Angeles is both the car and smog capital of the world. Pollution caused by cars has already prompted California to set a deadline of 2003 for 10 percent of vehicles in the state to be zero-emission. That means 100 thousand electric cars on the state's freeways, since only EVs will meet the strict rules on emissions. If people get really concerned about air pollution, global warming, and the environment in the twenty-first century, governments could start forcing car companies to make fewer and fewer conventional cars. Although no one is predicting that today, it could happen, in which case we may be driving electric cars after all.

"I still think that the car of the future will be an electric car. But the car of the near future is more likely to be a hybrid car than a pure battery electric or indeed a pure fuel-cell vehicle, at least in the next five years or so," says Rose. Adds Bradford Bates, manager of alternative power source technology at Ford Research Lab: "I think it was only eighteen months ago that I was telling

Oops!

DUMB PREDICTIONS ABOUT TRANSPORTATION

The horse is here to stay, but the automobile is only a novelty, a fad. —The president of the Michigan Savings Bank in 1903, advising Henry Ford's lawyer, Horace Rackman, not to invest in the Ford Motor Co. Rackman bought $5,000 worth of stock anyway, eventually selling it for $12.5 million.

My imagination refuses to see any sort of submarine doing anything but suffocating its crew and floundering at sea.
—H. G. Wells, British author and futurist, 1901

Airplanes are interesting toys but of no military value.
—Marshal Ferdinand Foch, French military strategist, 1911

This fellow Charles Lindbergh will never make it. He's doomed.
—Harry Guggenheim, millionaire aviation enthusiast

In 1901, I said to my brother Orville that man would not fly for fifty years . . . ever since, I have distrusted myself and avoided all predictions. —Wilbur Wright, 1908

No airship will ever fly from New York to Paris. That seems to me impossible. . . . No known motor can run at the requisite speed for four days without stopping."
—Wilbur Wright, one year later

people I didn't think my grandchildren were going to be able to buy a fuel-cell car. Today, it would be quite surprising if they couldn't buy one."

THE FINAL FRONTIER

The early years of the twenty-first century could end up being the Golden Age of space travel. A new generation of "reusable launch vehicles" (RLVs) has the potential to completely change the way we shoot satellites into orbit, deliver cargo and packages—even the way we get from place to place all over the world. Plans are under way for "hypersonic" space planes that could put suborbital space flight within the reach of average people, even tourists. Some of the more ambitious ideas could reduce the flying time from New York to London to as little as twenty minutes. The United States, Japan, and Russia are all working on hypersonic aircraft that could reduce flying time between, for example, Japan and New York—currently a fourteen-hour marathon over the North Pole—to under two hours.

The coming revolution in space travel and transportation is being driven by the rush to "privatize" space. Throughout most of history, space programs and nearly all launches were run by the governments of the United States, the former Soviet Union, or other countries. The twenty-first century, however, promises the end of big, expensive, government-funded space missions and the beginning of an era of small, regularly scheduled flights of RLVs built and run by private companies. "Make no mistake," NASA administrator Daniel Goldin said recently, "it is the private sector that will finally build the machines and provide the access to space to make the dream a reality for all Americans."

The new space race then, will pit corporations, not nations, against each other. The competition is already heating up. In 1996, a St. Louis–based organization of space enthusiasts announced the ten-million-dollar "X Prize." The prize can be claimed by anyone who successfully launches three or more people in a suborbital flight at least sixty-two miles above the ground—beyond Earth's atmosphere and gravitational pull—return them safely to Earth, then do it again within two weeks. The prize is intended to encourage the development of a private space industry. Apollo 11 astronaut Buzz Aldrin is among the organizers of the X Prize, which is intended to find "a twenty-first-century Charles Lindbergh."

The goal of the X Prize is "to challenge the best engineers and innovators to build a spacecraft that eventually could be used to develop a commercial space-transportation and tourism industry." Organizers point out that while private companies are in the business of building rockets for commercial satellite launches, for example, no one is trying to get into the business of regularly sending people into space for transportation and tourism. The X Prize is an attempt to jump-start such an industry.

"It's time to go from NASA to the private sector," says Diane Murphy, spokeswoman for the X Prize Foundation. However, while $10 million sounds like a boatload of cash, it probably won't come close to covering the expenses of whoever wins the X Prize. But the organizers expect that the publicity that comes from the first privately funded passenger flight into space will lead to big bucks from satellite launches, passenger flights, and even space tourism.

It's worked before. Large cash prizes have a history of spurring important advances in flight. There were over one hundred aviation prizes announced from 1905 to 1935. In fact, Charles Lindbergh himself was competing for the Orteig International Prize, a $25,000 award offered by a wealthy Paris hotel owner, when he made the first solo flight across the Atlantic in 1927.

At least sixteen companies are competing for the X Prize. And while none of them have built a working launch vehicle yet, they all have different ideas about what the future of manned space flight will look like. Some companies are designing conventional rockets that launch straight up. Others think they can build a plane that takes off like an ordinary jet, then fires its rockets once it gets to 35,000 feet. Others plan to boost their spacecraft into the sky on the back of another plane. One company has designed a space plane that's towed into the sky behind a 747, like a giant glider.

It's anyone's guess which of these designs—if any—will be the one to win the X Prize, let alone become the model that makes RLVs a workable everyday transportation system. But the contest organizers have succeeded in creating a surge of next-generation space flight creativity.

"There's nothing about the technology that says this can't be done," says Norman LaFave, chief executive of Dynamicar Research, which is competing for the prize. "In fact, Nasa's X-15 rocket plane was flying at hypersonic speeds back in the 1950s and 1960s without any of the technical sophistication and materials technology that is readily available to us now." LaFave predicts reusable space vehicles that will travel at eight to ten times the speed of sound. At that speed, the Concorde would feel like a slow boat. LaFave predicts his space planes will ultimately reduce the travel time from New York to London to a mere twenty minutes.

That may sound like an exaggeration, and it probably is. Heck, it takes more than twenty minutes just to taxi to the runway at most major airports. But the designers and engineers working on reusable space planes speak about their work with a confidence that would make Lindbergh proud. "Compared to the difficulty, danger, and expense of flying in the teens and twenties, leaving the atmosphere is a piece of cake," says Burt Rutan, who made history in 1986 by piloting an experimental plane around the world without refueling. "And yet, we are not doing it." LaFave agrees. "It's just not as hard as people think it is."

Launching an RLV may not be technically difficult, but getting one ready to fly again in a matter of days certainly is. In order to usher in an era of cheap and regular space transportation, the companies that are trying to build RLVs will ultimately need to operate just like airlines, with regularly scheduled flights. NASA's space shuttle is a type of RLV, but right now it takes weeks or months of work to prepare the shuttle for another launch. The wear and tear of exiting and reentering Earth's atmosphere requires a rigid schedule of maintenance and inspections for maximum safety. Passenger planes, on the other hand, can be refueled and ready to fly again in a matter of hours. Each plane that an airline buys must be able to make thousands of flights—even tens of thousands—so that the cost of the plane can be spread out over every passenger who ever flies on it. While no one expects RLVs to ever provide a flight as cheap and affordable as the airlines do now from New York to Los Angeles, a viable RLV will have to be able to make many, many flights for affordable space transportation to become a reality.

In fact, most experts assume that the real payoff in hypersonic transportation will be cargo, not passengers. In other words, it's much more likely that you will someday send a package into space than take a ride yourself. Federal Express founder Fred Smith has often talked about his goal of offering overnight delivery service between any two points on the planet. That can't happen without hypersonic space planes. And since you can fit lots more packages than people on board an RLV, private space operators stand to make a lot more money from parcels, not people. Plus, packages don't lose their lunch when they go weightless in space. Further into the future, passenger transportation will probably be available, but at a premium price. At least in the early years of RLV travel, it will be reserved exclusively for wealthy business travelers and tourists.

With so much money to be made launching satellites, delivering packages and ferrying passengers around the globe, the era of RLVs certainly seems inevitable. Space buffs say RLVs will do for space what the railroad did for the American West. It's an interesting comparison. Before the transcontinental railroad was built, the West was settled by people traveling in covered wagons. Those Conestoga wagons brought settlers and all their possessions out West, but nobody ever came back in one. It's the same thing with most of today's space launches. They're designed to go out but not back. Once the railroad linked East and West, making it possible to go back and forth easily, trade and industry helped the West grow from a collection of frontier towns and seaports to—less than a hundred years later—one of the world's biggest cultural and commercial centers. "The first satellite lofted by a fully reusable, privately funded launcher," noted *Popular Science* in a 1998 article, "could be as important as the driving of the last spike of the transcontinental railroad."

Want to Know More about the Future of Travel and Transportation?

On the Web:

- Intelligent Transportation Society of America (www.itsa.org/)
- Union of Concerned Scientists (www.ucsusa.org)
- EV World—The World of Advanced Electric Vehicles (www.evworld.com)
- Global Positioning Systems (http://itre.ncsu.edu/gis/gps/)
- Single State Rocket Technology (http://gargravarr.cc.utexas.edu/ssrt/index.html)
- Space Transportation Programs (http://stp.msfc.nasa.gov/)
- X Prize Foundation (www.xprize.org/)

At the Library:

- *Charging Ahead,* by Joe Sherman (Oxford University Press, 1998)
- *Islands in the Sky: Bold New Ideas for Colonizing Space*, by Stanley Schmidt and Robert Zubrin (John Wiley & Sons, 1996)
- *History of the Electric Automobile: Hybrid Electric Cars,* by Ernest Henry Wakefield (Society of Automotive Engineers, 1998)

CHAPTER 8

Can Earth Support Nine Billion People?

The earth is a beautiful place, but it has a pox called man.
—Friedrich Nietzsche

Sometime in October 1999 an important milestone in human history took place. We don't know precisely where or when, but somewhere in the world, a baby was born who was the six billionth human being on Earth. And as you read this, Baby Six Billion is out there somewhere, kicking, crying, crawling, and trying to find a little room to grow up in the new millennium.

This baby is going to have to have pretty sharp elbows, because he or she will have lots of company. Baby Six Billion will live to see the birth of Baby Seven Billion by 2012. By his or her thirtieth birthday, Baby Eight Billion will be born. And finally, sometime around his or her fiftieth birthday, Baby Six B may even have a grandchild called Baby Nine Billion.

To give you a sense of how quickly our population has been growing, consider this: The number of people added to Earth's population in the 1990s *alone* was greater than the entire population of the planet in 1600, notes Bill McKibben, a well-known environmental writer. And the population grew more since 1950 than it had for the entire previous history of mankind. How many people is that? "We add a New York City every month, almost a Mexico every year, almost an India every decade," says McKibben.

According to projections by the United Nations, the earth's population will continue to grow rapidly in the first half of the new century until it peaks at about 9.4 billion people in 2050. Keeping all of these people fed, dressed, sheltered, employed, and moving from place to place will put a tremendous strain on the planet's resources. It will almost certainly mean a lot of changes in the way we live if we expect to take care of that many people without destroying our environment. We're going to need every smart idea we can come up with to take care of Baby Six Billion—and her 3.4 billion brothers and sisters who are on the way.

IMPACT ON THE PLANET

Right now, you're sitting down and reading a book. So you're not taking up too much space or using too much energy, right? Wrong. The oil to heat the room you're sitting in was pumped out of the ground thousands of miles away by an oil rig that takes up a lot of space, then shipped, probably on board an oil supertanker, to a massive refinery (more space) to be turned into heating oil. Then it was delivered via a gas-guzzling truck to your oil company, which transferred it to another truck, which loaded up the tank in your cellar. Is there a light on in the room? The electricity to run the lamp is probably also generated by oil or gas at a power plant miles from your home, and brought to you over a giant power grid. The clothes you're wearing may have started as a cotton plant, perhaps grown in Mexico, soaking up lots of water and chemical fertilizers. A factory turned the cotton into cloth, another factory turned it into the clothes you wear, and everything had to be transported to a store where you found them and bought them. That's a lot of space and energy for one pair of underwear. Nice sneakers. Any idea how many *centuries* they're going to sit in a landfill after you wear 'em out? The book in your hands was once a tree. It had to be chopped down, pulped, bleached and turned into paper, consuming more water and energy in the process. Did you shower this morning? The average shower consumes between twenty-five and fifty gallons of water. Each of us uses nearly two hundred gallons of water per day! And unless you took a cold shower, you used more oil or gas to heat the water. Is that your stomach rumbling? Maybe you went to McDonald's for lunch. Your burger started out as a cow that needed a whole lot of grazing land and water before meeting her destiny as a Happy Meal. You want fries with that? The potatoes for the fries took up space and water in Idaho. McDonald's alone uses 25 percent of the U.S. potato crop each year.

No, I'm not suggesting that you should sit naked and shivering in the dark and starve yourself. I'm merely pointing out that all of us take up a lot more space and use a lot more energy than we probably realize. Everything you own, everything around you, had to be grown, harvested, mined, produced, refined, manufactured, assembled, bottled, packaged, shipped, stored, and displayed before it got to you. The point is that you take up a lot more space than just the four walls around you, and your share of the world's resources goes far beyond the gas, oil, and electricity your family uses at home and in your car. Simply put, it takes a lot to keep you running. It has been calculated that the average American uses up three hundred shopping bags of raw material every week.

If everyone on Earth consumed at the same rate as Americans do, it would take *three* Earths to keep us all alive.

When environmentalists look at population, they see more than mouths to feed. They look at "sustainability"—the ability of the planet to provide for us all, and to continue to do so year after year without running out of resources. Our growing population will present us with two serious problems in the twenty-first century. Not only will there be more of us, but nearly all of the 9.4 billion people on Earth will consume more than previous generations. A Washington State University professor once tried to figure out how much energy modern man uses up compared to prehistoric man. He estimated that back when we were all hunters and gatherers, we consumed about 2,500 calories a day, all of it food. As McKibben points out in his book *Maybe One: A Personal and Environmental Argument for Single-Child Families,* that is the daily energy intake of *a dolphin*. "A modern human being uses 31 thousand calories a day, most of it in the form of

THE FACE OF CHANGE

The sheer number of people will only be part of the story in the next century. The type of people on Earth and where they live will also shift dramatically. In the developed world—Europe and North America, for example—the number of births has gone down. That's because of changes in the way people live in those countries. Generations ago, when most people lived on farms, large families were desirable. More kids meant more farmhands. But as people gave up farming for cities and suburbs, and as we moved from farms to factories to so-called information work, large families became an expense, not a benefit.

The birthrate in countries like Germany, Italy, Spain, Russia, France, and Japan has slowed to the point where those countries will actually *lose* population in the first half of the twenty-first century. All told, developed nations will add only 100 million people by 2020, according to U.S. Census data, while so-called developing nations will produce 2.2 billion—twenty-two times as many.

In the United States and Europe, expect to see lots more gray hair, too. Within the first few decades of the twenty-first century, more than one out of every four people will be over the age of sixty-five. Just a decade ago, that figure was only one in ten! With many people living longer, healthier lives, by 2050, there will be nearly1.5 billion people over the age of sixty-five—three and one half times as many as today. Not only that, but as adults decide to have children later in life, the number of children will also go up significantly. The result will be what the United Nations Population Fund calls "the sandwich generation." They will be squeezed between having to provide medical and financial care for older relatives while raising and educating kids of their own.

fossil fuel," he notes. "That is the intake of a pilot whale. And the average American uses six times that—as much as a sperm whale." Our rate of consumption—not just food, but water, natural resources, and raw material—is one of the most crucial environmental issues facing the world in the new millennium.

"We appear to be the same species, with stomachs of the same size, but we aren't," says McKibben. "It's as if each of us were trailing a big Macy's-parade balloon around, feeding it constantly."

CAN EARTH SUSTAIN EVERYBODY?

OK, so we're looking at a future with billions more people taking up more and more space and consuming more and more food, water, and natural resources. So, to make a long story short, we're doomed, right? Well, it depends on whose crystal ball you're looking into.

There have been predictions that the human population would outgrow Earth's ability to support and sustain it almost as long as there has been a civilization on the planet. The ancient Greeks Plato and Euripides worried that we would run out of food if the population kept growing. The most famous doomsayer was an English economist named Thomas Malthus. Two hundred years ago, Malthus wrote his famous "Essay on the Principle of Population," which predicted that the number of human beings on the planet would grow faster than the earth's ability to produce food. He expected that hunger, disease, and famine would be the inevitable result. To this day, the word *Malthusian* can be found in most dictionaries to describe prophecies of doom and gloom.

The good news is that Malthus, so far at least, was wrong. Writing two hundred years ago, there was no way he could have known that advances in agriculture and technology would lead to a much more abundant supply of food. Human ingenuity triumphed over the limits of nature that were known to Malthus. Most dire predictions about population—and estimates of how many of us can live on Earth at any given moment—tend to fail. That's because the people making those predictions assume that the number of people will increase, and that everything else, including the supply of food and water, will remain the same. But most changes are unpredictable. Back in 1800, for example, when the population of the United States was five million, if you told someone that over 270 million people would one day live in the United States, they would say, "That's impossible! Where will they all graze their horses?" They had no idea that cars would one day transform our lives. One hundred years later, the biggest environmental crisis facing the United States was the alarmingly rapid depletion of its forests. The move away from heating with wood along with the development of new materials and methods for building construction averted disaster.

Fears of a population explosion exhausting Earth's natural resources have been with us continually since Malthus. In the 1960s, Paul Ehrlich's terrifying book *The Population Bomb* triggered a new round of fear. Like Malthus, Ehrlich warned that Earth would soon be populated beyond the planet's ability to feed itself. "The battle to feed all of humanity is over," he wrote. "In the 1970s, the world will undergo famines—hundreds of millions of people will starve to death." But that was thirty years and 2.5 billion people ago. Like Malthus, Ehrlich's doomsday warnings were themselves doomed by technology—in this case, the "Green Revolution" in farming that produced more than enough food to feed the world. While hunger is still very much an issue, and malnutrition still plagues too much of humanity, food production has *tripled* since the Second World War, growing even faster than the population.

So far.

It would be foolish to assume that every problem presented by our growing population is going to be solved by sheer brain power and ingenuity. Indeed, there is no shortage of modern Malthusians who believe that we are on the brink of environmental disasters, from global warming to burying ourselves in our own garbage. Some argue that focusing only on food misses the larger point. Sure, we might always be smart or clever enough to find ways to feed ourselves, no matter how many people crowd the planet. But what about our runaway consumption of natural resources like oil or even water? What about mankind's destruction of natural habitats like the rain forests and all species that live there? What about the damage billions of humans do to the air and oceans? Malthus was wrong, but even if we find ways to feed ourselves, the twenty-first century promises serious challenges to the environment and our ability to do something about it.

If Malthus had written his essay in 1998 instead of 1798, he might have been even gloomier. He might point out how our current population of just six billion is depleting the supply of drinkable water on every continent. How our appetite for seafood is pushing ocean fisheries to the point where we are harvesting more fish than nature can replace. How the earth's temperature is rising as humans pump carbon dioxide and other greenhouse gases into the air. And how our need for more space is resulting in the biggest disappearance of plant and animal species since the dinosaurs were wiped off the face of the earth millions of years ago.

OUR TROUBLED PLANET

Let's hope that history repeats itself, and that human cleverness once again finds a way to overcome nature's odds. Because the simple fact is that at the dawn of the twenty-first century, the threats to our environment have never been greater or more frightening.

For all of the technological advances of the last one hundred years, you could argue that the twentieth century was a disaster for the environment. Mankind has prospered, but the natural world paid a steep price. The ancient old growth forests that once covered the globe have largely vanished and hundreds, if not thousands, of plant and animal species have disappeared. Holes have been torn through the earth's layer of ozone that protects us from the sun's damaging rays. The reasons for this are many, but two statistics tell much of the story: We ended the twentieth century with five billion more people and over half a billion more cars than we started with.

Today, global warming threatens to wreak havoc on Earth's climate and raise the level of the oceans. As much as one-third of the world may face shortages of fresh water within the next twenty years. And, of course, the population hasn't stopped growing. By the midpoint of the coming century, we could have twice as many people as we had just ten years ago. It's certainly possible that history will prove our modern Malthusians wrong. But if not, you can expect to hear lots more about the following problems in the years ahead:

Global Warming

Global warming will almost certainly be the single biggest environmental issue of the twenty-first century. "The greatest threat to the long-term health of our planet, as the danger of nuclear war declines, is probably global climate change," says Dr. James Hansen, director of the NASA Goddard Institute for Space Studies. "For most climate scientists, it's no longer a question of whether global warming will occur, but when."

To understand the global warming debate, you need to understand something called the *greenhouse effect*. Like a glass house that traps sunlight and warms the inside, the earth's atmosphere traps heat and warms the planet's surface. Critics of the idea of global warming like to point out that far from being a threat to the environment, the greenhouse effect is what makes life on Earth possible. Without it, the planet would be 60 degrees colder and covered with ice. Gases in the atmosphere, especially carbon dioxide, keep the sun's warmth from radiating back into space. The global warming debate, however, concerns whether we now have too much of this good thing, and are raising the earth's temperature to dangerous levels by pumping too much carbon dioxide and other greenhouse gases into the air.

The number-one cause of increased greenhouse gases is burning fossil fuels—coal, oil, gasoline, etc. The human race now produces 30 billion tons of carbon dioxide every year, two thirds of it from burning fossil fuels. That's four times more than we produced just fifty years ago. The amount of carbon dioxide in the air has been steadily increasing since the Industrial Revolution, but it really took off once cars and trucks became a staple of everyday life. The average car gives off five tons—ten thousand pounds—of carbon dioxide (CO_2) every year. "It's like tossing a five-pound bag of charcoal briquettes out my window every twenty miles or so," writes John Ryan in his book *Over Our Heads: A Local Look at Global Climate.* CO_2 builds up in the atmosphere and contributes to global warming, many scientists believe, wreaking havoc on the climate all over the world.

While the increased amount of CO_2 in the atmosphere is not in doubt, its effect on the environment is at the center of the global warming debate. Most scientists think that the earth's temperature has risen about 1 degree Fahrenheit over the last century. And environmentalists point out that five of the ten warmest years on record since 1860 have occurred in the 1990s—proof positive, they say, that global warming is underway. Others continue to insist that we are seeing nothing more than natural fluctuations in the earth's temperature. The fact that some of the most vocal critics of global warming come from the coal, oil, and electric industries, however, raises questions about their motives. It seems safe to say that while the case has not been proven conclusively and the debate will linger for some time, the weight of scientific opinion is shifting the question from whether or not global warming is real to what should be done about it.

"To truly address the climate crisis we need to embark now on large-scale energy efficiency and conservation programs," says Ross Gelbspan, the author of *The Heat Is On.* "Ultimately we need a global project to replace coal-burning power plants, oil-burning furnaces, and gas-burning cars with low-carbon and renewable energy."

In 1997, leaders of 160 nations met in Japan to negotiate the Kyoto Protocol, which calls on most developed nations to cut emissions by the year 2012. The United States, for example, is supposed to reduce its greenhouse gas emissions to 7 percent below 1990 levels. Developing nations are supposed to reduce their emissions in the second phase of the treaty. President Clinton signed the Kyoto Protocol, but fearing it would be rejected, the administration had not yet sent it to the U.S. Senate for ratification in late 1999.

What will happen if nothing is done? There will be "more frequent and more intense heat waves, causing thousands more heat-related deaths. Severe droughts and floods will become more common," predicts Carol Browner, the administrator of the U.S. Environmental Protection Agency. "Tropical diseases, like malaria, will expand their range. Agriculture will suffer. The oceans will rise, perhaps by several feet over the next century—swamping many coastal areas."

Many environmentalists are concerned that nothing will really be done about global warming until it's too late. "We have the evidence, we hear the whistle blowing, but most ordinary Americans, in their day-to-day lives, cannot yet see the train coming," says Browner. "In human terms, the costs are incalculable—farmers put out of business, coastal areas under water, fresh water turned to salt water, medical advances lost to extinction."

Many scientists estimate that by the end of the twenty-first century, the average global temperature will increase as much as 5 degrees if emissions of carbon dioxide and other greenhouse gases aren't reduced. That may not sound like much, but it's enough, they say, to melt the polar ice caps so quickly the sea level would rise several feet, flooding coastal cities all over the world.

"There's no question that if you add CO_2 to the atmosphere you're going to change the climate, it's just a question of how fast and how soon," says James Baker, the Administrator of the National Oceanic and Atmospheric Administration (NOAA). "I think that we're starting to see what we call the fingerprint of global warming."

Maybe, but whether it's enough to scare us into seeking real alternatives to the fossil fuels that run our cars, heat our homes, and drive our economy could end up being one of the most important stories of the twenty-first century.

Food and Water Shortages

As we saw in Chapter 5, advances in biotechnology are helping farmers squeeze higher and higher yields out of the same acreage. And when all is said and done, that's probably for the best, since the amount of available farmland on Earth is steadily decreasing. Erosion, caused by the clear-cutting of trees and brush, takes millions of acres of farmland out of production every year. In fact, depletion of water resources and slash-and-burn foresting is blamed for turning more than fifteen million acres of farmland into unusable desert every year.

Even with advances in productivity per acre, the world's annual grain harvest has stayed the same for the last ten years, while the planet's population has grown by nearly a half billion people. A study by the EPA found that worldwide production of wheat, rice, and other important food grains is likely to fall 7.6 percent by 2060, while the population rises to over nine billion. The situation offshore isn't much better. A 1995 United Nations report said, "About 70 percent of the world's marine fish stocks are heavily exploited, overexploited, depleted, or slowly recovering." Nine of the world's seventeen major fishing grounds are being depleted of fish, with four "fished out" altogether. "Despite rising affluence, our likely world population of ten billion people won't be able to live as high on the food chain as the average American," says Lester Brown of the Worldwatch Institute. "There simply won't be enough food." For every alarmist, however, there is an optimist who believes that advances in farm productivity will more than keep up with the growing population. "There is no real threat of famine," says Dennis Avery of the Hudson Institute's Center for Global Food Issues.

More alarming is the possibility of water shortages around the world. "Water scarcity is the sleeping tiger of our environmental problems, but the tiger is waking up, and we had better wake up too," says Sandra Postel, director of the Global Water Policy Project in Amherst, Massachusetts, and author of *Last Oasis: Facing Water Scarcity.* The Nile River is the world's longest river, sustaining much of humanity in northern Africa; Postel estimates that the equivalent of twenty more Niles could be needed over the next thirty years just to keep up with the needs of the world's projected population. That's obviously not possible, so it's important that we learn to live with the water resources we have. In the years ahead, you're going to hear the phrase *water-stressed countries* more and more. It refers to parts of the world where groundwater is vanishing, rivers are drying up, and salt build-up in the soil hurts a country's ability to feed itself.

Like most crises, the shortage of drinkable water is felt most severely in the developing world, where even now more than a third of all people lack access to clean water. It's possible that we will see wars fought over water, as rivers shared by more than one country are depleted by irrigation and the construction of dams.

Deforestation

You've no doubt heard a lot about how the earth's rain forests are disappearing, but you may not know why it matters. Covering only two tenths of 1 percent of Earth's surface, the rain forests are an important source of food and wood, natural fibers and materials used in fabrics, rugs, ropes, and other products. They are also vital to the regulation of our global climate. But, perhaps most important, they represent our most significant example of *biodiversity*—a word that refers to the incredible variety of plant and animal life on Earth. Human beings consume an estimated seven thousand different plant and animal species for food, and scientists have catalogued nearly 1.5 million species. But there may be as many as forty million in total. Since 1960, more than 20 percent of the planet's rain forests have been chopped down and burned in Asia, South America, and Africa. One of the reasons people are so concerned about the loss of the rain forests is the possibility that plants that grow there could hold the key to important medical breakthroughs. Over two thousand tropical plants have been identified as having properties that could fight cancer in humans, for example. However, according to the Rainforest Alliance, scientists have only tested one in ten tropical forest plants for such properties, and only one in one hundred have been intensively screened. It is possible that we will destroy potentially helpful species before we even know they exist. The famous biologist E. O. Wilson said in a recent interview that the world's biodiversity is "a largely unmined trove of new substances" that has the potential to be of incredible value to humanity. "The loss of biodiversity," he says, "is the folly our descendants are least likely to forgive us."

Other threats to our environment in the twenty-first century include:

WASTE The United States has 5 percent of the planet's population, and produces nearly 20 percent of its waste. A majority of Americans support recycling in theory, but 96 percent of our plastic ends up in landfills, along with two thirds of our paper. Optimists expect this to improve. "When people see how well recycling works over the course of time," insists Evelyn Haught of the Institute of Scrap Recycling, "the demand will increase."

INFECTIOUS DISEASE Despite incredible advances in medicine, infectious diseases like malaria, tuberculosis, and AIDS still kill more people than wars, car accidents, and cancer combined: more than seventeen million people every year. Scientists say many of the causes are environmental, from contaminated drinking water to overcrowded cities where disease spreads easily.

TOXINS Greenpeace has estimated that 70 percent of Earth's habitable space has been ecologically disturbed. Dangerous levels of pollution from toxic wastes and chemical poisons from landfills and factories have been linked to a wide variety of illnesses. One of the most serious problems is lead contamination: an estimated 200 million people worldwide already have dangerous levels of lead in their blood. Pollutants like lead affect the intelligence of as many as 90 percent of children in some African countries.

With all these environmental problems facing us, it can sometimes seem as if humanity is facing down the barrel of a very big gun. Allen Hammond, the author of *Which World? Scenarios for the Twenty-first Century,* sees three different possibilities for life in the immediate future. His first prediction is what he calls "Market World," in which a global economic boom eliminates most poverty. Continued improvements in agricultural technology lead to huge increases in the amount of food produced. Population growth is brought under control, the average lifespan increases, and pollution is mostly eliminated. The people of Market World are a true global village. The result is not just prosperity for all, but, says Hammond, "a cultural and educational renaissance."

Hammond's second, gloomier scenario is called "Fortress World." In Fortress World, we live in on a planet that's divided among haves and have-nots. Surging populations and environmental problems lead to terrible health conditions in Africa, Latin America, and India, with depleted farmland, polluted water, and skies filled with smog. Forests are chopped down for wood, fish are depleted from the oceans, and entire species are wiped off the face of the earth. Worse, the terrible conditions in the Third World lead to increases in terrorism and crime, much of it aimed at the developed world, which remains healthy and prosperous. Fortress World is a scenario that Malthus may have come up with if he were alive today.

The third and final scenario is Hammond's most radical, if least likely. "Transformed World" is an environmental utopia, where mankind develops a strong desire to protect and preserve the environment, corporations embrace ecologically sound business practices, waste is eliminated through recycling, and energy consumption is stabilized. The rain forests are saved, global warming comes to a halt, and the planet's biodiversity is no longer in danger. Even our urban areas become healthy places to live as mass transportation grows and the internal combustion engine disappears.

Market World, Fortress World, or Transformed World. You can clearly see the beginnings of each of these scenarios in the world today. The big question is, Which world we will be living in by the end of the twenty-first century?

THE COMING AGE OF MEGACITIES

Right around the time Baby Six Billion was born in the Fall of 1999, another milestone was reached. The odds are a little better than fifty-fifty that he or she was born and lives in a city somewhere in the world, not in a small village or rural area. In the twentieth century, the human race went from being a mostly rural species to a mostly urban one. In 1900, only 14 percent of people lived in cities. But more people worldwide now live in cities than in the countryside. Why is that a big deal? Cities have a much deeper impact on the environment. Higher concentrations of people in the same place mean more waste and more pollution, in much less space than the environment can usually absorb. And it's not just cities that will affect the environment in the future, it's the *type* of cities. The twenty-first century will see the emergence of the "megacity": a sprawling, densely populated urban area teeming with millions—even tens of millions—of people.

To understand the environmental impact of a megacity, consider this: In 1800, the biggest city on Earth was London. It was the only city that had more than one million people. Today, well over three hundred metropolitan areas have populations of a million or more, and sixteen cities, including Tokyo, Mexico City, and New York, have more than ten million. By 2015 there will be at least twice as many megacities of ten million people or more, most of them in the developing world—Asia, Africa, and South and Central America. By the time Earth's population hits eight billion, five billion of those people will be city dwellers.

The world's cities take up only 2 percent of the earth's surface, but according to the *International Herald Tribune,* account for roughly 78 percent of the carbon emissions pumped into the atmosphere and 60 percent of the water used by people. Megacities represent environmental disasters waiting to happen. The earth has had billions of years to develop ecosystems that maintain a balance among species. And in the 170 thousand years since humans first appeared, we have spread our environmental impact around by living mostly on the move as nomadic hunters and gatherers. It took the Industrial Revolution, two hundred years ago, to get people to concentrate in cities. Compared to the relative age of the earth, cities first appeared a few seconds ago. The earth hasn't evolved a way to handle them. When cities become fast-growing megacities—especially in poorer parts of the world where environmental concerns take a backseat to day-to-day survival—water supplies can get quickly fouled, and diseases are easily transmitted.

A recent report from the Council on Foreign Relations warned that no one "has the faintest idea of how to provide adequate food, housing, health care, education, and gainful employment to such exploding numbers of people . . . as they crowd into megacities like Mexico City, Cairo, and Calcutta."

Can we cram billions of people into the world's exploding cities without upsetting the environmental apple cart? That will be one of the biggest environmental questions of the twenty-first century. "Over the millennia, humanity has proved to be an artful dodger of fate . . . a master escape artist from traps laid by nature," notes environmental writer Eugene Linden in his book *The Future in Plain Sight: Nine Clues to the Coming Instability.* "Still, it is very late in the game."

BLUE SKIES AHEAD?

If it seems like all the environmental news from the future is bad, don't despair. While the modern day Malthusians have plenty of warning bells to sound, there are those who see much sunnier days ahead.

The late Julian Simon, an economist at the University of Maryland, wrote a book called *The State of Humanity,* in which he made two predictions. "The material conditions of life will continue to get better for most people, in most countries, most of the time, indefinitely," he wrote, "and many people will continue to think and say that the material conditions are getting worse."

Simon was the best known of a school of economists known as *cornucopians,* who insist that population growth is a good thing because it actually increases the amount of useful knowledge available to benefit mankind. More people equals more ideas. If we run out of oil, coal, copper, or iron, these economists argue, someone will invent a substitute. "The main fuel to speed our progress is our stock of knowledge, and the brake is our lack of imagination," Simon wrote. "The ultimate resource is people:

skilled, spirited, and hopeful people who will exert their wills and imaginations for their own benefit, and so, inevitably, for the benefit of us all."

Take that, Malthusians.

Certainly there is cause for optimism. The Kyoto Protocol, for all the problems faced in putting it to work, shows world leaders are concerned about global warming and taking it seriously. The move to cleaner forms of energy and alternatives to the internal combustion engine is a real response to environmental concerns. Biotechnology and genetics promise further abundance and the kind of human cleverness that makes the cornucopians so optimistic. "In the long term, the trends are clearly positive," says futurist John Petersen, founder of the Arlington Institute, a research and policy study group. "We have a generation of kids growing up around the planet who are much more sensitive to the environment. They see people as part of the whole system we live in, not as outside that system."

The optimists have one very big thing going for them: They have been right so far. But the pessimists have always been with us, and no doubt always will. What they have going for them is a future of which no one can be certain. When someone says a pessimist is wrong (or an optimist is right) you can always answer with "so far." The pessimists were wrong when the earth's population went from one to two billion, from two to four billion, and four to six billion. But would they still be wrong if the population hit ten billion? Twenty billion? Fifty billion? With luck, we'll never have to find out. In the end, it may be that we need both optimists and pessimists. We need the pessimists to sound the alarms, and the optimists to answer them.

"It's the task of those of us alive right now to deal with this special phase, to squeeze us through these next fifty years," concludes McKibben. "That's not fair—any more than it was fair that earlier generations had to deal with the Second World War or the Civil War or the Revolution or the Depression or slavery. It's just reality. We need in these fifty years to be working simultaneously on all parts of the equation, on our ways of life, on our technologies, and on our population."

Want to Know More about the Future of Earth and the Environment?

On the Web:

- United Nations Population Information Network (www.undp.org/popin/)
- Committee for the National Institute for the Environment (www.cnie.org/)
- Earthwatch Institute (www.earthwatch.org/)
- EnviroLink Network (www.envirolink.org/)

At the Library:

- *The Future in Plain Sight: Nine Clues to the Coming Instability,* by Eugene Linden (Simon & Schuster, 1998)
- *Maybe One: A Personal and Environmental Argument for Single-Child Families,* by Bill McKibben (Simon & Schuster, 1998)
- *Which World? Scenarios for the 21st Century,* by Allen Hammond (Island Press, 1998)
- *The State of Humanity*, Julian Simon, editor (Blackwell, 1996)
- *The Heat Is On,* by Ross Gelbspan (Perseus Books, 1998)
- *Last Oasis: Facing Water Scarcity,* by Sandra Postel (W. W. Norton & Co., 1997)

CHAPTER 9

Is Anybody Out There?

I find nothing more tantalizing than the thought that radio messages from alien civilizations in space are passing through our offices and homes right now, like a whisper we can't quite hear.

—Dr. Frank Drake, president of the SETI Institute

Sixteen million years ago, a huge comet or asteroid slammed into the planet Mars. The enormous impact blasted chunks of rock and debris through the Martian atmosphere and out into space. One piece of rock floated around silently for millions of years. Then, about thirteen thousand years ago, the four-pound chunk of Mars drifted into Earth's gravitational field and fell to the surface in Antarctica. And there it lay, covered with snow and ice, until meteorite hunters found it in 1984.

In 1995, a small section of this humble Martian rock, sliced, catalogued, filed, and renamed ALH84001, wound up under a microscope at the Johnson Space Center in Houston. Close inspection seemed to indicate something remarkable—the presence of fossilized life. If the tiny wormlike structures were what they appeared to be, evidence of past life on another planet, then this sliver of rock might hold one of the most important scientific discoveries of all time.

While the discovery of life on Mars is by no means universally accepted—a long, loud debate continues to rage over whether the fossils are what they appear to be or not—scientists are becoming increasingly convinced that life is a frequent phenomenon in the universe. They believe that life is likely to occur on other planets that like Earth, have environmental conditions suitable to it. Recent discoveries of planets revolving around other stars outside our solar system have only strengthened the belief that where there are other planets, there may be life.

Of course there is a huge difference between finding life on another planet and finding *intelligent* life. As important a discovery as it would be, finding microbes on Mars is not quite the same thing as finding an advanced civilization in a galaxy far, far away. If it were to occur, contact with intelligent life elsewhere in the universe would be, quite simply, the most shocking piece of news in the history of mankind. It would raise thousands of profound questions for our civilization, questions that would be both troubling and inspiring.

How does mankind fit into the grand scheme of life in the universe? Is intelligent life—or any life at all—a rare event, or is the universe filled with life, from simple microbes to advanced civilizations? And if there are other races of intelligent creatures out there, do they last for a long time, or do they die out in just a few years? Scientists are tantalized by these questions and are trying, against very long odds, to find the answers. The search for intelligent life in the universe is a lonely and frustrating task, but if successful, it would rock our world like no other news since Copernicus proclaimed that the earth revolved around the sun, and not the other way around.

There are potentially billions of planets outside our own solar system that could possibly host some form of life. For years, scientists have trained powerful listening devices to the stars in the hopes of picking up evidence that we're not alone in the cosmos. The more optimistic of these scientists believe that intelligent life elsewhere in the universe is a mathematical near certainty. And in the coming century, they expect to prove it to a skeptical world. Just five hundred years after Columbus discovered America—a mere hiccup in time, cosmically speaking—scientists are hoping to discover distant worlds of which Columbus could not have even dreamed.

LIFE ON MARS?

Dr. David McKay and a group of NASA scientists from the Johnson Space Center in Houston stunned the world in August 1996 with their announcement that they had found fossils of microscopic critters in the Martian meteorite from Antarctica. The discovery was seen as so important that NASA Administrator Daniel Goldin personally rushed to the White House to inform the president and his top deputies of what they had found. "We are not talking about 'little green men," said Goldin. But the little gray worms that McKay and his team had discovered were big enough news all by themselves. If the Big Question is Are We Alone?, the samples from Mars seemed to say the answer was no.

The Martian microbe and the rock it rode in on created a sensation. ABC's Peter Jennings called it "the most spectacular discovery since human beings began looking up." The cover of *TIME* magazine simply declared "Life on Mars." President Clinton spoke to the nation from the White House: "Today Rock 84001 speaks to us across all those billions of years and millions of miles. It speaks of the possibility of life. If this discovery is confirmed, it will surely be one of the most stunning insights into our universe that science has ever uncovered." All this over a piece of piece of rock no bigger than a potato. It was as if this supposed microscopic critter from Mars had pulled a ray gun and said, "Take me to your leader."

The scientific community, however, was not as excited as the media, and not quite as prepared to take McKay's word for it. Other scientists who looked at the samples were less eager to conclude that this piece of the Fourth Rock that crashed into our Third Rock carried evidence of *anything.* The shapes that looked like microbes, skeptics argued, were simply natural crystals. And besides, they said, any evidence of organic materials, originally believed to be left by Martian critters, was probably caused by contamination while the meteorite cooled its heels on the Antarctic ice cap.

"They found these lovely pictures of bacteria-shaped objects that looked for all the world like bacteria," said Dr. Allan Tremain—one of the leading skeptics—of Houston's Lunar and Planetary Institute. Lovely but small, even for bacteria. "From the very beginning, biologists were quite concerned that they were way, way too small for bacteria as we know them. The shapes they showed were about a tenth of the length of a usual bacteria," Tremain wrote.

McKay and his team stuck to their guns. In fact, in March 1999, McKay claimed to have discovered fresh evidence of Martian life in two new meteorites, a 1.3-billion-year-old chunk of space rock that fell to Earth in 1911 near Nakhla, Egypt, and a 165-million-year-old meteorite, that was found in India in 1865. Both samples showed the same microscopic forms that turned up in the 4-billion-year-old Antarctica meteorite. If the findings of McKay's team can be proven, the big difference in age of the two meteorites would prove that life has been present on Mars, at least in bacterial form, for over a billion years of Martian history.

While the size of the "bacteria" fossils in the Antarctica meteorite was the biggest point of criticism when McKay and his team announced their discovery a few years ago, the Egypt and India discoveries are different. The apparent fossils in these two samples are exactly the same size as some familiar Earthbound bacteria. "They're essentially dead ringers for many types of fossil bacteria that we see here on Earth," said McKay. And while that has not silenced all the critics of the life-on-Mars theory, it has made their case just a little tougher to argue.

Indeed, because some of the newer samples are fairly young compared to the age of Mars in general, McKay remains convinced that not only has he found evidence of life on that planet, but that it's *still there today*. "We still have life on Mars. It's still underground somewhere, where there is liquid water, and all we have to do is go there and find it," he told an interviewer recently. "That's my prediction, that we will find living forms on Mars."

To boost the case for life on Mars and elsewhere, scientists are currently exploring life in the harshest and most extreme climates here on Earth—in vents on the ocean floors where bacteria live in water hot enough to boil if it was on the surface. These otherworldly microbes eat hydrogen sulfide, which would kill most life forms on Earth. Weird-looking white spider crabs three feet across and other strange critters feed on the bacteria, creating a food chain unlike any other on the planet. Scientists also are searching in Antarctica, where simple organisms have been found living in the ice. "What we're interested in is understanding the limits of life, understanding the ability of life to survive in cold and dry environments," says Dr. Chris McCay, a NASA scientist who studies microscopic bacteria and algae living in sheets of ice in Antarctica. "It's interesting here on Earth, but it's even more interesting when we consider the possibility of life on Mars or Europa, one of the moons of Jupiter." If simple organisms can live in terrestrial climates once thought completely incapable of supporting life, why can't they live on other planets?

Despite the skepticism over the specific findings of fossilized life from Mars, a consensus seems to be forming among astronomists, biologists, and others that life may indeed be a common phenomenon, on Mars and elsewhere in the universe. If you asked most experts, "Do you think there was life on Mars three and a half billion years ago?" many—perhaps most—would say yes. "The earth and Mars were very similar in terms of liquid water on the surface, temperatures in the atmosphere and everything," observes Seth Shostak, a radio astronomer with the SETI (Search for Extraterrestrial Intelligence) Institute in Mountain View, California. "And life got started on the earth three and a half billion years ago, and it seemed to happen very quickly. And if it happened here, why not on Mars? Is the earth just a miracle planet? Or could what happened here happen more or less anywhere you had the same conditions?"

A definitive answer may come in the first decades of the twenty-first century. Energized by these hints of extraterrestrial life, NASA is mounting several missions to the Red Planet. Ultimately, in 2005, a spacecraft will go to Mars to pick up fresh, uncontaminated samples of Martian rock and carry them back to Earth for analysis, returning to our planet in 2007.

The stakes in the Mars debate have profound implications. If it can be proven that simple life forms exist—or once existed long ago—on our nearest planetary neighbor, we will be forced to rethink much of what we now believe about our universe. "It would give us more confidence that there's life elsewhere beyond Earth, not only on Mars, but in other solar systems, and on other planets," says McKay. "Because if life is present on Mars, that tells us that life in fact may be very common elsewhere."

The stakes in such a discovery couldn't be higher. Scientists from biologists to astrophysicists are working hard to discover the origins and the fundamentals of life in the universe. So far, they have one really good example to study—life on Earth. But, being a skeptical bunch, scientists would like another example, thanks very much. Finding a second instance of life in the universe would answer some of our most important questions. Is life a miracle? Or is it common? Are we alone in the cosmos? Or is life as common as, say, microbes on Mars?

Fresh samples from Mars could also settle another burning question about our origins. Because the supposed Mars microbes are so similar to Earth microbes, some scientists theorize that life on Earth may have *started* on Mars and was transported here inside meteorites like the one McKay and company are studying. That could explain the similarities. It could also mean that you and I—and every other living creature on Earth—are, in fact, Martians. Take *this* to your leader!

"In the first billion years after the solar system was formed, when Mars had a warm climate and abundant water, asteroid impacts were much more frequent than they are now," wrote physicist Freeman J. Dyson, in the November 1997 issue of *The Atlantic.* "We should not be surprised if we find that life, wherever it originated, spread rapidly from one planet to another. Whatever creatures we may find on Mars will probably be either our ancestors or our cousins."

FREEZE-DRIED FISH FROM JUPITER

If Mars proves to be barren, scientists have another contender in the life-is-elsewhere sweepstakes: Europa, one of Jupiter's four largest moons. Pictures taken from the Galileo spacecraft show the surface of Europa to be smooth and covered with ice, with large cracks apparently caused by shifts in a liquid ocean beneath the frozen surface. "The pictures are strikingly similar to some pictures of the ice that floats on the Arctic Ocean," says Dyson, who is the president of the Space Studies Institute in Princeton, New Jersey. "It would not be surprising if Europa had a warm ocean underneath the ice."

Dyson has suggested a novel approach to looking for life on Europa: he advocates searching for freeze-dried fish in orbit around the planet. "Every time a major impact occurs on Europa, a vast quantity of water is splashed from the ocean into the space around Jupiter," he wrote in the *The Atlantic.* "Creatures living in the water far enough from the impact have a chance of being splashed intact into space and being quickly freeze-dried. . . . Even if we did not find freeze-dried fish in Jupiter's ring, we might find other surprises—freeze-dried seaweed, or a freeze-dried sea monster."

Laugh all you want. The man's a legendary physicist and a futurist's futurist. The idea of finding freeze-dried fish in orbit around Jupiter is fanciful, the wildest of long shots. But it illustrates a serious point about searching for life elsewhere in the universe. Nature is full of surprises, and we shouldn't be surprised by anything we discover. As Dyson points out, nobody in Europe had ever seen a duck-billed platypus before explorers brought one back from the New World, and even then, many experts thought it was a hoax. "Many of nature's most beautiful creations might be dismissed as wildly improbable if they were not known to exist," says Dyson. "When we are exploring the universe and looking for evidence of life, either we may look for things that are probable but hard to detect or we may look for things that are improbable but easy to detect. In deciding what to look for, detectability is at least as useful a criterion as probability. Primitive organisms such as bacteria and algae hidden underground may be more probable, but freeze-dried fish in orbit are more detectable." To have the best chance of success, Dyson argues, we need to keep our minds and our eyes open to all possibilities.

If life in the universe is as varied and unique as life here on Earth, then suddenly the cantina scene in *Star Wars* doesn't seem so crazy. It's certainly no more bizarre than giant crabs dining on hydrogen sulfide–eating microbes in 350-degree water miles beneath the surface of the ocean. One thing seems certain. The twenty-first century will offer conclusive proof one way or the other as to whether life, small and humble as it might be, exists on our next-door neighbor as well as elsewhere in our solar system and perhaps beyond. If the answer is yes, one of mankind's oldest and most profound mysteries will at last be solved.

Proof of life on Mars, Europa, or elsewhere could jump-start an age of space exploration unlike any we've seen since the days of the Apollo missions to the moon. Why? Because if life exists on Mars, then, some scientists argue, it must not be unique to our solar system. Just look at the amazing variety of life on Earth—everything from single-cell organisms to plants and animals to human beings. If that's the case on one lonely planet, imagine the variety the universe may hold! Some scientists argue that if intelligent life is common throughout creation, then not only are we not alone, we might not even be especially advanced. What if there are others out there that are like us, or completely different, but intelligent. Could we find them?

Could they find us?

ARE WE ALONE?

Nearly every kid who has ever lived has, at one point, lain down on the ground on a warm summer night and stared out at the billions of stars in the sky, wondering, "Is anyone out there?" Each point of light we see—and billions more we can't see—is a sun. If even a fraction of those suns have planets, and if even a few of those planets have life, then we can't be alone, can we? With all those stars and all those planets, some of them must have intelligent creatures on them—creatures who stare at the sky and wonder if they're the only ones in the universe.

If you've ever had that thought, then without realizing it, you have come very close to expressing something called Drake's

Equation—a formula that has convinced astronomers of something that every kid can feel in his or her bones—that we're not alone. The formula can be used to estimate the abundance of life in the universe based on the number of sunlike stars, the fraction of those stars with orbiting planets, the number of *those* planets capable of sustaining life, the small fraction of those planets where life actually appears, how often intelligent life evolves and how long intelligent civilizations actually last, and so on. Drake's Equation assumes that the human race and its technologies are actually one of the younger civilizations, and that we may well be able to detect radio signals from distant planets that are, technologically speaking, much older than our own.

Now, if Drake's Equation makes it sound as if a lot of factors—stars, planets, etc.—have to line up just perfectly in order to produce intelligent life, you're right. But when you do the math, the equation gives you some appreciation of how vast the universe is—and how likely it is that life exists elsewhere. For example, the Milky Way galaxy, the cloudy band of stars that you see arcing across the sky on a clear summer night contains billions of stars, of which our sun is only one. And the Milky Way is one of billions of galaxies in the universe.

Dr. Frank Drake, who in 1961 devised the famous equation that bears his name, has no doubt that we're not alone. "There are approximately ten thousand advanced civilizations in our Milky Way Galaxy alone," the astronomer and astrophysicist estimates. And if you apply Drake's Equation to the entire universe, which contains perhaps 100 billion other galaxies, there could be *4 trillion* intelligent civilizations out there.

Drake's Equation is the inspiration for dozens of astronomers, physicists, and mathematicians who have devoted their careers to scanning the stars for stray signals from distant civilizations. If the Mars meteorite hinted that life is not unique to Earth, and Drake's Equation indicates that there are large numbers of detectable civilizations out there, then the men and women involved in the search for extraterrestrial intelligence (SETI) are determined to find proof.

"In the end it just boils down to a numbers argument. There

are more stars out there than grains of sand on all the beaches of the earth," observes Seth Shostak. "It would be pretty special if this were the only grain of sand where anything interesting was happening. If astronomy has taught us anything in the last four hundred and fifty years, it's that anytime we thought there was something special about our situation, we were wrong. So to assume that we're not astronomically special, but we are biologically special, is probably wrong too."

"Personally, I find nothing more tantalizing than the thought that radio messages from alien civilizations are passing through our offices and homes, right now, like a whisper we can't quite hear," writes Drake in his autobiography, *Is Anyone Out There?* "In fact, we have the technology to detect such signals *today,* if we only knew where to point our radio telescopes and the right frequency for listening."

Detecting those signals, however, is an immensely difficult task. Ancient explorers set sail in wooden ships to explore distant worlds. The size of the universe makes it impossible to take to the stars in spaceships on a journey of exploration. Even the closest stars are too far away to mount an expedition. The most advanced rockets travel at a brisk 10 miles per second. At that rate, to travel to the star nearest to Earth, Alpha Centauri, would take 60 thousand years! But a radio signal from Alpha Centauri, traveling at the speed of light, would reach us in only 4.2 years. The only way we will ever know if we have company in the universe (in our lifetimes, at least) is by listening for radio signals from distant worlds. There are about one thousand stars within one hundred light years of Earth. These have been the focus of most SETI research so far.

So, today's explorers stay in one place and do their exploring via remote control. The tools of the trade for intergalactic explorers are massive radio telescopes and computers that search tens of thousands of radio frequencies for signals. There are two basic methods scientists use to search the sky for alien radio signals. The first approach is to use giant radio telescopes to search a single star at a time. A radio telescope is similar to the backyard TV satellite dish on a massive scale. The world's largest radio telescope, in Arecibo, Puerto Rico, is a one-thousand-foot-wide aluminum bowl set in a huge hole in the ground.

The second approach is to sweep the heavens using lower-power dishes, hoping to pick up a stray signal. This sounds simple, but it's not. The universe, it seems, is a pretty noisy place. Researchers listening for radio signals from distant worlds have to sort through all sorts of background noise, from radar to telecommunications satellites. Imagine trying to listen in on a conversation between two people halfway across a crowded room, and you have some idea how difficult it is. SETI researchers rely on a second telescope hundreds of miles away from their main telescope to sort out the interference. Because of the earth's rotation, signals from deep space would appear to have a slightly different frequency at the two different locations. Looking for that shift helps scientists judge if something they hear is from Earth, or Earth's orbit, or if it is truly extraterrestrial.

If a signal is detected that might be coming from someplace far off in the galaxy, and if two different antennae thousands of miles apart detect it coming from the same place, then the odds that it is extraterrestrial are far greater. The next step is to move the antenna back and forth in the sky. If the signal is coming from a fixed, far-off point, the signal will go away when you move your focus away from the source. If it's a signal creeping in from the earth, it won't disappear when you do this.

The problem with SETI research, of course, is knowing where to look. With billions of galaxies containing billions of stars, finding extraterrestrial radio signals is truly like searching for a needle in a haystack. How do you know where to point the telescope and what frequency to tune into? Imagine tuning into every radio station in the world trying to find the one playing a specific song. Drake says organized SETI efforts through the late 1980s "was like looking for the needle by strolling past the haystack every now and then. We weren't embarked on a search that had any real chance of success."

SETI scientists are by nature a skeptical bunch. None of them expects—or will admit to expecting—cosmic E-mail anytime soon. But if Drake's Equation is right, and we humans are not alone, evidence of extraterrestrial intelligence could come at any time—today, next week, within a few years. It is entirely possible that you will see proof positive of intelligent life on a distant planet in your lifetime. And if that happens, it will change everything mankind thinks about our place in the grand scheme of things. It will be, quite simply, the most important scientific discovery *ever.*

ARE THE ALIENS LISTENING TOO?

SETI is concerned almost exclusively with listening for broadcasts from other worlds, not broadcasting *to* other worlds. Why not? For one thing, we've been sending signals into space for decades in the form of TV and radio broadcasts. Such broadcasts may be strong enough to be picked up by aliens, but if *I Love Lucy* reruns are being shown on Alpha Centauri, we'd never know. "Our system could not pick up Earth at the distance of the nearest star," Shostak admits. "Our TV broadcasts are not designed to entertain aliens. They're designed to entertain earthlings."

Still he defends the idea of listening to the stars instead of trying to hail others. "I find it an incredulous thought that *nobody* is broadcasting. If I go to a party and I don't feel very sociable, I might decide not to say anything to anybody. But I've never been to a party where no one says anything at all to anyone else," he says.

One of the questions SETI researchers wonder about is how long other civilizations might be able to broadcast. "Once they invent radio, how long do they stay on the air before they, for example, blow themselves up?" Shostak asks. "We've had radio for about one hundred years. That's not a very interesting length of time in terms of the age of the galaxy. It may be that you invent the H-bomb about the time you invent radio. Maybe everybody does that and they're not on the air for very long. Radio signals may be like flashbulbs going off in the galaxy. We may never be looking in the right place at the right time to see one, because they're not on very long."

THE WOW! SIGNAL

Searches for electronic signals from space have been going on since 1960, when Drake himself spent several months searching Epsilon Eridani and Tau-Ceti, two nearby stars, using an eighty-five-foot antenna in West Virginia. And in the forty years since we first tuned into the cosmos, there has been complete silence. Just the usual cosmic background noise and terrestrial interference.

Except once.

In 1977, researchers at Ohio State University detected *something* that remains unexplained to this day. Dr. Robert Dixon, the astronomer running the OSU search recalls, "the signal was unmistakably strong and had all the characteristics [that astronomers would expect] of an extraterrestrial signal." It lasted seventy-two seconds and was so strong that Jerry Ehman, the scientist who observed it, wrote "Wow!" in the margin of the computer printout generated by the signal. The incident is famous among SETI researchers and became known as the "Wow! signal."

What was it? We still don't know. The researchers trained their receivers in the direction of the Wow! source, but heard nothing further. Hundreds of searches in that direction turned up nothing further. "We never found the signal again. It was gone," says Dixon. "In fact, while we were receiving the signal for the first time, it turned off as we observed it." Ehman recalls, "Bob and I speculated extensively about the signal and lists of known sources, including satellites and ground-based transmitters, and found no matches. Hence, the identification of this signal has not been found and probably will never be found."

"Since the possibility of an extraterrestrial origin has not been able to be ruled out," Ehman says, "I must conclude that an ETI (extraterrestrial intelligence) might have sent the signal that we received as the Wow! source." Note that Ehman says "might." Like all scientists involved in the search for extraterrestrial intelligence, Ehman wants additional signals to be received and analyzed by many observatories before coming to the conclusion that

ET has phoned home. "The origin of the Wow! signal is still an open question for me," says Ehman. "I choose not to draw vast conclusions from 'half-vast' data."

Ehman's comments say something very important about the seriousness of SETI research. The men and women who scan the heavens for signs of life are not UFO buffs looking for reasons to believe in extraterrestrial life. They are serious scientists who understand that a high standard of proof must be met in order to convince anyone that life exists elsewhere in the universe. Many SETI searches have found unexplained signals, but unless they can be confirmed by other telescopes, they don't meet the test for proof of intelligent life. Only independent verification will prove that a signal originated from beyond our solar system.

"All of us at SETI are skeptical people," notes project manager Kent Cullers. "We don't just start by saying 'this is the real thing, prove it isn't.' We start by saying 'What could this be? Could this be a system problem? Could it be a satellite? Could it be a communications link that we don't know about?' We have a whole database that's supposed to let us know when some kind of incidental signal happens."

What if a signal proved to be the real thing? What would it tell us? "We wouldn't learn a lot right away. You'd have to go back and build a much bigger setup to see if you could find any message," says Shostak. "And if there's a message, then there are two possibilities. One is that you understand it, and the other is that you don't. If you do understand it, then you're in touch with a civilization that's way ahead of ours, and they tell you all sorts of nifty stuff—all of physics, all of astronomy, the cure for cancer, how to get along, whatever. You just short-circuit a bunch of history and jump into the future, like giving the Amazons a key to the Library of Congress." The other possibility, of course, is that you *don't* understand it. But even then, says Shostak, it would be very interesting. It would put mankind in its place, so to speak, offering instant perspective on where we stand in the cosmos.

Given the laws of physics, however, don't expect a two-way

conversation anytime soon, if ever. Signals could come from spots in the galaxy that are thousands, even millions, of light years from Earth. "If our understanding of the universe is right, there are signals touching you and me right now, already transmitted from distant civilizations, and they've now had time to be transmitted and arrive," says Cullers. "But anything that we receive today, tomorrow, or in the future will be old news for that civilization."

Ultimately, detecting any verifiable signal would be like discovering the New World, only even more profound. "We've been told for four hundred fifty years we're not astronomically special," says Shostak. "We keep getting hit over the head—'the earth's not the center of the universe, the sun's not the center of the universe, our galaxy is not the center of the universe'—but we still like to think that somehow humans are special. That we have a special relationship with the universe, we're unique, we're the crown of creation and all that. It will be interesting to find out if all of that's true."

Or not.

Oops!

WORST PREDICTIONS ABOUT SPACE

Man will never reach the moon regardless of all future scientific advances.

—Dr. Lee De Forest, inventor of the vacuum tube and father of television, 1957

Professor Goddard does not know the relation between action and reaction and the need to have something better than a vacuum against which to react. He seems to lack the basic knowledge ladled out daily in high schools.

—1921 *New York Times* editorial on the work of Robert Goddard, rocketry's pioneer

SETI RESEARCH TODAY

Compared with the cost of the space shuttle program, building a permanent space station, or putting a man on the moon, SETI research is a rock-bottom bargain. In 1993, the last year NASA ran a SETI program, the total budget worked out to about a nickel per American taxpayer—a fraction of the billions the space shuttle eats up. But Congress pulled the plug on SETI funding with a snicker. "Of course there are advanced civilzations in outer space," said one congressman. "But we don't need to spend six million dollars this year to find evidence of these rascally creatures. We only need seventy-five cents to buy a tabloid at the local supermarket."

SETI researchers call that kind of talk "the giggle factor."

The giggle factor is the name for the snickers that come from nonscientists who view the search for life elsewhere in the universe as a waste of time and money. And it's the giggle factor that currently determines how much money the government is spending in pursuit of the most important scientific discovery of all time: Zero. Zilch. Not one thin dime.

Today, SETI research is privately funded. Silicon Valley billionaires have been big fans and financial backers of the search. Movie director Steven Spielberg, the director of *E.T.* and *Close Encounters of the Third Kind,* donated $100,000 to a SETI program at Harvard University. And why not? Aliens, after all, have made him a *very* rich man!

Being a SETI researcher requires an almost unimaginable amount of patience. And not just because of the giggle factor. You sit for long hours, often in the middle of nowhere, looking at data from giant radio telescopes, waiting, as one researcher says, "for cosmic E-mail." In addition to having to explain to your friends and family that, yes, you really *do* look for evidence of intelligent life in the universe, you go to work every day almost certain to fail. Even the most optimistic people in the field say there's a 90 percent chance that they'll never live to see the first confirmed contact with another civilization. Along with the giggle factor, one of the other obstacles SETI researchers face is people who ask if there is life out there, why hasn't it been found by now? "I'm personally fairly optimistic," says Shostak "but mind you, this is a little like asking Christopher Columbus, 'You haven't found any continents yet and you've been sailing for a week. Are you *ever* going to find any?'"

Long odds, no money, little respect. Why would anyone devote their life and career to this? "There have been 100,000 thousand generations before us and, as you said, every generation had twelve-year-olds who would stand out in the backyard, look up at the sky, and wonder if there was anyone looking back. They could only wonder about it," says Shostak. "For the first time, we can do experiments [to find the answer]. That's a very privileged position. It's sort of like what happened in the late fifteenth century, where the first time you actually had the technology to cross oceans. That opened up vistas that changed the world."

SETI AND UFOS

Want to see a SETI researcher get mad? Ask him about UFOs. One of the difficulties serious SETI researchers like Drake, Shostak, and their colleagues face is that people who don't understand what they do tend to lump them in with UFO buffs and science-fiction fans. Actually, there are UFO buffs who are convinced that SETI is part of a conspiracy to keep alien life a big secret. "It would be much more interesting if you found them in the backyard instead of halfway across the galaxy," Shostak sighs. "Unfortunately, none of that evidence stands up, in my opinion and in the opinion of just about everybody I know."

Based on simple math and physics, SETI researchers have a hard time believing in UFOs. "Most of the public have no conception of the energy, time, and money required to send a spacecraft through the hundreds of light years of space, says Jerry Ehman. "The writers of *Star Trek* haven't helped here." A small spaceship traveling five light years to a nearby star at 70 percent the speed of light—*way* faster than anything mankind has built so far—would consume 500 thousand times the amount of energy used in the United States each year! The laws of probability indicate that there is almost certainly intelligent life out there. But the laws of physics indicate it is just as unlikely that they'll come knocking on our door.

"I can do a simple calculation that says that maybe every one hundred thousand years an advanced civilization might send a probe to this planet. And if that's what we were getting, I might investigate it," says Cullers. "But when we get one hundred thousand reports *a year,* that's a whole different thing, and most of those have got to be nonsense."

Yes, the truth is out there. But simple logic says that it's probably going to stay out there.

Some SETI researchers are concerned that UFO buffs and wild-eyed conspiracy theorists actually damage their reputation and hurt what they are trying to accomplish. "I constantly have to say, 'No, this is real physics. This is real astronomy,' and 'No, we want proof that everyone can confirm," says Cullers. "We don't have alien signals hiding in a closet somewhere."

The sense of wonder and awe with which many people view SETI research is both a blessing and a curse for the men and women who do it. But if the people at the SETI Institute succeed, the names Drake, Cullers, and Shostak will go down in history next to the names Columbus, Magellan, and Vespucci. That must make the giggles a little easier to endure.

Still, there are plenty of UFO buffs and conspiracy theorists who are convinced that there is already proof of intelligent life—even crashed spaceships and alien corpses in government warehouses—and that SETI researchers are all part of the coverup. "That's complete nonsense," Shostak says with a laugh. "Every time we get a false alarm—and that's happened two or three times in the past couple of years, where we've gotten a signal that for a while looked good—there's tremendous excitement, the newspapers start calling. I've never seen anybody with black hats and narrow ties show up saying 'We're going to shut you down.' I don't know where those guys are, but they never seem to pay any attention," he says.

Keep in mind that the first thing SETI scientists do when they find an unexplained signal is to call other observatories and ask them to try to confirm it. That means that within minutes, you'd have several observatories, each with dozens of astronomers—and within minutes their spouses, boyfriends and girlfriends, kids and dogs—who suddenly all know about the greatest discovery in history. Not much chance of keeping *that* a secret.

But as long as Hollywood can make hit movies out of aliens and UFOs, the problem won't go away. Frank Drake, one of the founding fathers of SETI research, has even been accused by UFO buffs of having performed autopsies on alien bodies. "I have no medical training at all," he laughs. "I wouldn't know how to dissect a frog, let alone an alien."

LIFE ON THE KUIPER BELT

Thinking farther out—a lot farther out—is it possible that one day mankind could live somewhere other than Earth? Could we one day colonize other planets, moons, or asteroids the way Europeans colonized the New World five hundred years ago? Quite possibly. Doing so, however, will probably require breakthroughs, not in space travel technology, but in biotechnology. The same breakthroughs that are today letting us genetically engineer plants and animals with desirable traits could one day be used to create plants and animals that can survive in alien climates.

Scientists and engineers are already at work on an experiment to build a small oxygen-making machine to be sent to Mars. Researchers at the University of Arizona's Aerospace and Mechanical Engineering Department are building an "oxygen generating subsystem" that will go aboard the Mars Surveyor 2001 mission, scheduled to land on Mars in January 2002. The device will produce small amounts of oxygen from the carbon dioxide in the thin Martian atmosphere. "This is a landmark experiment," says one researcher. "It is the first time in human history that we will produce a consumable of use to humans from extraterrestrial resources." If the experiment is successful, it could be the prototype for a larger system that, well into the future, could produce vast quantities of breathable oxygen for a human colony on Mars.

The other big hurdle to clear before we can begin colonizing space is cost. Colonizing the solar system might be doable, but given the current state of our technology it would be impossibly expensive. "No law of physics or biology forbids cheap travel and settlement all over the solar system and beyond. But it is impossible to predict how long this will take," says Freeman Dyson. "My guess is that the era of cheap unmanned missions will be the next fifty years, and the era of cheap manned missions will start sometime late in the twenty-first century," he writes. Dyson is making an educated guess based on history. It took 128 years from Columbus's first voyage until the Pilgrims landed on Plymouth Rock. "So I'm guessing that in 2085, one hundred and twenty-eight years after the launch of the first Sputnik, the private settlement of Pilgrims all over the solar system will begin," he predicts.

And don't be surprised—if you live long enough—to see human colonies sprouting up in some unlikely places. As Dyson points out, most of the habitable surface area in our solar system is not found on neighboring planets, but on asteroids, which are made of rock, and comets, which are made of ice. A large band of asteroids can be found between Mars and Jupiter. Comets are even better candidates, since they are made of ice. Where there's ice, there's water—a necessity for human survival. And there's a huge band of comets called the Kuiper Belt orbiting just beyond Neptune. Dyson estimates that the total surface area of the trillions of objects in the Kuiper Belt is about a thousand times the surface area humans have on Earth.

"Life in the Kuiper Belt would be different from life on Earth, but not necessarily less beautiful or more confined," Dyson wrote in a recent cover story in *The Atlantic.* "After a century or two there would be metropolitan centers, cultural monuments, urban sprawl—all the glories and discontents of a high civilization. Soon, restless spirits would find the Kuiper Belt too crowded. But there would be an open frontier and a vast wilderness beyond. Beyond the Kuiper Belt lies a more extended swarm of comets—the Oort Cloud, farther away from the Sun and still untamed."

Want to Know More About the Future of SETI and Space?

On the Web:

- SETI Institute (www.seti.org/)
- Space Studies Institute (www.ssi.org/)
- The Planetary Society (www.planetary.org/)

At the Library:

- *Other Worlds: The Search for Life in the Universe,* by Michael D. Lemonick (Simon & Schuster, 1998)
- *Is Anyone Out There?* by Frank Drake and Dava Sobel, (Delta, 1994)

CHAPTER 10

What Could Go Wrong?

It used to be a polarized world, good guys and bad guys, us and them. Now, it's a multipolar world. . . . The enemy is not a large bear, but a whole raft of snakes.

—Lt. Gen. Patrick Hughes, director of the U.S. Defense Intelligence Agency

So far, the future seems like a pretty cool place. OK, so it'll be a little more crowded. We'll have a few small ethical dilemmas with privacy and our ability to monkey with the gene pool, but that's a small price to pay, you might be thinking, for unlimited wealth, the end of all diseases, wiping out hunger and colonizing the solar system. The future? Bring it on, baby!

Well, maybe . . . just maybe . . . the future won't be all that it's cracked up to be. Something could go wrong. In fact, if you've been to the movies lately, you might have detected a slight case of the millennium jitters on the big screen, with one movie after another promising the end of the world (with spectacular special effects, of course). In a way, this is nothing new. Hollywood has always been great at knowing exactly what scares the bejeezus out of us at any particular moment in time—and pushing our buttons to make us sweat. In the 1950s, we were afraid of atomic war and nuclear fallout. So the movies gave us giant ants and grasshoppers, and lizards like Godzilla, all made massive, thanks to radiation. The 1970s gave us disaster movies by the dozen, on planes, in high-rise buildings, and on the high seas. More recently, the movies have played on our fears of crime, serving up a enough slashers, psychopaths, and serial killers to keep the police—and the undertaker—working overtime.

And it's not just the movies. Something about the turn of the century just put people in a morbid frame of mind. A poll by *USA Today* on the eve of the millennium showed three out of four Americans expected a deadly new disease to emerge in the next twenty-five years, while two out of three expect a "global environmental catastrophe." You think *that's* pessimistic? Try this: a majority—51 percent—agreed that it's at least somewhat likely that civilization will be destroyed by a nuclear or other man-made disaster during the twenty-first century. But why stop there? Thirty-eight percent said they expect the earth will be destroyed by an asteroid or other environmental disaster, while nearly four out of ten expect to see Judgment Day or some form of religious cataclysm. Phew!

On the other hand, 53 percent said they're optimistic that the quality of life for average Americans will be better by 2025. *Huh??!?* The only explanation is that those polled must think the average American is immune to comets, asteroids, plagues, and the holy wrath of God Almighty. Either that or these people are spending *way* too much time at the movies.

Our movies and public opinion polls do tell us something serious, however. They tell us that people are nervous. Just when things seem to be going great is when the pessimists among us start looking over their shoulders and waiting for—no, *expecting*—disaster to strike. The bad news is that there will be plenty of things to worry about in the twenty-first century. Most troubling is that many of the great advances of the twenty-first century that we've talked about so far—in biotechnology, genetics, information technology—have the potential to jump up and bite us in the, er, asteroids.

FROM Y2K TO TEOTWAWKI (THE END OF THE WORLD AS WE KNOW IT)

If you're an optimist, here's some advice to get you through the twenty-first century: Study hard, go to college, and get a good job.

Save lots of money. Take good care of your body, because you're going to live a really long time and you'll want to be in the peak of health to enjoy it all. It's going to be an era of miracles and wonders. Count yourself lucky to be alive!

And for you pessimists, here's some different advice: Train yourself in survival skills. Buy ammunition. Stockpile water, canned goods, and nonperishable food. Buy a shovel, and dig a deep bunker in your backyard. Get in. It's going to be one scary century.

Can we be talking about the same one hundred years? Absolutely. It just depends who you are talking to. If history is a guide, the truth won't be one or the other, but somewhere in between. The twentieth century brought us incredible advances in science, medicine, and technology—along with two World Wars, the atom bomb, ethnic and racial conflicts, and a big hole in the ozone layer. Likewise, the twenty-first century will undoubtedly bring both good and bad. And just as the emerging technological breakthroughs we have discussed seem too incredible and wonderful to be believed, some of the threats and dangers we face seem too terrible to be true.

First a word of warning: If you're the type of person who dives under the seats at the first sign of a movie monster, read no farther! Because we're about to look at the potential dark side of the twenty-first century—a world in which we may teeter between danger and disaster, grappling with problems that mankind has never had to deal with before. Problems that could change our lives in some pretty nasty ways.

If we survive, that is.

What can go wrong in the twenty-first century? Plenty. Global warming, food shortages, new and frightening epidemics of disease, overpopulation, chemical and biological warfare, "information terrorism," nuclear holocaust, widening gaps between rich and poor, catastrophic computer crashes—basically, the end of the world as we know it. And that's just for starters. The most interesting and potentially terrifying thing to consider, however, is that human beings are about to become "active choreographers of nature" on an unprecedented scale, as Michio Kaku points out in his book *Visions: How Science Will Revolutionize the 21st Century.* We stand on the verge of an era in which we have unprecedented ability to manipulate the world around us, using everything from genetics to nanotechnology. Our fate may ultimately depend on our ability to make the right choices, and to see far enough into the future to understand the consequences of our decisions.

One of the unfortunate facts of human history is that we have always had a gift for finding new and ever more efficient ways for slaughtering each other, and there will almost certainly be lots of "progress" on that front as well. Let's take a look at a few of the more likely, if depressing, potential nightmares of the next one hundred years.

TWENTY-FIRST-CENTURY WARS

The most powerful weapon in future wars won't be a nuclear warhead, cruise missile, or laser-guided smart bomb. It won't be a fighter, bomber, aircraft carrier, or submarine either. If military strategists are right, the most potent weapon in any arsenal in the twenty-first century is something that can be found in millions of homes. In fact, there's one sitting my lap as I type these words. It's the computer. Experts are increasingly convinced that future wars will be fought with bits and bytes, not just bombs.

Until recently, the people who sit up late at night at the Pentagon planning future wars threw around phrases like *mutually assured destruction, missile gap,* or *strategic and tactical nukes.* But the Information Revolution has them grappling with a new war vocabulary, including such terms as *data weapons, logic bombs, net war, virus insertion, cyberterror,* and *hacker warriors.*

The *biggest* buzzword military strategists throw around these days is *assymetries.* The United States, as the world's only superpower, has the military personnel, technology, and firepower to apply overwhelming force to win any conventional battle anywhere in the world. Don't worry about invaders landing on the beach and taking us over. It simply can't happen. Launching a conventional attack on the United States would be a suicide mission for anyone who dared to try. So they won't. Instead, a clever enemy will look for asymmetries, ways in which our technological superiority can be used against us.

Our very dependence on technology may be our biggest weakness. So the next big war, experts predict, will be aimed at bringing down computer and communications links and other vital electronic functions that keep the country and the economy running. The objective of this kind of warfare is to not to seize land, as in a traditional war, but to seize control of the things that make our society function and use them against us. The soldier of the future is not an armed warrior—it's a computer hacker.

Why attack with hackers instead of soldiers? Say, for example, you're in charge of an international drug cartel, a small country or a terrorist organization committed to bringing down the United States. It doesn't make sense to buy fighters, bombers, and aircraft carriers. First of all, they're expensive and almost no one will sell them to you. But more important, they're too easy to find and destroy. And how are you going to win a war against an armed-to-the-teeth superpower like the United States anyway? Instead, the goal will be to win at "information warfare."

But don't think for a second that future wars will be like video games—images splattering on a screen with no real-life consequences. War in the twenty-first century is more likely to be fought with weapons of mass *disruption* than of mass destruction, but the effects could be just as deadly. Information attacks might be aimed at disrupting vital communications, transportation, news and financial links, bringing everyday life to a halt and causing deadly chaos in the streets.

What would a "cyber war" look like? It might start innocently enough, with a few simple annoyances to throw us off balance. Imagine one morning that automated teller machines start malfunctioning. When people go to withdraw a few bucks, they find that their accounts have been emptied. Passengers might arrive at airports, only to find their reservations mysteriously have been canceled, or that they've been booked to entirely different destinations. Now imagine a wave of plane crashes as the nation's air traffic computers all go down. Ambulances and fire engines don't respond because they're off chasing a sudden rash of false alarms. Then the phones go dead everywhere. Computer failures hit the New York Stock Exchange, shutting down the market and triggering a worldwide financial panic. Chaos spreads. Hospital computers are jammed with nonexistent patients who are booked for emergency surgery, while real patients sit in waiting rooms and parking lots. Trains and ships carrying the goods we need to live from day to day get rerouted to wrong destinations. As it becomes obvious that something is very, *very* wrong, false emergency warnings are issued over radio and TV stations urging people to evacuate major cities. Now imagine that the nation's power grid gets hacked and suddenly, from coast to coast, everything *just goes black.* As night falls, rumors of biological and chemical attacks spread like wildfire. Within hours, the most advanced civilization Earth has ever known is reduced to panic, hysteria, and anarchy, as people turn into savages with only one thought in their heads: survival.

Not one shot has been fired.

As you can imagine, the deadly panic and chaos that would follow an attack on the nation's information and communications infrastructure would probably make the damage done by a bombing raid seem minor by comparison. Indeed, this kind of information warfare has convinced many military thinkers that some future wars may not be fought between armies on battlefields at all. By hacking into sensitive communications areas such as air traffic control centers, 911 calls, or military facilities, or crippling banking and financial computers or the electrical power grid, small numbers of people could do incredible damage and wreak unimaginable havoc.

How vulnerable are we? Do you really want to know?

A frightening report from the Center for Strategic and International Studies in Washington in 1999 warned that the United States "has erected immensely complex information systems on insecure foundations." Our economy, the report warned, "is totally dependent on these systems. America's adversaries and enemies recognize this dependency and are developing weapons of mass disruption and mass destruction." According to the study, for as little as $10 million, thirty computer hackers strategically located around the world "could bring the United States to its knees."

No invading army of millions of soldiers, no armada of warships, no airborne division of fighters and bombers. *Thirty people.* That's all it would take. In 1997, the Pentagon tested computer security in a virtual wargame called Operation Eligible Receiver. Hackers worked for two weeks trying to break into sensitive military and civilian computer systems. They succeeded beyond the wildest dreams—or worst nightmares—of military officials. They gained access to computers belonging to the U.S. Pacific Command in Hawaii, which oversees 100 thousand U.S. troops in Asia. More frightening still, they tapped into the U.S. electrical power grid system, showing that it could be sabotaged, and that the entire country could plunge into a power outage. "We found that we have a lot of work to do to provide better security," Pentagon spokesman Ken Bacon said. "We're not alone in this regard." The exercise led to congressional hearings on how to better prepare the United States to recognize and combat attacks on military and civilian electronic targets.

TERRORISM

The strategy and tactics of warfare will not be the only thing changing; so will the enemies. Until now, wars have generally pitted nation against nation, or governments against armed, well-organized rebels. But military theorists are now convinced that the greatest threats we face in the new century will come from "enemies without borders." These enemies could be rogue nations run by corrupt governments, drug cartels, or other organized criminals, terrorist organizations, or even doomsday cults. Even if we don't see all-out information wars, most defense experts seem to agree that we will see more terrorist attacks in the twenty-first century, and with frightening new weapons. Bombs, guns, and electronic disruption will be joined by horrifying biological and chemical weapons.

Even President Clinton has warned that it is "highly likely" that a terrorist group will launch or threaten a germ or chemical attack on American soil within the next few years. "If there is never an incident," the president told *The New York Times,* "nobody would be happier than me twenty years from now if the same critics would be able to say, 'Oh, see, Clinton was a kook, nothing happened.'" FBI director Louis Freeh has testified before congress that "as chemical and biological weapons of mass destruction become more accessible, we face the potential of even more catastrophic acts of terrorism." The protection of the United States and its people from acts of terrorism "remains one of our highest priorities," Freeh said.

As concerned as military planners and security experts might be about an Infowar, they are even more worried about the threat of terrorism on U.S. soil. The danger will almost certainly grow in the twenty-first century for two reasons: terrorists ranging from religious fanatics to individual crackpots like the Unabomber are likely to act for a much wider variety of reasons than ever before. Moreover, terrorists may gain access to weapons of mass destruction, including crude nuclear weapons, germs and biological agents, and poison gas weapons. Simply put, it's never been easier for so few people to do such massive damage—and for so little reason.

Experts worry that we could see a new type of "catastrophic terrorism" attack that will make previous horrors like the Oklahoma City and World Trade Center bombings seem mild by comparison. "A successful attack with weapons of mass destruction could certainly take thousands, or tens of thousands, of lives," notes the influential magazine *Foreign Affairs.* "If the device that exploded in 1993 under the World Trade Center had been nuclear, or had effectively dispersed a deadly pathogen, the resulting horror and chaos would have exceeded our ability to describe it. Such an act of catastrophic terrorism would be a watershed event in American history. It could involve loss of life and property unprecedented in peacetime and undermine America's fundamental sense of security, as did the Soviet atomic bomb test in 1949." Ominously, the magazine concludes that the danger of weapons of mass destruction being used against

America "is greater now than at any time since the Cuban missile crisis of 1962."

Can it be avoided? "I wish I could be optimistic, but I can't," Robert Blitzer, chief of the FBI's Counter-Terrorism Planning Section, said recently. "It's a continuing war."

DISASTERS FROM SPACE

OK, here's some relatively good news: Despite Hollywood's recent fascination with alien invasions, killer comets, and asteroid strikes, the chances of a giant piece of space junk crashing to Earth and ending life as we know it is remote. But the bad news is, it's not impossible either. In fact, on any given day, our planet is peppered with more than one hundred tons of space debris—mostly pieces so small they pose almost no threat to life on Earth. Of course, all it would take is one decent-size comet or asteroid to make things pretty grim for years to come, if not forever.

Can it happen? It already has. And not that long ago. On June 30, 1908, an object the size of a fifteen-story building, probably a piece of a comet, came crashing into Earth's atmosphere over a remote stretch of Siberia. It created an explosion as powerful as two thousand atomic bombs, flattening trees for hundreds of miles. The odds of probability say that a similar strike is likely sometime in the next several hundred years. And next time, we might not be so lucky as to have it hit an uninhabited part of the planet. Of course, the comet that hit Siberia was a pebble compared to the sixty-mile-wide object that slammed into Mexico's Yucatan peninsula 65 million years ago. Scientists think the dust and debris it released into the atmosphere killed off the dinosaurs and most other life on Earth.

"The possibility of a comet striking the earth "certainly exists, but it's decreasing," says Marina Fomenkova, a comet researcher at the University of California at San Diego's Center for Space. That's simply because there are fewer comets lurking out there with the potential to hit the earth. "There was a period of heavy bombardment in the first billion years of the earth's history, but there aren't as many now," she says. "The bigger it is, the easier it is to discover." Indeed, astronomers know of at least 1,700 comets that cross Earth's orbit from time to time, but none are considered a threat to hit the earth. At least not anytime in the next couple of decades.

Still, if medical science is successful in dramatically increasing our life span, there is a chance you could live long enough to see a close call with a comet when you are, oh, 140 years old or so. The International Astronomical Union issued a comet collision warning a few years ago for August 14, 2126. When comet Swift-Tuttle, which passed within several million miles of the earth in 1992, makes a return visit to our solar system then, the IAU calculates there is a one-in-ten-thousand chance it could strike the earth. Small odds, but people who buy lottery tickets pin their hopes on chances that are *way* more remote. If it hits, say bye-bye to just about every life form on Earth more sophisticated than a cockroach.

And if it misses us in 2126, well, there's always next time. Because the path of the comet crosses the earth's orbit, Brian Marsden, of the Harvard-Smithsonian Center for Astrophysics, says, "Sooner or later, it will hit us. Over a million years, there's an excellent chance of being hit." The risk of a collision next time it passes by, however, is "small enough that everybody shouldn't worry, but large enough that it should be taken seriously," he says.

The late Carl Sagan, one of the world's most famous astronomers, once said, "The earth lives in a bad neighborhood." Sagan was very concerned about the possibility of an Earth strike. "Orbiting the Sun along with us, there are an enormous number of asteroids and comets," he said. "Some cross the earth's orbit and sooner or later, the earth will be in the way, and impacts will occur. The chance of this occurring in the near future is extremely small, but it is at least as great as the chance of an individual dying on an airplane trip, and many individuals consider that chance great enough to take out special insurance for their trips."

One thing is for certain: If it happens, you want to be anywhere but here. When fragments of the comet Shoemaker-Levy slammed into Jupiter in 1994, the explosion was more powerful than every nuclear bomb on Earth combined. The black smears the impact left on the planet's surface were bigger than the earth itself. It's the most compelling reason possible for colonizing the solar system. Sooner or later, we'll have nowhere else to go.

GENETIC TAMPERING

In Chapter 6, we looked at the frightening but probably inevitable issue of "designer babies"—children whose parents would decide before they were born what traits and attributes they would have. If, as expected, genetic testing and gene therapy become standard features of having children, they have the potential to take us down a very disturbing path.

Princeton University professor Lee M. Silver, in his influential book *Remaking Eden,* describes a world 350 years from now, where society no longer struggles with issues of race or ethnic prejudice, but where there are two classes of people—Naturals and the Gene-enriched, or simply "GenRich."

"The GenRich—who account for 10 percent of the American population—all carry synthetic genes," writes Silver. "Genes that were created in the laboratory and did not exist with the human species until twenty-first-century reproductive geneticists began to put them there. The GenRich are a modern-day class of genetic aristocrats." He describes a world with GenRich athletes, with enhanced skills so extraordinary that they are clearly nonhuman. They can no longer compete against Naturals; it simply would be unfair. There are GenRich scientists, GenRich musicians, artists, and intellectuals, who control the economy, the media, entertainment, and knowledge industries. Their children attend elite private schools "rich in the resources required for them to take advantage of their enhanced genetic potential." The Naturals, meanwhile, whose skills and intellect are no better match for the GenRich than their athletes, hold down jobs providing services and manual labor while sending their children to public schools, where they learn only the skills they'll need to replace their parents in their marginal jobs.

Then one day, scientists make an amazing discovery. They find that among the rare intermarriages between GenRich and Naturals, there is a 90 percent infertility rate. In other words, genetic engineering has produced not just two different classes of human beings, but it's beginning to splinter mankind into two different *species.*

A mere science-fiction fantasy? Silver says no. "What has yet to catch the attention of the public at large," he writes, "is the incredible power that emerges when current technologies in reproductive biology are brought together in the form of *reprogenetics.* With reprogenetics, parents could gain complete control over their genetic destiny, with the ability to guide and enhance the characteristics of their children and their children's children as well."

Silver argues that in the end, the well-known nightmare scenarios in George Orwell's *1984* and Aldous Huxley's *Brave New World* got it all wrong. It's not Big Brother or an all-powerful government that will run our lives and seize control of human reproduction—it's parents. Couples who quite naturally want to give their children every advantage won't draw the line at correcting genetic defects that could lead to disease. They'll opt for genes that will increase their kids' chances for happiness and success.

It will never be allowed, you say? Who will stop them? In a society like ours that values individual freedom above all else, Silver argues, it is hard to imagine a reason parents would not be allowed to use reprogenetics to shape their lives and their children's. "And therein lies the dilemma," writes Silver. While each individual use of the technology can be viewed as a personal choice, "together they could have dramatic, unintended long-term consequences."

Biotechnology critic Jeremy Rifkin echoes Silver's concern. "Meritocracy," the idea that the person with the most talent and skills rises to the top, could give way to what he calls a *genetocracy,* with people stereotyped by their genes, making way, says Rifkin, "for the emergence of an informal biological caste system in countries around the world."

PLAGUES AND EPIDEMICS

The Black Death in the fourteenth century wiped out a third of the population of Europe. The diseases (along with gunpowder and bullets) that Europeans unwittingly brought to the New World wiped out as much as three quarters of the population of what is now Mexico, and the complete populations of some Caribbean islands. In 1918, a worldwide epidemic of influenza killed over 20 million people. Since the 1980s, the AIDS virus has killed nearly fifteen million people worldwide; over 25 million more have the virus that causes AIDS. Advances in medicine have made us lower our guard against many infectious diseases, but as the AIDS epidemic has shown, the threat of incurable viruses is still very much with us. And terrifying new bugs like Ebola, Marburg, and hantaviruses have a nasty habit of springing up from time to time. Plus, new strains of old diseases have emerged recently that are resistant to the antibiotics that have been used to hold them at bay for decades.

The most ominous piece of epidemic-related news for the twenty-first century is that AIDS, Ebola, and other new and terrifying diseases emerging from the tropics appear to be related to mankind's destruction of the rain forests. "In a sense, the earth is mounting an immune response against the human species," writes Richard Preston in *The Hot Zone,* a best-selling book about a near-miss outbreak of Ebola in suburban Washington, D.C. "Nature has interesting ways of balancing itself. . . . The rain forest has its own defenses. The earth's immune system, so to speak, has recognized the presence of the human species and is starting to kick in."

Could other lethal, uncurable diseases be lurking, waiting to make the jump from animals and other species of the rain forest to humans? No one knows for sure. But the most terrifying prospect is that an apocalyptic plague could be spread on purpose, as an act of war or terrorism. "Ebola is horrible enough," warns Preston, "but scientists are white-knuckled-scared about viruses coming out of laboratories. My fear of nuclear weapons has been transferred into my fear of biological weapons." These are not irrational fears either.

"We have every reason to believe that the first half of the twenty-first century will be dominated by a biological threat," says Steven Block, a molecular biology professor at Princeton University. "I hope it won't take the biological equivalent of Hiroshima for people to realize the danger." Several incidents in the last several years have demonstrated just how serious is the threat of a biological attack:

- September 1984, Dalles, Oregon. Members of the Rajneeshpuram cult spread salmonella bacteria in local restaurants in an attempt to make people too sick to vote on issues affecting the cult in local elections. More than 750 people fell ill—nearly a tenth of the town. Forty-five people were hospitalized.
- In 1989, Los Angeles, California. An organization calling itself the Breeders sent a letter to the mayor, claiming that they had spread Mediterranean fruit flies, a pest that harms citrus crops. The claim was later confirmed by the U.S. Department of Agriculture.
- May 1995, Tokyo, Japan. Members of the doomsday cult Aum Shinrikyo released nerve gas in subway cars at rush hour. Five thousand people were stricken; twelve died. It was later learned that the cult had its own microbiology lab, and that it tried to release deadly bacteria from the top of a Tokyo skyscraper. They also set up offices in New York and tried unsuccessfully to acquire the deadly Ebola virus.
- February 1998, Las Vegas, Nevada. A university-trained biochemist, once kicked out of his local militia for holding views that were too extreme even for them, was arrested in Nevada under suspicion of possessing deadly anthrax spores.

"It's the world in which we live," concedes Dr. James Hughes, director of the National Center for Infectious Diseases at the U.S.

Centers for Disease Control and Prevention. "There have been a lot of wake-up calls."

It's frightening enough to think of the harm that can be done by doomsday cults, zealots, and fanatics. More frightening still is the realization that several governments around the world have secretly developed and stockpiled biological and chemical weapons to use in attacks on other countries. The world got a frightening look at the threat of germ warfare between nations when a former Soviet biological weapons specialist defected to the United States in 1992. Ken Alibek served as deputy director of Biopreparat, the former Soviet Union's secret biological warfare program, until he defected to the United States. His work included creating bacteria and viruses for biological weapons, and overseeing the development of ways to launch such weapons, including bombs and ballistic missiles. Alibek has said that he worked on fifty-two different strains of deadly viruses and bacteria, and that his country's plans called for several different diseases to be released in American cities at the same time—in quantities great enough to wipe out the entire population of Earth several times over. Alibek says not much can be done to protect people from biological warfare. "Too much hope is placed in vaccines. Even if vaccines existed for every possible agent—and they do not—it would be impossible to inoculate every person in the United States," he wrote in a *New York Times* article. "And vaccines are of relatively little use if an attack has already occurred."

Experts say the most likely candidate for use in a germ warfare attack would be the deadly anthrax bacteria. Unless terrorists announced that they had spread anthrax, which is unlikely, experts fear we would not even recognize an attack until it was too late. "After a period of about three days, people would begin to notice—some of them—that there was some kind of a new cold going around the city," says Richard Preston. Unfortunately, antibiotics would have been needed on the first day of infection to save most people. "Then on about day four, you suddenly develop lethal anthrax pneumonia, and your lungs fill up," he says. "You simply stop breathing. These anthrax victims will be describing to the doctor how they feel, and they will die in mid-sentence."

The scariest thing about a germ warfare attack, public health officials and the FBI agree, is how simply it could be done and how quickly it would spread. For example, a lone attacker, vaccinated against smallpox, could release the virus on board a 747, infecting hundreds of people. Each passenger would leave the plane and come into contact with countless others, spreading the disease like wildfire before the original victims even knew they were sick. "I think it would be the closest thing to a living hell that I could imagine," Michael Osterholm, chief of disease epidemiology at the Minnesota Department of Public Health and a terrorism consultant, told *ABC News* last year. "This really is a doomsday scenario. I don't think many people could ever believe it would happen in modern-day medicine with all the tools that we have, but it's real," he said.

Genetically altered bacteria, or "superviruses," which experts like Alibek and others already believe exist, raise the stakes—and the potential terror—even higher. These are laboratory strains of anthrax and other bacteria that are vaccine-proof. Farther down the road, another potentially lethal side effect of the Genetic Revolution will be the ability to create and produce biological weapons that target specific ethnic or racial groups, a development that could have grim consequences in parts of the world where ethnic hatred periodically erupts in violence. "It will unfortunately be possible to design biological weapons of this type when more information on genome research is available," Dr. Vivienne Nathanson, head of science and health policy at the British Medical Association (BMA) predicted recently. The apartheid government in South Africa, for example, is reported to have stockpiled biological agents to use against its black population. One of the reasons germ warfare attacks have been so rare, in fact, is fear that such weapons would also kill the people using them, not just the intended victims. Genetically targeted weapons would reduce or eliminate that possibility, actually making it more likely that they will be used.

Oops!

WORST PREDICTIONS ABOUT DISASTERS

God Himself could not sink this ship.

—Unidentified steward aboard the R.M.S. *Titanic*

No matter what happens, the U.S. Navy is not going to be caught napping.

—U.S. Secretary of the Navy Frank Knox, December 4, 1941. The Japanese bombed Pearl Harbor three days later.

WAKING NIGHTMARES

Scared yet? Here are a couple more things to keep you up at night:

CRIME A study by the National Center for Juvenile Justice in Pittsburgh predicted that the number of murders and other violent crimes committed by kids would double by 2010. Much of the rise is expected to be caused by a new breed of young thugs, dubbed "superpredators" by Princeton University professor John Dilulio. "This new horde from hell kills, maims, and terrorizes merely to become known, or for no reason at all," says Dan Coburn, a former superior court justice and public defender in New Jersey. "These teens have no fear of dying and no concept of living."

INTERNATIONAL SECURITY Not all twenty-first-century national security threats will come from "infowar" and terrorism. "The gravest security problems for the U.S. would result from the criminalization of either Russia or Mexico," says Kori N. Schake of the Institute on Global Conflict and Cooperation, University of California at San Diego. "Organized crime has already reached worrisome proportions in Russia," she notes. That's a problem—

to put it mildly—in a country that still owns enough nuclear weapons to blow up the world many times over. Mexico, meanwhile, has enormous problems with crime, drugs, poverty, and political corruption—all along a thinly policed two-thousand-mile border with the United States. Government officials have described Mexico as "fighting for its very life against drug lords."

GOOD TECHNOLOGY, BAD INTENTIONS

Take nearly every technology known to mankind, add a dash of creativity and a healthy dose of bad intentions, and you've got the potential for disaster. Take the global positioning satellite system (see Chapter 7), soon to be available in most new cars. Pack a tiny Piper Cub airplane with explosives and a GPS system and you've created a poor man's cruise missile. "It doesn't take the free-floating imagination of a futurist to realize that such breakthroughs as direct-satellite TV broadcasts, morphing software, commercial satellite imagery, and super-computers on a chip all have possible military applications," notes Peter Grier, the defense correspondent for the *Christian Science Monitor.*

Television as a weapon? Think about it: The same computer graphics techniques that make dinosaurs appear real in the movies or that animate much of the cast of *The Phantom Menace* could be used to confuse people and destabilize a government. Imagine turning on the TV one evening and seeing the president of the United States warning you to evacuate your city because there was about to be a nuclear attack by terrorists—and to disregard all subsequent broadcasts because the television networks were under attack by those same terrorists. Then imagine that seconds later, the president is back on TV, telling you to disregard what you had just heard because that was a message broadcast by terrorists. Confusing? You bet. And millions of Americans, not knowing which was real and which was disinformation, would probably head for the hills. "This is not science-fiction," said George Stein, a professor at the Air War College, in a report to the U.S. Air Force in 1997. "These are the capabilities of existing or rapidly emerging technologies. . . . The mastery of the techniques of combining live actors with computer-generated video graphics can easily create a 'virtual' news conference, summit meeting, or perhaps even a battle which exists in 'effects' though not in fact. Stored video images can be recombined endlessly to produce any effect chosen. Now, perhaps, pictures will be worth a thousand tanks."

Every new technology brings the potential for some kind of unintended consequence. We've already discussed a number of these in this book: the possibility that genes designed to create herbicide-resistant crops will find their way into the wild, creating superweeds that can't be killed. Or that genetic testing and engineering techniques used to eliminate birth defects will be used to create designer babies, genetically engineered to be physically and intellectually superior. One of the more far-fetched but nonetheless frightening examples of unintended consequences concerns nanotechnology. It's raised by Eric Drexler in his book *Engines of Creation,* in which an "accidentally created, omnivorous, bacteria-size robot spreads like blowing pollen, replicates swiftly, [and] reduces the entire world biosphere to dust in matter of days."

Self-replication of everything from nanobots to machines endowed with artificial intelligence could be a breakthough technology in the twenty-first century. And that makes some technology watchers a little bit nervous. "Victor Frankenstein refused to give his monstrous creation a bride for fear of their reproductive potential," observes Colin McGinn, a professor of philosophy at Rutgers. "Maybe we should be thinking hard now about the replicative powers of intelligent machines. If the twentieth century was the century of nuclear weapons, then the twenty-first might be the century of self-breeding aliens of our own devising."

Happily (perhaps) most unintended consequences don't take the form of sudden disasters, like Drexler's hungry nanobots. They take time to develop and grow. One thing is nearly certain, however: Great changes in science and technology often bring about equally great changes to which societies have a hard time adjusting. The Industrial Revolution, for example, brought wealth and higher standards of living for many. But it also gave us crowded, unhealthy cities, and child labor abuses. The second Industrial Revolution at the end of the nineteenth century brought us the automobile, electricity, and a wave of prosperity unlike anything before it. But it too had a downside: high unemployment and rampant materialism. We are now in the midst of a transformation to the Information Age and an extraordinary era of biological and medical breakthroughs. What will their unintended consequences be? We've already heard concerns about the creation of a two-tiered world, with information haves and have-nots. Could we be about to create a permanent, technology-deprived underclass? Could the Genetic Revolution bring new forms of discrimination? It's safe to say that not every segment of society will be happy with many of the changes the twenty-first century will bring. The big, unanswerable question is What will they do about it?

As our taste in movies show, we like to scare ourselves (nearly) to death. It is comforting to consider that the human race just emerged from a century that saw two world wars, the detonation of nuclear weapons, famines, floods, earthquakes, and scores of disasters, natural and man-made. Yet somehow we emerged with the earth in one piece, higher standards of living for many people, longer life expectancy and civilization more or less intact. There have been bumps in the road, to be sure, but we seem to keep moving forward. There's no reason to think that won't continue. Is there?

Pleasant dreams.

Want to Know More?

On the Web:

- Terrorism Research Center (www.terrorism.com)
- The Hacker News Network (www.hackernews.com/)
- Outbreak (www.outbreak.org)

At the Library:

- *The Next World War,* by James Adams (Simon & Schuster, 1998)
- *The Hot Zone,* by Richard Preston (Doubleday, 1995)
- *Biohazard,* by Ken Alibek with Stephen Handelman (Random House, 1999)

CHAPTER 11

The End of the Job: Twenty-first-century Careers and How to Prepare for Them

The old definition of working nine to five for one employer for fixed pay is dead. Everybody's an entrepreneur in the new world.

—William Halal, George Washington University professor of management

THE END OF THE JOB

For centuries, the directions for living for most of us have been pretty simple: Wake, work, eat, sleep, repeat. We have structured much of our lives—our daily routines, where we live, where we go to school, what we study—around our need to hold down a job and bring in a paycheck. If business and employment experts are correct, however, this fundamental formula could undergo a dramatic change in the twenty-first century. You may have a career, perhaps even several careers, but you may never have a job.

For your parents and grandparents, losing a job was a traumatic experience. But many people entering the workforce in the twenty-first century will not only lose their jobs, they'll lose the entire *concept* of a job. Yes, we will all still work for a living, but the idea of a "job"—show up at the same place every day, work the same hours, do the same thing—slowly will disappear. Why?

Because the traditional idea of a job, just like the traditional school year, may have outlived its usefulness.

In the same way that the traditional school year resulted from the need to free kids to work on the family farm in the summer, the job as we know it today is a direct product of the Industrial Revolution. Companies built huge factories filled with massive machinery, then hired people to operate it. In order to get the most value out of a factory, they had to run those machines twenty-four hours a day, and staff up with three shifts of people, each shift working eight hours. If people didn't show up at the right time to do the right job, the whole thing would grind to a halt.

But what if the only machine you have to worry about is your computer, and it's portable? Suppose your job is to write plans, reports, and presentations, and they're due on the first of the month. Does it matter if you work on it from nine to five? You can wake up in the middle of the night and work in your underwear and no one will know. Does it matter where you work or when you work? Labor and business experts say it doesn't even matter if it takes you two hours to do something it takes others twenty to accomplish. It's all about you, the skills you have to offer, and who is willing to pay for them.

Say hello to the worker of the twenty-first century: in other words, you. You'll be willing to work flexible hours to keep up with global, round-the-clock demands of the Internet-driven economy. You'll be technology-savvy, having grown up with computers, cell phones, and the Internet. You won't be intimidated by rapid changes in technology, since this will be all you've ever known. This will be especially crucial since, looking into the new millennium, the hottest career market will almost certainly be in the field of Information Technology. Your reward will be top dollar for your talents, and the ability to work when you want, where you want, and for whom you want.

This new breed of worker is already starting to emerge. The Bureau of Labor Statistics calculates that 27 percent of today's workforce keeps flexible schedules—nearly double the number of "flex-time" workers in 1991. The shift is being driven by the dramatic rise in what experts call "knowledge work"—earning our living with brains, not brawn. Just as the Industrial Revolution lured workers from farms to factories, the Information Age is driving employees from factories to desks. And once liberated by mobile communications and the miniaturization of phones and computers, that desk can be virtually anywhere.

"Technology really drives this," William Halal, professor of management at George Washington University, tells the *Minneapolis Star Tribune.* "You're holding people accountable for their performance so they can do it any time they want, anywhere they want—as long as they get the job done. This will be a commonly accepted way of structuring work."

FROM 9 TO 5 TO 24/7

As the nature of work changes in the twenty-first century, many experts believe we will see an even more dramatic shift, as the traditional relationship between employer and employee will be retooled. For people of your grandparents' generation, there was an understood "contract" between workers and employers. If you worked hard and did a good job, you pretty much expected to keep your job as long as you wanted—even for your entire career. My father, for example, worked for American Airlines from the day he got out of the army until the day he died. But for people of your parents' age, the contract started to change, then slowly to disappear. Many young people today have grown up watching their parents switch jobs frequently, get downsized out of a company or leave to pursue other, better opportunities elsewhere. They "will harbor a distrust of the employer-employee contract and will rebel against the rigid rules of the conventional workplace," argues employment expert John Challenger. "It's a redefinition of the employment contract."

What will replace the old contract is something Daniel H. Pink has called the "free agent nation"—a system where most workers think of themselves as hired guns. You'll sell your talent to the highest bidder, perhaps for as little as a few weeks or months at a time, then move on to your next assignment which might be in a completely different business or industry. Many experts see the change as inevitable, and desirable for both workers and employers. Businesses will save money on expensive insurance and benefits, and by having only as many people as they need on the job at a given moment. Workers will gain by selling their skills to the highest bidder, and they'll be able to tailor their lives to spend as much time as they want doing things other than work. Talented free agents will have the opportunity to try new things, take risks, change careers, and look for work in new businesses and industries that interest them without worrying about climbing the corporate ladder. "This shift is about both economics and values," says Pink, who left his job as a speechwriter at the White House to become a free agent writer. "It's the economics of work, but it's also people deciding what's important in their lives, and redefining loyalty, and risk and security and success."

Today's teens will be at the forefront of this revolution, becoming a workforce unlike any other we've ever known—one that is thoroughly comfortable with technology and able to perform many different job-related tasks. "The upcoming generation of self-employed will redefine the concept of 'office' and become an ultra-mobile workforce which will live by a palm-top unit that is mailbox, fax, cellular phone, and notebook," Challenger predicts. "They will work on the road, taking their special niche of expertise directly to the customer or client."

In other words, it's quite likely that by the time you enter the working world, you won't be somebody's employee. You'll be a highly skilled free agent who will sell his or her services to the highest bidder to work on a project or assignment, then move on to the next opportunity. How will you find work? "There will be huge databases on the Net of jobs that people want other people to do," predicts web pioneer Mark Andreesen. "'Edit this manuscript for me, write this computer program, or translate this into another language.' And you'll be able to bid on those jobs and you'll be able to do them and be paid for them online. There's all kinds of different commerce and business that become possible." John Challenger agrees: "I can see a time when the traditional want ad will be replaced with 'situation wanted' ads," he predicts. "Workers will place these ads on the Internet or other media and wait for companies to call them."

We're already well on our way to the free agent nation. Today, as many as twenty million people don't work for a specific company, but rather move from project to project. Some experts even predict that as many as 90 percent of us will be free agents in the next century. "I don't want to say that no job will exist in twenty years," says William Bridges, the author of *JobShift,* an influential 1995 book that was among the first to put forward the idea of free-agent employees. "For example, nuclear power plant workers should have clear job descriptions—no messing around. On the other hand, there are whole industries, such as filmmaking and consulting, in which job descriptions don't play any real role. Jobs are not the way work gets done."

Of course, jobs will never disappear altogether. We will always need doctors and nurses, and police officers and firefighters, for example, who come when we call—not just when they feel like working. But it's safe to say that advances in mobile communications and computing technologies will radically change the working world of the twenty-first century, giving us huge new numbers of people whose work will come to them, instead of their going to a factory or office every day.

PREPARING FOR THE TWENTY-FIRST-CENTURY WORKFORCE

The end of the traditional employer-worker contract upsets and frightens some people, who like the stability, regular paychecks, and health and retirement benefits traditional jobs offer. The idea of an honest day's work for an honest day's pay is something many people not only believe in, but build their lives around. It may help to consider, however, that the whole idea of a "job" is, historically speaking, a fairly recent invention. To people of the pre-Industrial era, the whole idea of set work hours, vacations, and paychecks would have seemed bizarre. In our not-too-distant agricultural past, people worked at home all the time, tending to crops, raising livestock, cooking, cleaning, sewing. People didn't think of these things as jobs, although all of it was certainly work.

These were just things that needed to be done. When all is said and done, the job as we know it today may prove to be nothing more than an historical curiosity—a custom that existed for a brief time before the Information Age took off. In the end, many experts say, both sides will be better off. "Few employers will guarantee jobs to everyone, and few workers can afford to rely on employers to develop their skills and careers," says Challenger.

Taking charge of your career development will be another big change in the future. If you've been counting the years, months, semesters, days, or minutes until you graduate, so you can kiss school good-bye once and for all, I've got bad news for you. Like a horror-movie beast that refuses to stay dead, you'll probably never be completely done with school. You can look forward to a career full of training and retraining, as rapid advances in technology quickly makes old skills obsolete. Regular return trips to the classroom will give you the skills you'll need to stay competitive as a free agent.

That's the bad news. The good news is, unlike previous eras where a job for life often meant the *same* job for life, you'll have the opportunity to change careers as often as you like, and to get trained in new skills that are even more rewarding and profitable.

Education will be the key to staying competitive—and employed. Until now, job security has pretty much depended on finding work in a good company and living by the rules of the employer/worker contract. In the future, however, job security will be almost completely in your hands. In a way, this is nothing new. The link between education and pay has been well established for a long time. Twenty years ago, the average college graduate earned 38 percent more than the average high school grad. Today, college graduates earn 71 percent more, according to the U.S. Department of Labor. As we move to a employment model where we are all auctioning off our skills on a constant basis, the gap between educated, skilled workers and those without special training is expected to grow much wider still.

Adapting to life as a free agent will be fun and natural for some—it will give them greater flexibility to spend time with friends and family, for example. But it will also present some new headaches for twenty-first-century workers and employers. The lines between being on the job and off duty have already become very blurry for some people. If you work from home, you'll never be in the office, but you'll always be at work. Thanks to E-mail and cell phones, some workers are already available to their bosses, customers, or clients nearly around the clock. Most experts expect this to get even worse as more and more of us move to flexible schedules.

Labor experts also worry that workers in a company full of free agents will feel lost, isolated, and out of touch with their companies and their colleagues. That's because those coworkers may end up not as familiar faces around the water cooler but as names on E-mail messages and voices on telephone conference calls. "People want to connect with other individuals, not just electronic message pads or laptop computers," says Challenger. "That will be just as true in 2020 as it is today."

Even technology boosters agree. "The reality is that telecommunications is doing for the travel industry what the computer did for the paperless office," jokes British Telecommunications' Peter Cochrane. "We insist on traveling and meeting people, because, the truth is, telecommunications is only a partial solution. In fact, telecommunications promotes a desire and need to travel for that vital human contact we find so necessary and enjoy."

OTHER TWENTY-FIRST-CENTURY WORKPLACE TRENDS

Flexible schedules and free-agent workers will be two of the most important trends of your future careers. But there will be plenty of other differences between your work life and that of your parents and grandparents. Other workplace trends to look forward to in the twenty-first century:

- Women will at long last begin to approach equal representation on the job. It's been over a generation since the women's movement really took off. During the *Father Knows Best* days of the 1950s, only 32.4 percent of women were working. Now, according to the Bureau of Labor Statistics, it's 57.3 percent and rising, compared to nearly 72 percent of men.

- The idea of "man's work" and "woman's work" will disappear. Traditionally male-dominated jobs like manufacturing and construction increasingly will be performed by women, as muscle power gives way to robotics and computer-assisted work. "Manufacturing jobs that depended upon a strong back will be replaced by jobs conducted from a computerized workstation," predicts Challenger. And men will pursue careers in fields that are often dominated by women, including health care and "service" jobs.
- One thing that may not change—or at least change fast enough—is the wage gap between men and women. Women still earn about 75 cents for every dollar earned by men, according to the U.S. Department of Labor. As women continue to gain equal representation with men in experience and education and take jobs in traditionally male occupations, labor experts predict that the wage gap will get smaller, but slowly. "It is clearly a work in progress," labor secretary Alexis Herman told the *Christian Science Monitor* last year, "but we've come a long way."
- Higher education will be a key to almost all types of work, even traditionally blue-collar jobs. "Employees must possess the skills to program and operate high-tech tools such as robots," predicts Challenger. "The traditional blue-collar worker with only a high-school diploma will sometimes be squeezed out," he says. "Workers of tomorrow can no longer rely on brawn to get them a job. The days of unskilled manual labor will be gone."
- The only office you ever know (other than your home) may not belong to your employer. It may be a corporate "hotel" where you work in an office furnished with a phone, fax, and data port for your computer or other office equipment. Just like today's hotels, you may stay for a day, a week, or months at a time. The people around you may work for the same company, or for completely different companies. You'll

plug in, work on your most recent assignment, and check out when you're done. You might even change jobs without changing your hotel space.

HOT CAREERS FOR THE TWENTY-FIRST CENTURY

If you check the Help Wanted ads, it's kind of depressing to see how infrequently the really cool jobs show up. I've looked for years and years, and not once have I seen an ad for "Rock Star." And the next time I see any major-league baseball team place an ad looking for a second baseman will be the first. So, like it or not, we all need something to fall back on just in case the NBA scouts, movie directors, and record labels are less than impressed with our talents. It might help in creating your "Plan B" to know where most of the real-world opportunities will be by the time you're out of school and looking for work.

When the Class of 1999 graduated from college, the departing seniors who were most in demand were—surprise, surprise—those with degrees in computers and information technology. A study by the National Association of Colleges and Employers of over three hundred college planning and placement offices across the United States found that the average salary for a 1999 grad with a computer science bachelor's degree was over $45,000.

The explosive growth of technology and the Internet is already having a huge impact on the career choices of students. According to the Lemelson-MIT program's 1999 "Invention Index" survey, 57 percent of students said they were "extremely interested" or "very interested" in careers in information technology—tops on the list. The fact that nearly two thirds of high-school students say they want careers in a field that barely existed a few years ago shows how rapidly the world of work might change in the next several years. "One of the interesting things about America is how rapidly our youth, when they are planning their careers, rush toward what they think are the new opportunities and away from those they think are old," says Lester C. Thurow, the economist and professor who oversaw the study. "In a short period of time, the vision of being a doctor or financier has been replaced by the vision of invention and technical entrepreneurship."

Careers involving the Internet and computers are expected to stay white-hot in the early years of the twenty-first century. "As the world gets wired, the demand for professionals in technology or communication will intensify," predicts Gerald Celente, author of *Trends 2000: How to Prepare for and Profit from the Changes of the 21st Century,* and director of the Trends Research Institute, based in Rhinebeck, New York. In fact, some companies want newly minted computer majors so much that they're not even waiting for them to graduate. They're hiring students before they graduate and paying for their education! And "signing bonuses," which promising professional athletes get when they sign with a major-league team, are now routinely being doled out to new hires in computer and technology fields.

Incredibly, the wheelbarrows full of money that employers are dumping at the feet of computer and technology grads doesn't seem to be driving huge numbers of kids into the field. Students "know that computers are where the money is, but when they see that they have to do all that math, they say 'Ooooh,'" says Marlaine Mowitz, of the University of Northern Colorado career center. "If their skills or interests aren't there, they're not going into it. They're still choosing majors based on their interests."

The good news for non-techies is that the job market has rarely looked stronger for young people, no matter what their skills or interests. According to the U.S. Bureau of Labor Statistics, the total number of jobs in the United States is expected to increase by 18.6 million between now and 2006. But the total number of workers age 16 and over will only increase by about fifteen million over the same period. That means an overall labor crunch, which should make it relatively easy for qualified workers to find employment. The Bureau, which studies specific jobs that are in demand, says the ten fastest-growing occupations between now and 2006 will all be in the computer or health-care fields. Those ten will be database administrators, computer support specialists, computer scientists (+118 percent); computer engineers (109 percent); systems analysts (103 percent); personal and home-care aides (85 percent); physical therapy assistants and aides (79 percent); home health aides (76 percent); medical assistants (74 percent); desktop publishing specialists (74 percent), physical therapists (71 percent); and occupational therapy assistants and aides (69 percent).

Here are some of the other hottest fields for the twenty-first century:

HEALTH/MEDICINE The Bureau of Labor Statistics says that nearly one out of every five new jobs created between now and 2005 will be in health care. With the baby boom generation well into middle age and quickly approaching senior status, demand for health-care services is expected to skyrocket in the twenty-first century. And, with hospitals and insurance companies demanding shorter hospital stays for recovery, more emphasis will be placed on in-home health care—among the hottest jobs will be personal and home health aides and physical therapists to take care of the increasing number of elderly people.

EDUCATION The demand for teachers is very strong right now, and is expected to grow over the next five to ten years. Many teachers who began their careers in the sixties and seventies are getting ready to retire (look around your school and you'll probably see a lot of gray hair), and colleges aren't graduating enough new education majors to fill all the available jobs. Plus, the school-age population is on the rise, fueling a demand for more teachers. The best opportunities will exist in the short-term for secondary school, special ed, and adult education teachers. People who go into education are usually motivated not by money but by their desire to work with kids and do something noble with their lives. And that's good, because average salaries for teachers are still pretty low—about $37,000 as of 1997.

BUSINESS Accounting and finance are the hottest specialties for business majors at the moment. The average starting salary for economics and finance majors last year, according to the National Association of Colleges and Employers, was $35,668.

Banks, brokerages, and insurance companies have been hiring plenty of management trainees in the last couple of years. You'll start out picking up the boss's dry cleaning with a salary of $25–30K, but you could triple that in a few years. Other hot business fields include venture capital, the art of finding the next Yahoo! or Amazon.com working out of somebody's garage, and marketing, the art of inventing new ways to separate customers from their money.

ENGINEERING Many colleges report their engineering graduates are getting five or more job offers apiece—and many more at top engineering schools. The demand varies within the field, however. Computer (again) and electrical engineering students have the most offers to choose from. Chemical and civil engineers are not as much in demand.

MEDIA AND ENTERTAINMENT There are two types of people in this world: those who work on the Internet, and those who will. The explosion of so-called new media is creating a huge demand for web designers, producers, programmers, and others to produce on-line "content"—and sending traditional print and broadcast employees scurrying for cover. New media isn't just about the entertainment industry, however. Most big companies have corporate intranet and E-commerce web sites that need to be kept up and running.

DEAD-END JOBS

A recent issue of *Forbes* magazine put the dilemma facing people in some careers in pretty clear terms. "Imagine. It's 1901, Ransom E. Olds is about to introduce the automobile assembly line, and you are a blacksmith. What should you do? (1) Put the horses on amphetamines. (2) Change your line of work. Correct answer: (2). Faster horses wouldn't have saved the day for the blacksmiths." In other words, if you're interested in a line of work that is threatened by the Internet, now would be a good time to start making other plans.

WHERE THE CLASS OF 1999 WENT TO WORK

The National Association of Colleges and Employers compiles data every year on where college graduates are going to work and how much they're getting paid. Here's a sample of the most popular jobs of the Class of 1999, the most recent year for which there are statistics, and their average starting salaries:

Public accountant	$34,778
Insurance claims agent	$28, 714
Graphic artist	$29,100
Reporter	$22,725
Market researcher	$33,272
Law enforcement officer	$29,007
Member of armed forces	$33,429
Software designer	$46,249
Environmental engineer	$34,388
Nurse	$31,366
Social worker	$21,654
Architect	$30,115
Management trainee	$30,602
Teacher	$24,941

SOURCE: National Association of Colleges and Employers

Here's an easy rule of thumb for figuring out whose jobs are in trouble in the Information Age: Can the line of work you're interested in be done faster, cheaper, or more easily on-line? If the answer is yes, you can bet it will be. As a result, here are some of the jobs that could dwindle or disappear over the next several decades:

TRAVEL AND INSURANCE AGENTS The Internet represents a huge threat to middlemen—anyone who brokers a deal between a customer and a company. Travel agents, insurance salesmen, and . . . um, er . . . reporters and writers (gulp!) are just a few of the types of middlemen who may need to start looking for other work. As more and more people become comfortable using the Internet, and learn to use intelligent agents and software to ferret out information and comparison shop for the best deals on air travel, hotels, insurance, and other products and services, it will soon be easier—and cheaper—to do it yourself. There will always be a small percentage of people who pay for the convenience of having someone do it for them, but this kind of work will become increasingly rare.

RETAIL WORKERS As more and more shopping becomes E-commerce, retail stores and shopping malls will lose customers to the Internet. Fewer real-world stores means fewer jobs for store clerks. As long as shopping remains one of the best loved American pastimes, however, malls and stores will never disappear altogether.

STOCKBROKERS The explosion of on-line stock-market trading through services like E*Trade and Charles Schwab has turned millions of Americans into stock market do-it-yourselfers. Brokers are still prized for their investment advice, but as more and more financial advice is generated by intelligent agents and on-line brokerages, even that may not be enough to keep large numbers of brokers in business.

BANK TELLERS There are two big threats to bank tellers: automatic teller machines and direct-deposit paychecks. "Today's teller function will become totally obsolete within the next twenty-five years," predicts banking expert Arnold Danielson. Most of the people who make regular visits to bank branches are older customers who prefer to deal with a person instead of a machine. But future customers may visit a branch once in their lives—when they open their account.

ASSEMBLY AND MANUFACTURING WORKERS As the United States continues to leave its industrial past behind, fewer and fewer people will be able to make a living assembling things. The only exception is the construction industry, which is expected to grow slightly in the first decade of the century. According to the Bureau of Labor Statistics, nearly all the job growth in the United States between now and 2006 will come from "service" jobs.

One thing is absolutely certain: Rapid advances in technology are having a profound impact on the world of work. It's almost unthinkable that your career and working life will be anything at all like those of your parents. New businesses and industries are being born at an astonishing rate, and most experts expect the pace of change will only get faster. Some types of jobs—even entire professions and industries—could disappear altogether. Sure, being in one of today's endangered professions might feel like being a blacksmith in the early days of the automobile. But it's important to remember that, in the long run, the auto industry created far more jobs than were lost by buggy whip, carriage and wagon-makers, the people who ran stables, and blacksmiths combined. And today's Information Technology industry is creating far more jobs and opportunities than it is displacing. If anything, jobs are being created faster than the tech world can find bodies to fill them. "Our skilled-worker shortage is a crisis," Harris Miller, the president of the Information Technology Association of America told the *Washington Post* recently. "It's as if we had run out of iron ore in the middle of the Industrial Revolution."

Want to Know More about the Future of Jobs?

On the Web:

- FutureScan (www.futurescan.com)
- College Board Career Search (www.collegeboard.org/career/bin/career.pl)
- Career Counseling for Teenagers (www.tfs.net/~gbyron/)
- The Princeton Review (www.review.com/careers)

At the Library:

- *JobShift: How to Prosper in a Workplace Without Jobs,* by William Bridges (Perseus Press, 1995)
- *I Could Do Anything if I Only Knew What It Was,* by Barbara Sher (Dell, 1995)
- *Free Agents: People and Organizations Creating a New Working Community,* by Susan B. Gould, et. al (Jossey-Bass Publishers, 1997)

CHAPTER 12

Changes from A to Z: Thirty Things That Will Be Different in the Twenty-first Century

Fifty percent of new products and services to be sold in the twenty-first century have not been invented yet.

—Dr. James Canton, Institute for Global Futures, San Francisco

In this book, I've tried to cover the big sweeping changes that will change the world you inherit. But life is also made up of lots of familiar, everyday things. Here is a collection of familiar objects, products, services, ideas, and institutions that will be very different in the years ahead.

ADVERTISING

MIT Professor Michael Dertouzos predicts that "reverse advertising" will largely replace advertising as we now know it. You—or an intelligent agent or "shopbot" that represents you—will go on line and describe what you want to buy. Companies that make those products or offer such services will come forward with offers to sell you what you need. "Though we are familiar with this practice for used items—that's what the want ads are in newspapers—we do not yet use it for new goods and services," writes Dertouzos in his book *What Will Be.* "Instead of wandering from store to store, looking for the right pair of shoes, you publish a precise description of what you're after and make the sellers come to you."

BIOSENSORS

Imagine a tiny chip inside your body that constantly monitors your health and alerts you if something is going wrong. Today, patients with diabetes have to prick their fingers anywhere from four to sixteen times a day to check their blood glucose levels. A biosensor inserted under the skin could take a reading every couple of minutes, sending signals to a wrist-worn computer if medical attention is needed. Such a device is being developed now by researchers at Sensors for Medicine and Science in Maryland. Also known as medical chips, or "medchips," they could be used to monitor the health of chronically ill patients. A tiny sensor implanted in your arm will constantly monitor your pulse, blood pressure, temperature, blood chemistry, and immune system responses. Working medical chips, already being tested, could be a reality in five to ten years.

BIONIC BODY PARTS

A device called a cochlear implant, an embedded chip attached to a microphone and a mini-computer, allows some deaf people to hear again. Work is under way on similar implants that would artificially stimulate the optic nerve, allowing the blind to see. Medical research on artificial organs and body parts suggests that we are quickly moving toward the day when many worn-out body parts can be replaced. Artificial hearts, skin, kidneys, lifelike limbs, and more are on the drawing board. One Japanese researcher, who is developing an artificial lung, even foresees going beyond replacing our own body parts to developing new ones. Noriaki Matsuda of Tokyo's Waseda University is working on an artificial gill that will enable people to breathe underwater, taking oxygen from seawater like a fish.

BRAINCAPS

Forget the Walkman. Your kids will have something *way* more cool: the *Braincap.* The brainchild, so to speak, of the great science-fiction writer and futurist Arthur C. Clarke, the Braincap will allow direct inputs to all five senses. "Anyone wearing this helmet, fitting tightly over the skull, can enter a whole universe of experience, real or imaginary—and even merge in real time with other minds," Clarke writes in *Asiaweek* magazine. The Braincap, he predicts, will be a reality by 2025. "Apart from its use for entertainment and vicarious adventure, the Braincap is a boon to doctors, who can now experience their patients' symptoms," says Clarke. "It also revolutionizes the legal profession; deliberate lying is impossible. As the Braincap can only function properly on a completely bald head, wig-making becomes a major industry."

CASH

People have been predicting a cash-free society for years. If you say something long enough, eventually it becomes true, and in the twenty-first century we may finally see the demise of paper money. "It seems remarkable that metallic and paper tokens (money) are still used in a world of information technology and electronics," notes Peter Cochrane in his book *Tips for Time Travelers.* Eventually, some experts predict, we will carry a single smart card that will be embedded with all our vital information—passport, driver's license, medical information, credit card, and bank account information. "Logically, a better scheme would be a chip implant," says Cochrane, the head of research for British Telecommunications Laboratories. "Just a small slice of silicon under the skin is all it would take for us to enjoy the freedom of no cards, passports, or keys. Put your hand out to the car door, computer terminal, the food you wish to purchase, and you would be instantly recognized and be dealt with efficiently. Think about it—total freedom, no more plastic."

Good idea, Mr. Cochrane. You first.

CATS AND DOGS

Technology will soon solve one of the most traumatic experiences of childhood—the lost dog or cat. Computerized tracking chips are available right now that you can have implanted beneath the skin of your pet. A special collar tag alerts the pound to the chip, so they can use a scanner on the animal. Within ten to fifteen years, chip implants may be done automatically when you have Spot or Socks neutered. "Actually today, my dog has a chip in it," Web pioneer Mark Andreesen told me recently. "If my dog gets picked up by the dog catcher or gets turned in to the pound, they can actually use a bar-code scanner. They can scan him and they see he's in a database, and they can tell who he is. The next step will be putting a chip in our dogs and they'll be connected to the Internet. And you're going to be able to check on a Web page and find out exactly where your dog is." Man bytes dog!

CLOTHING

Throw open your closet a few decades from now and clothes might look and feel familiar, but there will be lots of new technology behind your gear. Everything from new fabrics that resist dirt and stains to wrinkle-free shirts and pants (I hope made of something other than polyester) will be part of your wardrobe. Your clothes will do more than make you look good. Devices embedded inside will warm you in winter and help keep you cool during heat waves. Clothes will even change color to coordinate with your environment—or your mood. Within a few decades, "antisoiling agents will neutralize sweating, limiting the discoloration and olfactory embarrassments that have offended sensibilities since the dawn of sartorial civilization," reports *TIME Digital.* "Ultraviolet blockers will ward off skin cancer; antibacterial fabrics will protect the little ones in your life from the microbes lurking in day-care centers. Fabrics embedded with scented chemicals will emit fragrances to calm you."

CEMETERIES

Unless someone comes up with a way to make us immortal (see Chapter 6) in the next few years, the number of people who have died since the United States was founded in 1776 will surpass the number living, sometime around 2030. That may pose an unusual problem: where to put them all. Cremation is expected to gain in popularity in the United States as the cost of funerals continues to rise and space for burial plots grows scarce. In 1997, only 23 percent of all Americans who died were cremated, according to industry figures. By 2010, the figure is expected to hit 50 percent. The United States is below average in its current cremation rate. The world leader is Japan, where 98 percent of the dead are cremated.

DAY CARE

If both of your parents worked when you were small, it's possible that they may have occasionally brought you to work and dropped you off at on-site day care facilities run by their companies when they couldn't arrange a babysitter. Believe it or not, before your careers are over, you may return the favor, bringing your parents to work and dropping *them* off at an eldercare facility run by your company. According to the Family and Work Institute, more and more employees are leaving jobs today to take care of elderly parents or relatives. By 2020, when the senior citizen population hits record levels (see "Parents" later in this chapter) the problem will be even worse. In order to hire and keep good workers, some labor experts predict, companies may have to run facilities to take care of the parents of their employees.

DIGITAL SIGNAL PROCESSORS

Every time there's a disaster—an earthquake, a tornado, a building collapse—you see pictures on the news of rescue teams with dogs combing through the wreckage, looking for trapped survivors.

In the future, the dogs will have to look for other work. Superfast *digital signal processors* (DSPs) will be used to create a whole range of life-saving products like sensors that will quickly and easily detect a heartbeat underneath a pile of wreckage. The same technology could one day be used to make a device like a hearing aid that could, when combined with the proper software, instantly translate a foreign language, letting you have real-time conversations with people even if you don't speak the same language. "We're definitely at the threshold of more natural capabilities in that area," says Dr. Lee Caldwell, director of internet technology, strategy, and standards at IBM. "I think we've got basic competent language translation now. I think you'll see a lot of improvement in that area."

DINOSAURS

In the movie *Jurassic Park,* scientists clone dinosaurs from DNA found in the blood of a mosquito preserved in amber. Could the Genetic Revolution bring back the dinosaurs? Or more recently extinct species? Could you take a tissue sample from a long-dead human being—Abraham Lincoln or Thomas Jefferson, for instance—and create his or her clone? Highly unlikely, say the experts. It would only work if the genetic material of the dinosaur, dodo, or dead president had been extremely well preserved by freezing. "I don't think it would be possible to clone from an extinct animal," said research scientist Dr. Colin Stewart in an interview with *TIME* magazine, "because the whole nucleus will have disintegrated, losing all structure and causing all the DNA to degrade. Once that happens, you'll never get anything from it." Ah, but what about woolly mammoths, the prehistoric forerunner of the elephant, whose frozen corpses occasionally turn up in melting Siberian glaciers? Sorry. Ice crystals in the beasts' cells would have destroyed the genetic material. When scientists want to freeze tissue samples for storage, they take great pains to keep crystals from forming. They don't just throw them in a walk-in freezer. Or a glacier.

DRIVER'S LICENSES

Most kids know down to the hour how long it will be between now and when they can go for their driver's license. But imagine a future in which you didn't have to be sixteen or eighteen to drive. Imagine a world where you could drive at virtually any age. In Chapter 7, we talked about smart cars and smart highways that would automatically drive you where you wanted to go. Taking that concept to its logical conclusion, Vincent P. Barrabba, general manager of corporate strategy and knowledge development for General Motors, has described a world in which "autopilot has made driver's licenses obsolete, and children use vehicles on their own. Parents can control routes and vehicle functions from home or any remote location."

FABRICATORS

The tech wizards at MIT have on their drawing boards the ultimate digital toy: the Fabricator. Think of it as a 3-D printer for on-line shopping, only it's not filled with an ink cartridge. It's chock full of polymers, metals, silicon chips, and other material used for building small objects. The idea is to let you download blueprints for computer parts and electronic gear that would be assembled right on your desktop. "Someday soon, we could download hardware from the Net," says James Ellenbogen of Mitre Corp., a federally funded research center near Washington, D.C., "just like we download software today."

GLASSES

Even if your vision doesn't need correcting, you will probably own a pair of glasses in the twenty-first century. How will you be able to watch TV without them? Video glasses could become as common as a Walkman is today. A small wireless receiver will pick up video signals from direct-broadcast satellites, projecting the image onto the inside of your glasses, where it will appear to float a few feet in front of your face. The same devices will also let you shop or read your E-mail—or, inevitably, video "V-mail"—wherever you are. Farther down the road, British Telecommunications' head of research Peter Cochrane predicts contact lenses that will do exactly the same thing, allowing you to take in video with your eyes closed.

LETTERS

As more and more personal communication is handled via voice, E-mail, and their video-based successors, "snail mail" will become increasingly rare. Nearly everything that is now sent through the mail—letters, bills, direct-mail pitches, catalogues, and magazines—has already begun a transition to electronic delivery. Once the majority of the country is connected to a E-mail, the volume of personal letters will drop dramatically. The best hope for the U.S Postal Service? E-commerce. As more and more purchases are made on-line, someone will have to deliver the goods. Eventually, many experts predict snail-mail delivery will drop from six days, to as little as twice a week. The Postal Service is pushing a shift to "centralized" delivery, where the postal carrier delivers to clusters of mailboxes in a single location instead of visiting each individual home on the route.

MALLS

The sky's the limit for on-line shopping. Some analysts expect on line sales and E-commerce to hit nearly $200 billion a year by 2002. Anything that can be delivered to your house can now be purchased on the Web. There are now even supermarkets in some areas that let you shop on line and deliver groceries to your door. Could this mean the end of the mall? Yeah, right. Needless to say, teens know something that E-commerce mavens seems to have forgotten. The mall is *so* not about buying stuff. As long as that remains the case, the mall will probably remain safe. One possibility, however, is that malls will become hangouts for more than just teenagers. "Malls are going to have to reconfigure to meet the needs of an aging society," predicts futurist Gerald Celente. "Instead of the department stores anchoring the mall, you're going to have malls for more than just buying clothes. It's for health, fitness, and nutrition as well."

OCEAN EXPLORATION

We've explored every square inch of dry land, we've landed men on the moon, and sent space probes to our planetary neighbors and beyond. So what's left for mankind to explore? How about the oceans? "I think there's a perception that we have already explored the sea," marine biologist Sylvia Earle, founder of Deep Ocean Engineering, told *TIME* magazine recently. "The reality is we know more about Mars than we know about the oceans." Indeed, twelve people have walked on the surface of the moon, while only two have been to the bottom of Challenger Deep, seven miles below the surface of the Pacific Ocean near Guam—the deepest point on Earth. The ocean holds huge deposits of valuable minerals. And the medicinal value of deep-sea fish, plants, and bacteria could rival what's found in tropical rain forests, leading to an untold number of wonderdrugs. Bruce Robison, of the Monterey Bay Aquarium Research Institute (MBARI) in California tells *TIME,* "I can guarantee you that the discoveries beneficial to mankind will far outweigh those of the space program over the next couple of decades. If we can get to the abyss regularly, there will be immediate payoffs."

PARENTS

Advances in health, medicine, and life expectancy will mean the baby boomer generation—in other words, your parents—could be around for a long, long time. Today there are 35 million Americans aged sixty-five and over. That should more than double to nearly 80 million in 2050. There will also be at least 20 million Americans over eighty-five—four times the number we have today. The sheer numbers of elderly are less important than their percentage of the population. Fifty years ago, there were roughly the same number of college kids in the United States as elderly, about nine to ten million each. But by 2040, the U.S. Census

Bureau estimates there will be about 20 million college-age youth and 75 million people age sixty-five and over. The number of elderly will have a profound impact as younger Americans—you—try to find ways to make sure the aging boomers have their economic, health, housing, and transportation needs taken care of. Look for more products, services, entertainment, and even job opportunities for the elderly, who, because of their good health, will be active much longer than previous generations of aging Americans. Plus, their sheer numbers will give the elderly a tremendous amount of power as a political force, as candidates promise programs and policies to win their votes.

POLITICS

The Internet is changing everything, and politics is no exception. On-line voting, proponents argue, could lead to the first increase in generations in the percentage of Americans who vote. The leaders of the future, moreover, may be those who can harness the communications power of the Net and ride it into office. "Each new wave in the technology of communications tosses up leaders who ride the medium," observes veteran *Newsweek* political commentator Howard Fineman. Washington and Jefferson, he points out, were experts with a printed pamphlet. Lincoln's great speeches were designed for the early days of the telegraph. FDR's "fireside chats" were made for radio, while John F. Kennedy and Ronald Reagan were perfect TV presidents. "Now what?" asks Fineman. "The president as Webmaster-in-chief? As hologram? We are racing toward a time in which there will be virtually unlimited channels of fully digital, interactive virtual reality transmitting data, entertainment, and news." He predicts a rise of digital grassroots activism where the Web becomes "the walkie-talkie and the bulletin board" where political issues take root and grow. Other political observers have wondered if the wired world can give us *too much* democracy. Instead of leaders, they fear, we may end up with politicians who see which way the digital wind is blowing and do nothing more than ride public opinion, instead of trying to direct it. "The "netizens" of the future will have to take their jobs seriously," says Fineman. "Are we ready for this much democracy? Let's hope so."

PRIME TIME

Not only will communications devices change (see Chapter 3), but we will see a gradual evolution in what comes out of them. Right now, if I say "computer" you think of the PC. If I say "television" you think of the box in front of the couch. Strange as it may sound, it's highly unlikely that your kids will see any difference whatsoever. Television shows—news, sports, sitcoms, and dramas—will be delivered over the Internet, just like what we now think of as "Web content." More important, it will be delivered not "Thursday at ten, nine central time" but when you want it, on demand. Each program that we now get over the air or from cable will soon be stored on computer servers that we will access either over the Web from a massive server, or on a set-top box that stores all our favorite shows. This will totally change our relationship with television. It could even change our culture. The days of millions of people gathered around the TV watching the same show—and talking about it the next day at school or work—may disappear, except for major breaking news stories or live sports events.

RELIGION

The Internet is changing the face of nearly every institution, and the church is no exception. By 2010, as many as 20 percent of Americans may attend religious services on-line. And while the United States is expected to remain a religious country, the face of spirituality here could change dramatically. The Roman Catholic Church, the largest denomination in the country, faces a decline in the number of men entering the priesthood (only men are permitted to be Catholic priests). That could mean a shortage of priests in the twenty-first century. Judaism faces a membership decline; 54 percent of Jewish children in the United States are being raised as non-Jews. On the other hand, one out of every seven people on Earth is Muslim, and Islam is one of the fastest-growing faiths in the United States. Experts also predict a rise in "syncretistic" or blended religions—borrowing customs from different faiths. "People are less tied to institutions," says Richard Cimino, the author of *Shopping for Faith: American Religion in the New Millennium,* "and more free to experience their faith, rather than just to observe. Religion will be more informal, more intimate, and more meaningful."

SINKS AND TOILETS

What would the smart home of the future be without a smart sink or toilet? Michael Dertouzos predicts every home will one day have a device he calls the "sink doctor." It could be used to automatically diagnose health problems. The sink would contain sensors that might detect small traces of blood from your gums, for example, when you brush your teeth. You might spit, says Derouzos, and hear a voice from the sink say: "At the rate you are going there is a fifty-fifty chance that you will have a periodontal incident in twelve to fifteen months and a loss of half your teeth by the time you are fifty-five years old."

SOCIETY

The face of America will change in the twenty-first century. The U.S. Census Bureau projects that by 2050, Americans of European descent will probably make up only half of the country's population of 500 million—down from about 75 percent today. The number of African Americans will rise slightly, from 12 percent to 14 percent of the population, while the number of Hispanics and Asians will rise dramatically. The Latino population of the United States will climb from one in ten today to one in four by 2050, while nearly ten percent of Americans will be of Asian descent. America's complexion will not be the only thing to change. Where we live will also be different. The biggest population boom will occur in the South and West. With the exception of a few big states like New York, New Jersey, Michigan, and Ohio, the number of people living in the Northeast and Midwest states may actually drop. And California will be the biggest state by far, with an estimated 63 million people by 2040.

SHIPS

The future of transportation will bring us smart highways and space planes (see Chapter 7) but for the foreseeable future, the sea will remain a vital transportation link. Right now, ships deliver 90 percent of all the imported products that arrive on our shores. A new generation of "megaships" already under construction is expected to handle over half the world's cargo by 2010. More than 1,100 feet long and carrying nearly seven thousand containers of cargo, some new megaships are so big that no U.S. port can handle one fully loaded. Los Angeles and Long Beach harbors will be able to handle the megaships within about five years, but on the Atlantic Ocean side, no U.S. harbor will be ready soon. Only Halifax, Nova Scotia, in Canada, has a natural channel deep enough for the megaships. Also on the drawing board: new designs for ship hulls that could be twice as fast as today's lumbering giants.

SUPERPOWERS

In the Cold War years, the United States and the Soviet Union used to be referred to as *superpowers.* This word for an especially powerful nation meant that each of those two countries had the ability to use their nuclear weapons to blow the world to smithereens at a moment's notice. As a result of this awesome power, many nations of the world aligned themselves with either the United States or the Soviet Union because of the protection—or threat—that they represented. In the twenty-first century, we may see the emergence of a new kind of superpower: an environmental one. An environmental superpower is a country whose environmental impact on the planet is simply so great it affects every other nation in the world. Nations like the United States and China are environmental superpowers because of the enormous influence they have over the global environment. In the case of the United States, it's because of its massive consumption habits (see Chapter 8). In the case of China, it's the sheer number of people. International agreements on things like greenhouse gas emissions will not succeed unless environmental superpowers play ball. If the environment continues to decline, the idea of environmental superpowers may affect the way we view the world, in much the same way that tensions between nuclear superpowers colored everyone's view of the world from the 1950s through the breakup of the Soviet Union.

TELEPORTATION

Every kid who has ever seen *Star Trek* understands teleportation. Kirk says, "Beam me up, Scotty," and is transported, bit by tiny bit, back aboard the *Enterprise*. It may surprise you to learn, however, that teleportation is scientifically possible. In fact, it's been done. Don't get too excited, though. Physicists have managed to successfully teleport a tiny light particle known as a photon. A few years ago, a team at the University of Innsbruck in Austria teleported a photon from one place to another. Transporting a living creature, even a simple one such as a bacterium, is not practical, because even the simplest beings contain overwhelming amounts of information. Think of how long it takes to download a large file or program over the Internet. Transporting Captain Kirk would be the mother of all downloads. It would take, oh, 100 million *centuries* for Scotty to beam Kirk up. By that time, the *Enterprise*, the crew, and all life everywhere in the universe would be long gone. The science behind quantum teleportation could, however, be useful in creating a future generation of computer billions of times faster than today's speediest silicon-chip–based machines.

THEME PARKS

Big theme parks like Disney World, Universal Studios, and Six Flags may lose their hold on our imagination. In fact, the theme park of the future may be all in our heads. "Virtual reality will live up to its name for the first time in the next ten years," movie director Steven Spielberg predicted in an interview with *USA Weekend.* "You'll be able to have experiences that, in fact, don't require forty-foot palm trees and thirty-eight-foot T-Rexes. But the experience will be just as enthralling. Even more so, because you'll be surrounded by images." As the director of classic special-effects fests such as *E.T.* and *Jurassic Park,* Spielberg probably knows what he's talking about. "You'll feel the breezes. You'll smell the smells. Yet when you stand back and turn on a light to look at where you've been standing, you're just in a dark room with a helmet on."

TRAINS

The U.S. is the world's transportation king. America builds more cars, trucks, planes, and ships than nearly every other country combined. But when it comes to trains, well, the United States sucks wind. Like a child who grows tired of an old toy, car-crazy America just didn't keep up with cutting-edge railroad technologies. The high-speed future of train travel already exists in places like France, Germany, and Japan. The French *Train à Grande Vitesse* (TGV), the train in the helicopter chase scene at the end of *Mission Impossible,* has been hurtling passengers along at nearly two hundred miles an hour since the late 1980s.

In the twenty-first century, America may finally be getting up to speed when it comes to train travel. Amtrak will soon debut a 150-mph train between New York and Boston. Florida is planning to build a 186-mph "supertrain" by 2006 that will connect Miami, Orlando, and Tampa. The real cutting edge of train travel is magnetic levitation trains. "Maglevs" are the closest thing imaginable to flying on the ground. In fact, riding a maglev, you are literally floating just above the track and at speeds of up to 300 mph! Germany is planning the world's first maglev passenger system between Hamburg and Berlin.

VIDEO PHONES

AT&T developed the first "picture phone" in 1956. A model demonstrated at the 1964 World's Fair allowed you to make video phone calls for a mere $27 for three minutes (no wonder they never caught on). But thanks to digital technology and the Internet, video phones are poised to become a staple of personal communications in the first decades of the twenty-first century. The "convergence revolution" (see Chapter 3) is leading to the development of a digital infrastructure that can handle the tremendous amount of data needed to stream video into the home over the Net. This fat new pipeline is being built to handle movies, video on demand, and other entertainment content, but it will also give us video telephones, which will probably have an even bigger impact on our lives than access to more entertainment. In fact, the biggest hurdle to video phones in the coming years will not be technology or price, but people's possible lack of desire to use them. Says technology pundit John Dvorak: "True success will never be seen if people don't want to be seen. Until that changes, video phones will remain a technological curiosity."

WRIST RADIOS

Our parents and grandparents grew up reading Dick Tracy comics in the newspaper. He wore a trademark two-way wrist radio. "It's the most remarkable invention of its age," gushed the cartoon detective well over fifty years ago. "It's miraculous. It both sends and receives!" Ever since, inventors have tried to bring the wrist radio to life, but most efforts have either been too big, too fragile, or too hot to wear comfortably on your wrist. Until now. Engineers at Lucent Technologies' Bell Labs have managed to cram tiny voice, video, and computer processors onto a single computer chip. *Voilà!* A wrist radio no bigger than an ordinary wristwatch. Actually, it will be a cell phone, not a radio, and future versions may be able to handle video calls. "Packing more functions on a single semiconductor chip is critical," says Peter Gammel, of Bell Labs, "The Dick Tracy watch is at the forefront of the digital parade." Look for affordable models in stores within the next couple of years.

INDEX

ABOUT THE AUTHOR

Robert Pondiscio (Rpondiscio@aol.com) is the Communications Director for *Business Week* and the author of a series of books for young readers about the Internet, science, and technology published by Avon Books, including *Kids On-Line*, *The Ultimate On-Line Homework Helper*, and *Get on the Net*. Robert began his career as a radio newsman in upstate New York while still a teenager. After working briefly for the NBC Radio Network, he joined Time Inc. Magazines in 1989, ultimately spending several years as the public affairs director for *TIME* magazine. While at *TIME*, he was part of the team that launched *TIME* Online in 1993, one of the first national magazines to go on-line. Robert lives in New York City and Medusa, New York, with his wife, Liza Greene, and their daughter, Katie.

MAY 9 2006
FEB

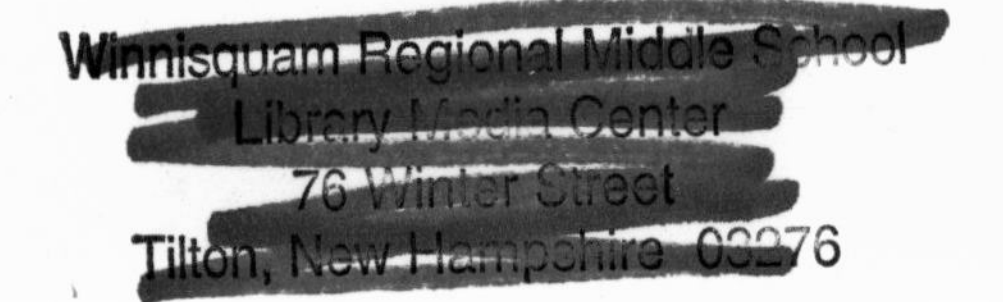
Winnisquam Regional Middle School
Library Media Center
76 Winter Street
Tilton, New Hampshire 03276